A MID-VICTORIAN FEMINIST,
BARBARA LEIGH SMITH BODICHON

Barbara Leigh Smith Bodichon (Mistress and Fellows of Girton College)

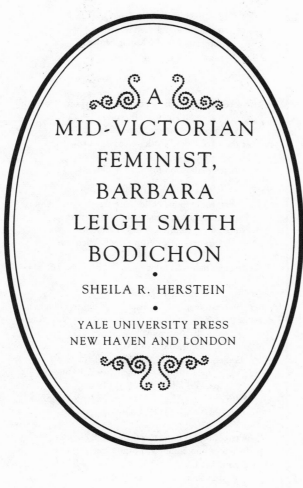

A
MID-VICTORIAN
FEMINIST,
BARBARA
LEIGH SMITH
BODICHON

·

SHEILA R. HERSTEIN

·

YALE UNIVERSITY PRESS
NEW HAVEN AND LONDON

Published with assistance from
the foundation established in memory of
Philip Hamilton McMillan of the
Class of 1894, Yale College.

Designed by Sally Harris
and set in Goudy Old Style type by
Eastern Graphics, Binghamton, New York
Printed in the United States of America by
Edwards Brothers, Inc., Ann Arbor, Michigan.

Library of Congress Cataloging in Publication Data

Herstein, Sheila R.
A mid-Victorian feminist, Barbara Leigh Smith Bodichon.
Revision of thesis (doctoral)—City University of New York.
Bibliography: p. 197
Includes index.
1. Bodichon, Barbara Leigh Smith, 1827–1891.
2. Feminists—Great Britain—Biography. 3. Feminism—
Great Britain—History. I. Title.
HQ1595.B63H47   1985   305.4′2′0924   85–8256
ISBN 0–300–03317–6 (alk. paper)

The paper in this book meets the guidelines for
permanence and durability of the Committee on
Production Guidelines for Book Longevity
of the Council on Library Resources.

10 9 8 7 6 5 4 3 2 1

FOR MY MOTHER,
CLARA PENKOWER HERSTEIN

CONTENTS

ACKNOWLEDGMENTS

Barbara Bodichon has been my constant companion for many years. The writing of her life has taken me to research libraries, archives, and personal collections in the United States and the United Kingdom. Every biographer does his/her research in hopes of finding just those special details that will bring the subject most vividly to life. My work owes its success to the assistance of a great many helpful and knowledgable people and I shall try to thank them here briefly.

Many librarians and archivists have shared their expertise and eased my way. I should like first to thank the interlibrary loan librarians Donald Petty and Helga Moody at City College of the City University of New York, who have tracked down a variety of esoteric and difficult references for me over the years. Mildred Surrey of the Fawcett Society Library in London and Margaret Gaskell at Girton College, Cambridge should also be mentioned. I thank the Mistress and Fellows of Girton College for providing me with photographs of Barbara Bodichon, Girton College, and Hertha Ayrton. The staffs of the Beinecke Library at Yale University, the London School of Economics Library and the Butler Library at Columbia University have all been extremely helpful. Upon occasion biographers are particularly priviledged and meet people who share their deep involvement with the subject and give special help. I wish to thank one such individual, Barbara Smith MacCrimmon, who wrote me many years ago to offer her personal collection of Bodichon letters for my use. Her enthusiasm was delightful and her collection proved most valuable.

Many persons read and commented on the manuscript during its various stages of development; each contributed to its improvement. Any flaws in the finished work are, of course, my own responsibility.

I must extend special thanks to Professor Gertrude Himmelfarb, who helped shape the initial version of this work, which was my doctoral dissertation at the Graduate School of the City University of New York. Her advice was invaluable, while the example of her own work provided me a model of the truly professional historian. To Professor Ann M. Burton go my warm thanks for her comments on the manuscript, but even more for her friendship and support throughout my graduate work. Professor Joel Wiener has given valuable advice on Victorian periodicals. I am particularly grateful to Professor R. K. Webb, who read the manuscript in its entirety and made many helpful suggestions.

To friends and family I owe many debts of gratitude for patience and support during the writing of this book. Barbara Dunlap and Eleanor Langstaff, who share my interest in Victorian history and literature, deserve special mention. My deepest thanks go to my mother, Clara Penkower Herstein, to whom this book is dedicated. Without her encouragement and enthusiasm I could not have completed this work. She has shown me throughout my life what it is to be an independent and truly liberated woman and has always been my best friend.

INTRODUCTION

In 1852 at the age of thirty-two, Florence Nightingale expressed her frustration at society's restrictions on female endeavor. Her fictional heroine Cassandra, whose agony was Nightingale's own, rejected woman's proper sphere: "Why have women passion, intellect, moral activity—these three—and a place in society where no one of the three can be exercised?"[1] Cassandra's cry echoed the dissatisfaction felt in drawing rooms throughout England. As middle-class women began to reject the passive role assigned them, the third quarter of the nineteenth century witnessed the beginning of reforms in women's legal status, education, and opportunities for employment.

Before 1850, the women's movement had been fragmented. It was not until 1848, the year of revolution in Europe, that the Christian Socialist Frederick Denison Maurice established Queen's College for women in London with the intention of improving the training of governesses. The following year, Bedford College was founded in London by Elizabeth Jesser Reid to give more women the opportunity to pursue secondary education. Many of the women later active in feminist campaigns attended lectures at these institutions. From 1850 onward the movement began to assume an organized shape. The first abortive attempts to gain the franchise date from this period. The movement brought men and women to-

1. Florence Nightingale, "Cassandra," in Ray Strachey, *The Cause* (London: G. Bell & Sons, 1928), p. 396.

gether in formal committees for the next fifty years. Feminist journals were established and societies devoted to women's issues began to function. The campaign to improve women's access to higher education opened and saw its first successes during these years.

The first organized feminist activities in Britain were the work of a small group of women from upper-middle-class social, economic, and religious backgrounds. Their efforts on behalf of their sex can only be understood in the context of the other social and political reform movements of the period. The participants in the mid-Victorian women's movement were for the most part members of a select group of families responsible for a variety of reform efforts. Their efforts were amateur in the best sense and reflected the attitudes of a unified, culturally concerned segment of society. The modern phenomenon of specialization had yet to develop and a real professionalization of society was many years in the future. The essentially amateur quality of Victorian reform efforts is demonstrated in the period's magazines and reviews, in the proliferation of local statistical societies, and in the committees and associations established for the study and improvement of the human condition. Every individual in reform circles served as his or her own historian and scientists, as well as doctor, philosopher, poet, and artist.[2]

The families that dominated the reform movements of the 1860s and 1870s made up an intellectual aristocracy.[3] The wives, daughters, and maiden aunts of this intellectual elite became the leaders of the women's movement. Evangelical, Quaker, and Unitarian families were drawn together by the humanitarian inspiration of the antislavery movement which opened the nineteenth century. Mingling, often intermarrying, in a world of culture and intellect and economically secure on the basis of manufacturing interests, Venns, Macaulays, Wedgwoods, Darwins, Gurneys, and Smiths considered themselves "gentlemen" but never confused their position with that of the true gentry. They worked for intellectual and

2. Robert Kiefer Webb, Harriet Martineau: A Radical Victorian (New York: Columbia University Press, 1960), p. 245.

3. Noel Gilroy Annan, "The Intellectual Aristocracy," in J. H. Plumb, ed., Studies in Social History: A Tribute to G. M. Trevelyan (London: Longmans, Green, 1955), pp. 241–87.

religious freedom and the recognition of merit and talent. By 1853 their ideals were expressed in the Trevelyan-Northcote report on civil service reform. In the sixties and seventies, they were drawn together in campaigns to extend voting rights and to open the universities to women and to people of all religious faiths. The women of this comfortable upper-middle-class world, whose lives were filled with European travel and brilliant dinner conversation, who were removed, in all but intellectual sympathy, from the experience of poverty and physical deprivation, organized and activated the first real changes in the legal and social status of Victorian women of all classes.

Little has been published on this early period of feminist activity, except for the exultant and understandably prejudiced histories and biographies produced by early twentieth-century feminists, who were themselves descendents of the nineteenth-century intellectual aristocracy. Ray Strachey's *The Cause*, 1928, and Barbara Stephen's *Emily Davies and Girton College*, 1927, are examples of this type of work. Before an understanding of this period can be reached individual feminist leaders must be studied, as well as organizations such as the Society for the Promotion of the Employment of Women, the National Association for the Promotion of Social Science, the Kensington Society, and other committees for promotion of employment, education, and women's suffrage. Periodicals such as the *English Woman's Journal* and the *Englishwoman's Review of Social and Industrial Questions* must be compared with the general periodicals of the day to determine how woman's legal and social status, as well as her self-image, was changing.

Barbara Leigh Smith Bodichon was considered by her contemporaries as the leader of the mid-Victorian feminist movement in the third quarter of the nineteenth century. Despite her important role, little has been written about her. L. P. Curtis noted in 1966 that biography "should seek to interpret the culture through the individual, just as it should reveal the individual through his culture."[4] Bodichon's personal history gains significance as it becomes an

4. L. P. Curtis, "The Queen's Two Bonnets," *Victorian Studies* 9 (1966): 272.

exploration of the political, social, and religious environment in which she lived. Her feminist work can only be understood by evaluating the influence of the radical Unitarian circle from which she came. Analyzing the family and philosophic connections of the upper-middle-class world in which Bodichon traveled will enable us to place feminism within the context of other mid-Victorian reform campaigns.

A MID-VICTORIAN FEMINIST,
BARBARA LEIGH SMITH BODICHON

THE SMITHS:
THREE GENERATIONS
OF PUBLIC SERVICE

Barbara Leigh Smith Bodichon was born on April 8, 1827, at Wat-
lington in Sussex, the eldest child of Benjamin Leigh Smith and
Anne Longden. The Smiths were wealthy, Unitarian, and active
reformers. The family originated on the Isle of Wight and had
owned a small estate there since the reign of James I. The Smiths
had been Dissenters since the seventeenth century. Barbara Smith's
great-grandfather Samuel Smith (born 1727) was a noted London
merchant. He and his brother Benjamin were partners in the family
wholesale grocery firm, in London, which for fifty years beginning
around 1761 netted its owners an average of four thousand pounds
per annum.[1] Samuel and Benjamin Smith broadened their business
investments by purchasing real estate in America, and for a time
owned a large portion of the city of Savannah, Georgia. However,
they sympathized so deeply with the cause of the American colo-
nists that they gave up title to that land and repudiated all claims
for property loss in an effort to make plain their support of American independence.[2]

Samuel's son William Smith (1756–1835) was generally acknowledged as the leading parliamentary spokesman for Dissenters
of all denominations. He served from 1805 to 1832 as chairman of
the Protestant Dissenting Deputies, a committee of laymen repre-

1. Richard W. Davis, *Dissent in Politics, 1780–1830: The Political Life of William Smith,*
M.P. (London: Epworth Press, 1971), p. 4.
2. Cecil Woodham-Smith, *Florence Nightingale, 1820–1910* (London: Constable, 1950),
p. 2.

senting Presbyterians, Independents, and Baptists, which had been established in 1732 to take care of the civil affairs of the Dissenters.[3]

The prosperity of the family business enabled William Smith to devote his life to public work. Elected first as M.P. for Sudbury in Suffolk in the general election of 1784, he served Norwich as M.P. from 1802 until his retirement from parliamentary life on July 24, 1830. Smith did not enjoy the political limelight, preferring to make his contributions quietly, behind the scenes, but in several of the reform efforts of his day he played a vital, if not dominant, role. And he emerged as the foremost public figure in the Dissenters' struggles to extend religious liberty and achieve real political equality.

The spirit of Rational Dissent continued to gain in strength throughout the eighteenth century. The doctrine asserted the right of individuals to employ reason in the interpretation of Scripture and insisted that the Bible, not the opinions of the Fathers, was the basis of Protestantism. The distinguishing sign of the Rational Dissenters was their insistence on the exercise of the natural right of freedom of inquiry.[4] Joseph Priestley, Theophilus Lindsey, and Thomas Belsham, former Rational Dissenters, assumed leadership in the Unitarian movement at the end of the eighteenth century, and William Smith joined the movement at this time. Eight-year-old William Smith had met Thomas Belsham, then fourteen, at a dissenting school at Ware. They continued a close friendship during their school years at Ware and Daventry and throughout their adult lives. Belsham and Smith chose Unitarianism amidst the social ferment of the French Revolution and despite general condemnation of the movement resulting from the fear of dissent and reform the Revolution had inspired.[5]

There is no record of precisely how or when Smith made his deci-

3. C. Gordon Bolan et al., *The English Presbyterians from Elizabethan Puritanism to Modern Unitarianism* (London: George Allen & Unwin, 1968), pp. 244–45.

4. Anthony Lincoln, *Some Political and Social Ideas of English Dissent, 1763–1800* (Cambridge: Cambridge University Press, 1938), p. 30.

5. Davis, *Dissent in Politics*, pp. 55–56.

sion, but he had been slowly moving toward Unitarianism since his years at Daventry. He was strongly influenced by Belsham, who had become an Arian at Daventry, resigning the post of principal there after adopting Unitarian views in 1789. The Arian movement also grew from an assertion of individuals' right to employ reason in interpreting the Scriptures. Critical examination of the Bible led Arians to the conclusion that there was little support for the doctrine of the Trinity. They considered Christ subordinate to the Father, but worshipped him as the Great Mediator. In 1791 Belsham joined Lindsey and Priestley in founding the "Unitarian Society for Promoting Christian Knowledge and the Practice of Virtue by the Distribution of Books."

In a sermon preached in 1790, Belsham emphasized the importance of truth and the obligation to strive always toward that sacred concept. He declared it the absolute duty of all "to bear testimony to it [truth] by diligent enquiry after it, courageous profession of it, faithful adherence to it, and by using every fair and honourable means of promoting its progress in the world."[6] Belsham's exhortation to search for truth became the basis of William Smith's personal and political credo. Smith's religious assertion in 1808— "Who but the infallible shall presume to arrogate to himself alone the title of orthodox or evangelical? Who duly conscious of the weakness of his reason and the strength of his prejudices shall claim to be exclusively rational?"—echoed also in his political speeches in defense of liberty and in his personal conduct of an urbane and tolerant household.[7]

Unitarians of the Priestley–Belsham school emphasized the function of reason in the search for truth, and refused to assert that they had reached ultimate truth, which forbade forcing their version of truth on others.[8] Excluded from Oxford and Cambridge because these institutions required subscription to the articles of the Church (Cambridge admitted Dissenters, but granted no degrees

6. Webb, *Harriet Martineau*, p. 68.

7. Davis, *Dissent in Politics*, p. 204.

8. Francis Edward Mineka, *The Dissidence of Dissent: The Monthly Repository, 1806–1838* (Chapel Hill: University of North Carolina Press, 1944), p. 22.

without subscription), the Dissenters developed independent academies such as Warrington and Daventry during the eighteenth century. In these academies the rationalistic spirit of the age exerted its strongest influence in religious as well as secular spheres. John Locke's *Essay Concerning Human Understanding* (1690), which was used as a text in the dissenting academies, strengthened the cause of rational inquiry into sacred truth: "I doubt not but to show that a man, by the right use of his natural abilities, may, without any innate principles, attain a knowledge of God, and other things that concern him."[9]

Participation in the political struggle for civil and religious liberty was a natural outgrowth of these doctrines. Dissenters of all sorts were politically active. They have been characterized as the most politically minded people of their time because the obstacles they met daily could only be justified or condemned in political terms.[10] Indeed, Defoe's biographer Walter Wilson asserted in a speech published in the *Monthly Repository* in 1823, "A dissenter, whatever may be his theological opinions, . . . is eminently a political character, being made so by the state. It is his duty therefore, never to lose sight of his situation, nor to forego any fair opportunity for urging its amelioration."[11]

One of the major political issues of the period between the American Revolution and the passage of the Reform Bill in 1832 revolved around the struggle between the old oligarchy, based on land and traditional privilege, and rising new talent, the aggressive and expanding middle class produced by the rapid commercial and industrial growth of the country. Because of the religious principles of the Dissenters, their commercial and industrial success, and their religious and civil disabilities, they formed a large and influential element in the new middle class who were naturally strong supporters of reform of the old oligarchical system.

Unitarians were particularly active, caught up in the political di-

9. John Locke, *An Essay concerning Human Understanding* (London: J. M. Dent & Sons, 1961), bk. 1, chap. 4, sec. 12.

10. Lincoln, *Ideas of English Dissent*, p. 17.

11. *Monthly Repository* 28 (1823): 394.

visions that arose over the French Revolution and condemned for overzealous devotion to political reform between 1790 and 1832. As late as 1825 the charge was made in the *Christian Remembrancer:* "The Unitarians are a political rather than a religious sect—radicals to a man."[12] It was certainly true that, while some sects of Dissenters fought reforms such as Catholic Emancipation, the Unitarians supported every movement toward greater political and religious freedom without prejudice.

William Smith was no democrat, however. Smith and Belsham were Whigs, albeit liberal ones. Smith did not have an overwhelming faith in the common man, nor did he foresee a radical change in the makeup of the House as a result of reform, as his support for a stiff property qualification for members attests. What might have developed into a profound conservatism in him, however, was tempered by the Unitarian doctrine of Necessarianism, advanced by Joseph Priestley and initially integrated in an academic curriculum by Thomas Belsham at Daventry.[13] The doctrine was fairly simple. The universe, moral and natural, worked according to laws set in motion by God. The laws were inevitable, but man could, by using the reason God had given, as scientists had clearly shown, understand the laws and conform to them. Man had a positive duty to understand and act accordingly, for by doing this he was advancing the divine plan. Necessarianism was not fatalism, however. The doctrine held that every man was the maker of his own fortune. Each person's actions and determinations were necessary links in the chain of causes and effects.[14] The doctrine led Smith to express an optimistic belief in a "progression of improvement" decreed by providence, hence his liberalism derived from his desire to assist providence. His ideas placed him in the ranks of the most liberal of the Whig politicians,[15] and in a letter to Charles James Fox dated November 15, 1801, he agreed with Fox's assessment of the most

12. *Christian Remembrancer* 7 (1825): 372.

13. Davis, *Dissent in Politics*, p. 96.

14. For a detailed discussion of the Necessarian doctrine see Webb, *Harriet Martineau*, chap. 3.

15. Michael Roberts, *The Whig Party, 1807–1812* (London: Macmillan, 1939; reprint, New York: Barnes & Noble, 1965), p. 277.

vital issues of the day—peace, Reform, the abolition of all religious tests in civil matters, and the abolition of the slave trade.[16]

The first important parliamentary debate William Smith took part in concerned Henry Beaufoy's motion in 1787 for a repeal of the Test and Corporation Acts.[17] Beaufoy, a Whig politician long associated with the politics of liberal Dissent, was the son of a Quaker wine merchant in London. He attended the dissenting academy at Hoxton and later the more famous Warrington academy. On March 1, 1791, Smith participated in a debate on a motion to bring in a bill for the relief of Catholic dissenters. He spoke twice on that same bill in April 1791 and participated in almost every discussion on religious disabilities until the repeal of the Test and Corporation Acts in 1828. Smith gave evidence of the strength of his convictions in 1790 in a speech defending Joseph Priestley. He was outspoken and gave no thought to his personal safety despite the violence against all kinds of religious and liberal opinion, that was brought on by fear of the French Revolution.[18] The length of his speeches, their earnest, righteous tone, and his prominent position as chairman of the deputies of the three denominations made him a target for satire in a political poem of the period:

> At length when the candles burn low in their sockets,
> Up gets William Smith with both hands in his pockets,
> On a course of morality fearlessly enters
> With all the opinions of all the dissenters.[19]

Smith's youth was spent in his father's house at Clapham, which offered a comfortable country retreat for London businessmen, as it was only about five miles by road from the Common to the City. Prominent among the Smiths' neighbors was a group of Evangelical families, the Clapham sect, which included men like banker Henry

---

16. Davis, *Dissent in Politics*, p. 97.

17. *Hansard's Parliamentary History of England from the Earliest Period to the Year 1803*, 25 (1787): 824.

18. Ibid., 28 (1790): 443.

19. Victor Bonham-Carter, *In a Liberal Tradition* (London: Constable, 1960), p. 37.

Thornton, Charles Grant, chairman of the East India Company, James Stephen, Zachary Macaulay, Granville Sharp, and William Wilberforce.[20] Smith developed close friendships with members of the sect, especially Thornton and Wilberforce. He supported Wilberforce in Parliament throughout the long campaign against slavery. In 1788 he supported Sir William Dolben's motion on the African slave bill, and in 1789 he made one of several passionate denunciations of slavery:

> Let no man here imagine himself sanctioned by example or defended by numbers; but let him ask himself, if his own wife or his own daughter were one of the trembling thousand, whom our ruthless and dirty vote is about to tear from their families and consign to all the horrors of foreign slavery? Were that the case, Sir, how would he then act? Would he then be satisfied with the flimsy pretences of slave dealers, or the cries for compensations from the whole West Indies?[21]

The strength of his conviction on the immorality of the slave trade was unfailing. In 1797 he dismissed the argument of expediency with contempt, declaring that no system of commercial policy which was repugnant to moral duty should be allowed to exist for a moment.[22]

Smith and Wilberforce held sharply differing religious views. A typical contrast between Unitarian and Evangelical reformers can be illustrated by a conversation between Major John Cartwright and Wilberforce. Cartwright, a Unitarian and a radical parliamentary reformer, met Wilberforce in 1801. Wilberforce expressed the hope that they would meet next in "a better world," but Cartwright replied that he hoped they would first correct the ills of this world.[23] Wilberforce and the Evangelicals were zealous reformers, but only in certain carefully restricted areas. They subscribed to a

20. Ibid., pp. 35–36.
21. *Hansard's Parliamentary History*, 29 (1792): 1255–56.
22. Davis, *Dissent in Politics*, p. 252.
23. Raymond V. Holt, *The Unitarian Contribution to Social Progress in England*, rev. ed. (London: Lindsey Press, 1952), p. 89.

conservative, strictly hierarchical, and class-conscious world view. R. K. Webb has noted that Victorian ideals of activity and service emerged not just from Evangelicalism, but also from the Necessarian doctrine of the Unitarians, which stressed the importance of the individual and "raised him to the towering pinnacle of master of his own fate through mastery of the laws of the universe." In contrast, the Evangelicals emphasized the insignificance of the individual.[24] But whatever impelled them toward social action, the Evangelical and Unitarian strands met and mingled in the efforts of Smith and Wilberforce to abolish the slave trade, and they established the humanitarian atmosphere which encouraged reform movements throughout the Victorian period.

Smith differed from Wilberforce, not only in his religion, but also in his politics, since Wilberforce supported conservative William Pitt and Smith was a staunch supporter of liberal Charles Fox. At Smith's Park Street house in London Wilberforce rubbed elbows with Fox, for by 1796 the house had become a meeting place for the Whig elite.[25] Smith provided a bridge between the Evangelical Saints of the Clapham sect and the liberal and radical supporters of abolition.

William Smith's household was large and cosmopolitan. William and Frances Coape Smith had five sons and five daughters. Patty was born in 1782, Benjamin in 1783, and Anne in 1785. Another daughter born in 1789 died at four months; Frances (Fanny) followed in 1788 and William Adams in 1789. Joanna was born in 1791, Samuel in 1794, Octavius in 1796, Frederick Coape in 1798, and Julia, the youngest, arrived in 1799.

Their upbringing was remarkably modern. For example, all the children were vaccinated against smallpox at a time when it was common for eight children out of twelve to succumb to the disease.[26] The Smiths traveled extensively. In Paris in 1802 Samuel

24. Webb, *Harriet Martineau*, p. 88.
25. See Samuel Rogers, *Recollections* (Boston: Bartlett & Miles, 1859), p. 31; and Morchard Bishop, ed., *Recollections of the Table Talk of Samuel Rogers* (Lawrence: University of Kansas Press, 1953), pp. 56–57, for descriptions of Whig dinners held at Smith's home.
26. Bonham-Carter, *Liberal Tradition*, p. 37.

Rogers took them to the Louvre and they watched Napoleon review his troops before being forced to return to England by the threat of war. At their country home in Parndon the family attended church services regularly and were encouraged to hear a noted preacher, whatever his theological views. Born and raised an Independent, educated a Rational Dissenter, during his adult life a member of the fashionable Unitarian congregation founded by the ex-Anglican Theophilus Lindsey in Essex Street, London, William Smith never entertained narrow theological views. His eldest son, Benjamin, was proud of his father's cosmopolitan outlook and reported to his sister Patty in 1806, after he and his father had visited Lord Holland, that their conversation had included discussion of the slave trade and the American political question. "I have never heard my father speak with more ease. I am not surprised that he has gained the affection of the Lady, if he always acts as he did this morning. There was nothing of the Presbyterian preacher in his manner of speaking."[27]

Smith was an avid collector of paintings and a patron the painters of John Opie and John Sell Cotman. He entertained Sir Joshua Reynolds at his home on numerous occasions. After a life of luxury, Smith lost the fortune that had provided his family comfort and culture. The family business failed and his eldest son, Benjamin, wealthy in his own right and owner of a successful distillery, took on support of his father. Benjamin financed the expensive, though uncontested, elections of 1820 and 1826 and insured his father's comfortable retirement. William lived with Benjamin's family in Blandford Square from 1830 until his death in 1835. Sir James Stephen eulogized him as a man sensitive to the sufferings of the world despite the comfort of his own surroundings. "If he had gone mourning all his days, he could scarcely have acquired a more tender pity for the miserable, or have laboured more habitually for their relief."[28] His religious convictions shaped his political and social attitudes and created within his family circle a sense of pub-

27. Davis, *Dissent in Politics*, p. 103.
28. Sir James Stephen, *Essays in Ecclesiastical Biography*, 2 vols. (London: Longman, Brown, Green & Longmans, 1849), 2:322–23.

lic obligation and openness toward ideas and individuals, which was the most important heritage passed on to his children and grandchildren.

Benjamin Leigh Smith, William Smith's eldest son, was born April 28, 1783. He went from Trinity to the distillery where he made a fortune. A bachelor until age forty, he was generous with his wealth, so that when his sister Joanna married John Carter (later Bonham-Carter) in 1816, he gave the couple his house at 16 Duke Street facing St. James Park, including in the gift all of its furnishings, and moved himself to a new home.[29] He became M.P. for Norwich on May 14, 1838 and held the seat until 1847. In addition to his London home he acquired property in Sussex. At forty he met Anne Longden, a milliner's apprentice, and, in the words of his eldest daughter Barbara, "notorious cohabitation as man and wife" followed.[30] He never explained his decision not to marry and almost nothing is known about Longden or her family background. Five children were born to the couple before Anne died in 1834 when Barbara was seven. Benjamin's youngest sister, Julia, helped raise the illegitimate brood (Barbara, Benjamin, Isabella, William, and Anne) in a household that echoed the hurly-burly of William Smith's Park Street and Parndon establishments.

Benjamin Smith was an active supporter of the Liberal party and of the repeal of the corn laws. He was a patron of William Hunt, the watercolor artist, and a firm believer in travel for his family. He exposed his children to political and philosophic discussion from babyhood. The household was irregular from the point of view of strict Victorian standards of education and social convention. Smith delighted in flaunting social mandates. He took his daughters for Sunday drives in their ordinary dresses and pinafores and went so far as to object to the shibboleth, as he regarded it, of baptism.[31] If the household was unconventional, it was also wealthy

29. Bonham-Carter, Liberal Tradition, p. 39.
30. Muriel Clara Bradbrook, Barbara Bodichon, George Eliot and the Limits of Feminism, James Bryce Memorial Lecture (Oxford: Oxford University Press, 1975), p. 4.
31. Matilda Betham-Edwards, Mid-Victorian Memoirs (London: John Murray, 1919), pp. 70–71.

and lively. Mary Howitt described the family to her sister after spending a seaside holiday with them at Clapton in 1845. She was struck by the excellent results that Smith's family regimen produced. She was entranced by the carriage he had had custom built like an omnibus to accommodate his five children and accompanying servants on trips through the country. Howitt was sure that the yearly journeys and informal family discipline contributed to the health and spirit of the young people whose company she found so invigorating.[32]

If the Smiths' traveling omnibus was a peculiar conveyance, their father's scheme for educating them was just as unusual. Rejecting schools, he kept his children at home and their early education came primarily from desultory reading. They had tutors, but no real structure was ever imposed to direct their course of study. Smith made his family part of an experiment in infant day education. He was a leading member of a committee of Whigs and Radicals, associated with Lord Brougham and James Hill, which set up an infant school at Brewer's Green, Westminster in 1818. His father, William Smith, had earlier joined with Brougham in the founding of the Royal Lancasterian Institution for the Education of the Poor in 1808 and had helped to transform it into the British and Foreign School Society in 1814.[33] These early Lancasterian schools ran on a monitorial system and were quite different from the experimental infant school established in 1818. The project grew out of discussions with Robert Owen and was modeled on Owen's infant school at New Lanark. Corporal punishment was outlawed there, teachers helped arouse the children's curiosity about everyday objects and spent a great deal of time organizing games and songs and stimulating infant conversation.[34] James Buchanan, who had taught at New Lanark since 1815, was sent to London to serve as master at

32. Mary Howitt, *Autobiography*, ed. Margaret Howitt, 2 vols. (Boston: Houghton Mifflin, 1889), 2:34–35.

33. Chester William New, *Life of Henry Brougham to 1830* (Oxford: Clarendon Press, 1961), p. 204.

34. Robert Owen, *The Life of Robert Owen*, 2 vols. (London: Effingham Wilson, 1857; reprint, New York: Augustus M. Kelley, 1967), 1:139–40.

Brewer's Green, and Brougham hailed the school as a unique experiment which extended Owen's ideas to a town population.[35]

James Buchanan's Swedenborgian philosophy and unorthodox
teaching methods embarrassed the members of the infant school
committee and, although Brougham assured the House of Commons after the school had operated for a year that "it was going on
in the most satisfactory manner,"[36] most of the supporters deserted
the cause, leaving Benjamin Smith to carry on alone. According to
Barbara Smith, "all the other gentlemen gave up the idea, when
they saw the queer fish Robert Owen had sent from Lanark."[37]
Smith approved of Buchanan's methods, paid his salary, bought another site at Vincent Square, Westminster, and built a two-story
building to serve as a school and a residence for the teacher. It included such amenities as a large playground and baths for the children.[38] The Vincent Square school accommodated about one hundred children, who came from the poorest classes in the area
nearby.

Buchanan's teaching methods stemmed entirely from his personality. He taught multiplication and grammar with rhymes and
games and used no books or slates in the school. Julia Smith was
greatly impressed by her first sight of his tiny figure in the classroom. She thought his expression angelic when he was playing the
flute and leading a band of marching children around the room.
"He was always alive, not mechanical, and I believe he could have
quieted the whole infantry at any moment when he chose with the
help of his wife and flute."[39] Barbara Smith remembered how
much the children loved him, "the poor little things clustering on
him like hiving bees, all trying to caress him."[40] Buchanan's wife
was a thrifty and efficient Scotswoman, a complete contrast to her

35. W. A. C. Stewart and W. P. McCann, *The Educational Innovators, 1750–1880*, 2
vols. (London: Macmillan, 1967), 1:243.
36. *Parliamentary Debates*, n.s. 59 (1819): 1199.
37. Barbara Isabella Buchanan, *Buchanan Family Records* (Cape Town: Townsend, 1923),
p. 25.
38. Ibid., p. 8.
39. Ibid., pp. 26–27.
40. Ibid., p. 22.

impractical, unworldly husband. Responsible for day-to-day details at the school, she was never more in her element than when she was bathing its hundred students.[41]

By the time Benjamin Smith's own children were born, the school had been operating almost ten years. Buchanan became the children's private tutor, spending time at Hastings and in London with the family, in addition to his duties at Vincent Square. The Smith children attended the school as soon as they were old enough to help with the younger pupils. Buchanan's extraordinary methods included a complete disregard for discipline. Barbara Smith recalled that he would pretend to teach her and her brothers and sisters to read, but actually spent most of his time in reading aloud to them from the three books he considered "sacred"—the Bible, the Arabian Nights, and Swedenborg.[42] The Smiths sometimes tyrannized their indulgent teacher. Barbara, even at the age of nine, demanded that he carry her upstairs. The family would refuse to allow him to eat, insisting instead that he read the Arabian Nights to them during meals. But doting on children as he did, Buchanan was unbending in his expectations of adults. He lectured Benjamin Smith severely about his behavior and political views and often stopped strangers on the street if he felt that their actions needed correction.[43]

The school at Vincent Square continued successfully under Buchanan's direction and Smith's sponsorship until 1839. In that year Buchanan, who never gained recognition for his educational experiment, emigrated to Cape Town. He had announced his Swedenborgian views to the representative of the London Statistical Society who visited the school in 1839, and, in the religious atmosphere of the day, schools conducted outside the orthodoxies of the established church were suspect.[44] Brougham, Buchanan's lifelong supporter, wrote in 1851 that "the shadow of Westminster Abbey fell

41. Ibid., p. 27.
42. Ibid., p. 23.
43. Ibid., p. 23–24.
44. See the London Statistical Society, "Second Report of a Committee Appointed to Enquire into the State of Education in Westminster," *Journal of the Statistical Society of London* 1 (1839): 193–215, for a description of the Vincent Square School and Buchanan's methods.

coldly on the dissenting teacher."[45] But although public recognition eluded Buchanan during his life, Barbara Smith was greatly influenced by his teaching. She carried his educational innovations into her own experimental Portman Hall School in 1854. Even at age fifty-seven, she acknowledged how profound his influence had been in a letter to her cousin Alice Bonham-Carter: "Oh Alice, I loved that man . . . that man had genius of the rare kind. My life was better for his life."[46]

The license allowed the Smith children by their tutor and by their father was unheard of in strict Victorian family circles, but was merely a concrete extension of Benjamin Smith's personal moral code, his dislike of pretension, and his commitment to social experiment and political reform. It should be acknowledged that there was considerable range in the styles of education of wealthy radicals and Unitarians. Smith's money was plentiful and he spent it on hospitals as well as schools, needy students, and political refugees. His nursery was not a separate and orderly sanctuary; rather, his children shared in all their father's activities, including his political campaigns and the dinner parties at which Lord Brougham and Harriet Martineau numbered among the stream of distinguished guests. The enthusiasm which characterized family activities was apparent in a Cambridge visit organized by Smith to provide a day's outing for the exiles he was sheltering. In May 1851, twenty-one refugees joined the Smiths and Mary Howitt for an enormous breakfast at Blandford Square and a visit to the younger Benjamin Smith at Jesus College. The day was spent in touring, conversation, and a series of sumptuous meals. Howitt tried to capture the animation of the event for her husband:

> If you could have seen the fun, freedom and jollity of those
> bearded and moustachio'd men who had been students up and
> down Germany, it would have delighted you. . . . What roars
> of laughter there were! When ample justice had been done to

45. *Westminster and Foreign Quarterly Review* 14 (January 1851): 397.
46. Barbara Bodichon to Alice Bonham-Carter, June 1884, Bonham-Carter Family Papers, Hampshire Record Office, Winchester, England.

the pickled salmon, ducks, fowls, tongue and pigeon-pie, we joined the rest of the party in the court of Kings. . . . All assembled at the Bull and our twenty-one with six handsome undergraduates added, sat down to a table covered with excellent and delicious dishes. You can imagine the speeches, the laughter, the wit![47]

Wealth gave the family independence; their father's natural dislike for conventions passed to the children. When chastized for unorthodox behavior in later life, Barbara Bodichon shrewdly pointed out that money could neutralize otherwise unacceptable attitudes: "I am a rich woman, and therefore, when I die there will be no fuss about burying an unbaptized person in consecrated ground."[48] Certainly their illegitimacy was a defiance of propriety that Benjamin Smith's five children were forced to come to terms with. None of them had any legal right to the family coat-of-arms or the name. Only by settling money on the children as each attained the age of majority could Smith insure their right to his fortune. The social stigma of their status could not be ignored. The Nightingales, their first cousins, did not acknowledge or call on the Smiths, and the "tabooed family," as George Eliot described them, must have known much inner turmoil, despite their great love and obvious respect for their father.[49] Elizabeth Gaskell saw many of the same qualities in Barbara Smith that she admired in Smith's first cousins Hilary Carter and Florence Nightingale. However, she found Smith difficult to like and explained her manner as a reaction to illegitimacy. "She is—I think in consequence of her birth, a strong fighter against the established opinions of the world—which always goes against my—what shall I call it?—taste (that is not the word) but I can't help admiring her noble bravery, and respecting—while I don't personally *like* her."[50]

47. Howitt, *Autobiography*, 2:78–81.
48. Betham-Edwards, *Mid-Victorian Memoirs*, pp. 74–76.
49. George Eliot, *The George Eliot Letters*, ed. Gordon Sherman Haight, 7 vols. (New Haven: Yale University Press, 1954–55), 2:45.
50. Elizabeth Cleghorn Gaskell, *The Letters of Mrs. Gaskell*, ed. J. A. V. Chapple and Arthur Pollard (Cambridge: Harvard University Press, 1966), pp. 606–07.

It is difficult to assess the impact of illegitimacy on Benjamin Smith's children, since they avoided mentioning the subject. Only after her marriage to Eugene Bodichon did Barbara Smith make an allusion to her birth, writing proudly to her aunt Julia that her husband wished only to meet those relatives who had acknowledged the Smiths as children: "When we were in London he said he would rather go to see you and Mr. Gratton than any of the relations who only knew us lately . . . he says he feels the relations who were good to us as children are the only relations to be treated as relations."[51] But despite these few exceptions, the family was not as widely shunned as one might expect given the strictness of Victorian social conventions, and they apparently experienced few barriers to their movement in respectable society as a result of their birth. Elizabeth Gaskell may have been correct in her assumption that illegitimacy was the basis of Barbara Smith's unconventional habits and ideas. It appears quite as likely, however, that the enlightened social and religious attitudes evident in William's and Benjamin's households molded family behavior. The Unitarian heritage cannot be underestimated as an influence on the Smith children. Although Barbara Smith and her brothers and sisters left the Unitarian church, drifting through intermarriage and broadening social connections into nominal acceptance of the Church of England, their courageous indifference to contemporary opinion was rooted in part in the Unitarian philosophy of their grandfather William Smith. For him faith had led politically to an aggressive Whiggism and strong stands on all issues of civil and religious disability. Morally it had determined his outspoken espousal of all just causes and his refusal to entertain the concept of expediency. The Unitarian insistence on a rational search for truth, necessitating freedom of thought and toleration, was passed from William to Barbara Smith, spiced by the touch of eccentricity that leavened Benjamin Smith's expansive nature.

There was certainly nothing orthodox about Benjamin Smith's eldest daughter. Barbara Smith dressed unconventionally, silenced any opposition with an indelicate "bosh!" and drove off visitors, if

51. Barbara Bodichon to Julia Smith, 3–5 June 1858, in Barbara Bodichon, *An American Diary, 1857–1858*, ed. Joseph W. Reed, Jr. (London: Routledge & Kegan Paul, 1972), p. 156.

she found them inconvenient, with "Devastators of the day, away, away!"[52] Writing to his sister Christina, Dante Gabriel Rossetti extolled the vitality and audacity of his new friend: "Ah if you were only like Miss Barbara Smith! a young lady I meet at the Howitts, blessed with large rations of tin, fat, enthusiasm, and golden hair, who thinks nothing of climbing up a mountain in breeches, or wading through a stream in none, in the sacred name of pigment. Last night she invited us all to lunch with her on Sunday, and perhaps I shall go, as she is quite a *jolly fellow.* "[53]

The young woman whom Rossetti found such an invigorating companion was as intense about ideas and causes as about her art. At the age of seventeen she began to keep a notebook in which she reflected on the books she read. The reflections are extraordinary, not merely because they are those of a very young woman, but because they indicate that Benjamin Smith's daughters were reading widely in materials quite different from the novels or religious tracts considered appropriate fare for the average Victorian daughter. Very few girls were actively encouraged to read widely and to discuss and write about the ideas they encountered. Elizabeth Barrett Browning recalled with some humor the restrictions placed on her in regard to her father's library and her evasions of the spirit, if not the letter, of paternal law:

> Papa used to say . . . "Don't read Gibbon's *History*—it's not a proper book. Don't read *Tom Jones* and none of the books on this side, mind!" So I was very obedient and never touched the books on *that* side, and only read instead Tom Paine's *Age of Reason,* and Voltaire's *Philosophical Dictionary,* and Hume's *Essays,* and Werther and Rousseau, and Mary Wollstonecraft . . . books which I was never suspected of looking towards, and which were not "on that side" certainly, but which did as well.[54]

52. Bradbrook, *Barbara Bodichon, George Eliot,* p. 4.

53. Dante Gabriel Rossetti to Christina Rossetti, 8 November 1855, in *Letters of Dante Gabriel Rossetti,* ed. Oswald Doughty and J. R. Wahl, 4 vols. (Oxford: Clarendon Press, 1965–67), 1:162–63.

54. Elizabeth Barrett Browning, cited in Percy Lubbock, *Elizabeth Barrett Browning in Her Letters* (London: Smith & Elder, 1906), p. 9.

Barrett never openly defied her father's dictum and so avoided further censorship of her reading. But Barbara Smith had no restrictions placed upon her reading. Having completed George Combe's *Moral Philosophy*, she concluded that "gaining knowledge is a moral duty," that "it is absurd to think that there is sufficient in the Bible to regulate our actions without using those powers of reason which God has given us," and asserted, "I agree with my whole soul in the positive belief of progression towards improvement and the ultimate perfection of man."[55] Smith continued to keep a journal marking the progress of her thought for a number of years.

Barbara Smith's first assertion of the inequities of laws concerning women is found in the pages of her journal. In 1849, at the age of twenty-two, she read John Stuart Mill's *Political Economy* and expressed her fervent hope that he would take up the issue of women's rights. She analyzed and reviewed the work, regretting that Mill had only briefly alluded to marriage and the laws affecting women:

> As far as he has let one see his views he thinks nobly rightly and liberally. And I wish with my whole soul that one who carries so much weight would put these things before men and I do not doubt that they would see the injustice of their laws to women and the absurdity of the present Laws of Marriage and Divorce. Philosophers and Reformers have generally been afraid to say anything about the unjust laws both of society and country which crush women. There never was a tyranny so deeply felt yet borne so silently, that is the worst of it.[56]

The woman question was not merely an issue for Barbara Smith's journal. Her aunt Julia Smith brought her directly in contact with the early movement for the improvement of education for middle-class women. In 1849 they enrolled in the new Bedford College for Women. Julia Smith was a friend of Harriet Martineau and of another Unitarian, the wealthy widow Elizabeth Jesser Reid. Mary

55. Barbara Leigh Smith, MS Abstract of Combe's *Moral Philosophy*, 184?, from her notebooks in Girton College Archives, Cambridge, England.
56. Barbara Leigh Smith, MS Abstract of Mill's *Political Economy*, January 1849, from her notebooks in Girton College Archives, Cambridge, England.

Mohl, another prominent woman in their circle, said of Reid that she would "push on womankind when womankind is unpushable."[57] Reid's father, William Sturch, an ironmonger in London, was an original member of the Unitarian chapel opened by Theophilus Lindsey at Strand in 1774. Sturch was a frequent contributor to the Unitarian journal, the *Monthly Repository*. Julia Smith was also interested in discrimination against women, so that when Reid established a college for women in 1849, Smith was appointed a member of its council. The journalist Henry Crabb Robinson met Smith when he visited Reid. He found her charming and "the most generous member of William Smith's large family," and although he thought "she and Mrs. Reid carry radicalism to a romantic excess," he felt "their moral worth more than outweighs a little extravagance in matters of opinion."[58] Barbara Smith, Elizabeth Reid, Mary Mohl, and Anna Jameson formed an intimate circle which revolved around Harriet Martineau. They spent their time engrossed in discussions of Martineau's ill health and social reform. Advocates of improved status for women, they were frequent visitors to the Smith home during Barbara Smith's youth and sponsored her early feminist activities. In 1849 they were instrumental in giving Bedford College its character.

Bedford contrasted sharply with Queen's college, founded only one year earlier in 1848. Queen's was founded to train teachers and grant them certificates of proficiency, an idea pioneered by the Governesses' Benevolent Institution in connection with a free registry service at its home for unemployed governesses. A Church of England institution, Queen's maintained close ties with the Anglican King's College, many of whose professors taught at Queen's. Bedford, in contrast, was without denominational bias. The college was created by Reid in connection with the nonsectarian University College, and women and men shared equally in its management. The curriculum included traditionally "masculine" studies as

57. *Letters of Julius and Mary Clarke Mohl*, ed. M. Simpson (London: Kegan, Paul & Trench, 1887), p. 162.
58. Margaret J. Tuke, *A History of Bedford College for Women, 1849–1937* (London: Oxford University Press, 1939), pp. 43–44.

well as the usual "feminine" subjects. Classes were taught by professors from University College. Like Queen's, Bedford took students from age twelve on. Students who followed the regular four-year course and passed the required examinations received certificates of general proficiency, while those who entered for individual courses of lectures obtained certificates in single subjects.

Barbara Smith attended lectures at Bedford, concentrating on art classes and devoting most of her time there to the drawing studio under the direction of Professor Francis S. Cary. Smith was a talented painter from childhood and later became well known for her watercolors. Bedford provided the first opportunity for women to obtain formal artistic training, including life classes. Julia Smith was active on the college's council during its first year, and she continued to serve the institution for some time as a lady visitor. Since in 1850 it was unthinkable for a young woman to attend a lecture given by a male professor unchaperoned, lady visitors, either married women or single women of advanced years, volunteered to be present at all college lectures.[59]

The founding of Bedford and Queen's Colleges represented a formal recognition of the inadequacy of education for middle-class women. In 1841 the Governesses' Benevolent Association was formed to assist private governesses in temporary financial difficulty. It soon became apparent that most applicants to the Association's employment register were unfit for their work. A diploma was proposed to certify competence, to be granted upon completion of an examination. Queen's and Bedford were founded to provide the rudimentary education necessary for middle-class women who wished to become governesses. These were the first systematic attempts to deal with the inadequacy of female secondary education. The constitution of Queen's stipulated that it was to be run entirely by men, whereas Bedford sought to involve women as equals in the management of their own educational institution. Bedford's step is of great significance, since female participation of this nature was

59. Ibid., p. 46.

unheard of at that time. Bedford's nondenominational character was also exceptional and aroused public suspicion and disapproval.

Barbara Smith's association with Bedford helped structure her later educational efforts at Girton College, Cambridge and brought her into contact with many of the women instrumental in the feminist campaigns of the next twenty-five years. Her association with the institution was brief, however. She did not pursue an organized course of study, but chose instead to take instruction in art and leave the completion of her education to life itself. The tendency to embrace a project briefly, albeit intensely, repeated itself throughout her life. Even at this early date we can begin to discern the glorious amateur, who shared with many in her upper-middle-class world insatiable curiosity, opinions on everything, and confidence in their ability to improve the human condition. Smith understood her own character quite well, realized her need for constantly changing experiences, and described her restless energy in a letter to her mother's sister, Dorothy Longden, before her marriage:

> I am one of the cracked people of the world, and I like to herd with the cracked such as A.M.H. [Anna Mary Howitt] and B.R.P. [Bessie Rayner Parkes], queer Americans, democrats, socialists, artists, poor devils or angels; and am never happy in an English genteel family life. I try to do it like other people but I long always to be off on some wild adventure, or long to lecture on a tub in St. Giles, or go to see the Mormons, or ride off into the interior on horseback alone and leave the world for a month. . . . I want to see what sort of world this God's world is.[60]

There is no question that financial independence allowed her the luxury of liberty and eccentricity. In 1848, when she attained her majority, her father settled £300 a year on her. By the time he died in 1860 this income had increased to £1000 a year. Some friends

---

60. Barbara Smith to Dorothy Longden, 1857, Bonham-Carter Family Papers, Hampshire Record Office, Winchester, England.

felt his unusual gesture would prove the ruin of his headstrong daughter.

Young women in the Victorian period were the responsibility of fathers, husbands, or brothers. The daughters in a middle-class household were not expected to pursue any goal other than marriage, nor to make any decision without the guidance of supporting males. Emily Shirreff noted the dependence of single women in her book on female education, published in 1858:

> It is common to see young women, and women no longer young, kept dependent in every movement, with a moderate allowance for dress from which not unfrequently they hardly dare to economize for any other object. They are without the power of making a journey, of asking a friend to stay with them—of making acquaintances—of engaging in any undertaking unless it is to cost nothing beyond their own trouble, and to square exactly with the most trifling arrangements of the rest of the family—without even a quiet room of their own in which they may if they choose enjoy solitude and their own pursuits.[61]

By giving his daughter financial independence Benjamin Smith was giving her a freedom of action not considered appropriate to "woman's sphere." For Victorians that sphere was rigidly defined and clearly stated in a multitude of manuals written for female edification and improvement. In *The Daughters of England*, one of a series of such books, the attitude proper for a woman is clearly outlined:

> I must now take it for granted that the youthful reader of these pages has reflected seriously upon her position in society as a woman, has acknowledged her inferiority to man, has examined her own nature, and found there a capability of feeling, a quickness of perception, and a facility of adaptation, beyond what he possesses, and which, consequently, fit her for a distinct and separate sphere.[62]

61. Emily Anne Eliza Shirreff, *Intellectual Education and Its Influence on the Character and Happiness of Women* (London: John W. Parker & Son, 1858), p. 409.

62. Sarah Stickney Ellis, *The Daughters of England* (London: Fisher, Son, 1842), pp. 6–7.

The feminine role thus clearly delineated made independence of thought or finance unnecessary and unthinkable. Some women in wealthy radical circles were independent-minded and quite unlike the pious angel portrayed so widely in Victorian literature.[63] Benjamin Smith's action was nevertheless unusual. It was meant in part to insure that her illegitimate birth did not deprive Barbara Smith of her rights in his fortune, but, more importantly, this gesture, which he repeated as each of his daughters came of age, demonstrated more concretely than any other might have done that he considered his twenty-one-year-old daughters responsible adults, with the same capacity for mature independent judgment and action which society accepted without question in young men.

A wealthy single woman at age twenty-one, Barbara Smith found herself in 1848 with unlimited vistas for action. Before we analyze her feminist efforts we must take time to understand women's status in England in the middle of the nineteenth century. Only then can we explore the feminist movement of the third quarter of the nineteenth century and Smith's role in it.

63. An excellent discussion of the validity of the stereotype "Victorian angel" is found in M. Jeanne Peterson's "No Angels in the House," *American Historical Review* 89 (1984): 677–708.

II

VICTORIAN FEMINISM:
A HISTORICAL PERSPECTIVE

The status of women in England in 1850 is not simply defined. Victorian women led lives that varied widely depending on their class, marital status, and occupation. To understand woman's status in general we must determine the legal and social restraints operating in common on a variety of groups including political hostesses, literary ladies, mothers, chain-makers, and factory hands, as well as ladies of the theater and ladies of the evening.

A woman in England could hold the highest office in the land, and as queen could exercise the same rights and powers as a king. A woman could be a peeress in her own right, and though not permitted to speak or vote in Parliament, she was entitled to be tried as a peer. Women were excluded from the electorate. During the feudal period, women were denied the franchise by custom, and the Reform Act of 1832, by the insertion of the words "male person," gave statutory sanction to the disfranchisement of women. The Municipal Reform Act of 1835 placed a similar disability upon women. Yet, although women were forbidden a parliamentary or municipal vote, they were not excluded from voting for members of the East India Company. This peculiar circumstance resulted because the East India Company was organized as a commercial venture, entitling its shareholders, regardless of sex, to a voice in its constitution and thus to a voice in the government of a large empire. In local government, women possessed of the necessary property qualifications could vote in vestry and for the guardians of the poor. A woman might serve as sexton, churchwarden, or overseer of the poor. This was not an anomaly, but merely reflected the low esteem in which such offices were held. In one case in which a woman was granted the right to serve as sexton the view was clearly stated: "This is a servile ministerial office which requires neither skill nor understanding . . . but this cannot determine that woman may vote for members of Parliament as that choice requires an improved understanding."[1] No woman could serve on a commission of the peace nor as an ordinary juror, except in rare cases regarding the pregnancy of a prisoner.

Women did participate actively in the anti–Corn Law campaign. The Anti–Corn Law Circular of 1841 congratulated the women of Manchester, who "have set a noble example to their sisters throughout the country. They have already obtained more than 50,000 signatures to the memorial adopted at the Corn Exchange."[2] Even this modest extraparliamentary activity was undertaken with hesitation and concern that contact with the world outside the home might damage delicate feminine natures. In 1853, Archibald Prentice, chronicler of the Anti–Corn Law League, felt the need to justify female participation in the campaign as consonant with woman's proper sphere in private and domestic life. Women's participation in these public events, claimed Prentice, was appropriate because it stemmed from a feminine concern for starving millions. "The ladies rendered effectual service to a cause endeared to them by the full confidence that it was the cause of humanity and justice . . . I offer no apology for the course they took, for I never had the least doubt of its perfect consistency with the softer characteristics of female virtue."[3] Women had also been associated with the Chartist movement, a large number of women's political associations having formed to forward the Charter. Similar associations had developed earlier, during the Reform Bill campaign, but they were sporadic and short-lived. By 1842 all such or-

1. Erna Reiss, *Rights and Duties of Englishwomen: A Study in Law and Public Opinion* (Manchester: Sherratt & Hughes, 1934), p. 41.

2. Ibid., p. 188.

3. Archibald Prentice, *History of the Anti–Corn Law League*, 2 vols. (London: W. & F. G. Cash, 1853; reprint, New York: Augustus M. Kelley, 1968), 1:170.

ganizations had disappeared. Clearly, in 1850 women's public activities were severely restricted, their responsibilities defined solely
in terms of domestic functions.

The middle-class woman provided the symbol of Victorian respectability, the figure around whom the most important of Victorian institutions, the family, was built. She stood in the status scale
above the army of working women, ranging from the girls in the
cotton mill to the genteel governess in her quiet school room. With
the industrial and technological changes of the nineteenth century,
the conditions of life for all women changed a great deal. If the Industrial Revolution brought working-class women into the factory,
it also helped to solidify the middle-class ideal of the idle woman.
"A lady to be such, must be a lady and nothing else," wrote Margar-
etta Greg in her diary in 1853. "She must not work for profit, or en-
gage in any occupation that money can command, lest she invade
the rights of the working classes, who live by their labour."[4] The
enormous increase in domestic servants during this period was a
concrete result of the idealization of the totally leisured middle-
class woman. Idleness represented entry into the gentry. Greg's
comment characterizes the goal of middle-class men as well as
women. To work for profit was to soil one's hands, figuratively if
not literally, and a gentleman or gentlewoman never worked for a
living. The idle woman, placed upon a pedestal by her male protec-
tor, served to enhance his status, to demonstrate his success and
ability to provide for her.

The practice of female idleness spread through the middle class,
until work for women became a sign of misfortune and disgrace.
This is not to suggest that the management of large households did
not provide responsible and challenging occupation for many Victorian women. However, the ideal middle-class woman was a stan-
dardized product, whose only suitable objective was courtship, marriage, and motherhood.[5] Physiological arguments were used to

4. Josephine Elizabeth Butler, ed., *Memoir of John Greg* (Edinburgh: Edmonston & Doug-
las, 1869), pp. 326–27.
5. Wanda Fraiken Neff, *Victorian Working Women* (New York: Columbia University
Press, 1929), pp. 186–87.

sustain the image of women as childlike creatures requiring the shelter of male support. Men were portrayed as protectors by virtue of superior muscular and intellectual power. They were considered the natural governors. Women, seen as feeble and timid, were constitutionally ordained to obey. Physiology dictated woman's maternal role and excluded her from legislative or philosophic pursuits.[6]

Since marriage was the only socially acceptable occupation open to middle-class women, their early lives were organized for the achievement of that end. "Women don't consider themselves as human beings at all," wrote Florence Nightingale in a note indicting family life in 1851. "There is absolutely no God, no country, no duty to them at all except family."[7] The marriage market was highly competitive and young girls were trained for it like race horses. It was not the job of a girl to be clever, but rather to have accomplishments; a little music, dancing, sketching, needlepoint, perhaps a smattering of French or Italian. "If you happen to have any learning," advised Dr. Gregory in his *Legacy of a Father to His Daughter*, which was reprinted eight times between 1793 and 1838, "keep it a profound secret, especially from men, who generally look with a jealous and malignant eye on a woman of great parts and a cultivated understanding."[8] Thackeray, in *The Newcomes*, speaks of woman as "well-broke." In *Middlemarch*, George Eliot wrote, "A woman dictates before marriage in order that she may have an appetite for submission afterward."[9]

The limited capacities of women and the possibility of offending men by unfeminine displays of independence were ideas emphasized in the many manuals describing proper behavior for women published throughout the period. Mrs. John Sandford's *Woman in Her Social and Domestic Character*, first published in 1831, ran through four editions in three years and held an honored place in many middle-class family libraries for the next quarter century. It put

---

6. Alexander Walker, *Woman Physiologically Considered as to Mind, Morals, Marriage, Matrimonial Slavery, Infidelity and Divorce*, 2d. ed. (London: A. H. Baily, 1840), p. 129.

7. Woodham-Smith, *Florence Nightingale*, p. 93.

8. Reiss, *Rights and Duties of Englishwomen*, p. 42.

9. George Eliot, *Middlemarch* (Boston: Houghton Mifflin, 1956), bk. 1, chap. 9.

women clearly in their place in the great chain of being: They had been assigned a subordinate role by nature and were advised to accept the inevitable in order to insure domestic tranquility. Independence was a sign of indelicacy and sensible women would be quick to realize that weakness was an attraction, not a flaw.[10] In an 1841 edition of *The Women of England: Their Social Duties and Domestic Habits,* Sarah Stickney Ellis cautioned gifted women against exhibiting their talents. Women's happiness depended on husbands remaining convinced of their own superiority. Ellis warned that women exercising their intellects risked permanent destruction of marital happiness. Even the sovereign had moments of doubt about her dual role. "I am every day more convinced," she wrote to her uncle Leopold in 1852, "that we women if we are to be good women, feminine and amiable and domestic, are not fitted to reign."[11]

The fact was that upper- and middle-class women saw their lives in terms of the men who supported them, whether father, husband, or brother. Even an impassioned appeal against the boredom and frustration of idleness such as that contained in Charlotte Bronte's *Shirley,* written in 1849, is directed at men. Bronte believed that action would be taken only if men were convinced of the necessity for change. She therefore made no attempt to inspire women to help themselves:

> Men of England! Look at your poor girls, many of them fading around you, dropping off in consumption or decline; or, what is worse, degenerating to sour old maids, anxious, backbiting, wretched, because life is a desert to them: or, what is worst of all, reduced to strive, by scarce modest coquetry and debasing artifice, to gain that position and consideration by marriage, which to celibacy is denied. Fathers! cannot you alter these things? Perhaps not all at once; but consider the matter well

10. Aina Rubenius, *The Woman Question in Mrs. Gaskell's Life and Works* (Cambridge: Harvard University Press, 1950), pp. 2–3.

11. Arthur Christopher Benson, ed. *Letters of Queen Victoria, 1837–1861,* 3 vols. (London: Murray, 1907), 2:444.

when it is brought before you, receive it as a theme worthy of
thought; do not dismiss it with an idle jest or an unmanly
insult.[12]

Idleness was an increasing source of dissatisfaction for middle-
class women at mid-century. Their individual protests increased
and stimulated the organization of the women's movement during
the mid-Victorian period. In 1850, however, a girl could rise to a
higher rank only through marriage. Marriage gave a woman a viable
social position, a household of her own to preside over. The preservation of the family was woman's proper sphere, the sanctity of the
home her only legitimate concern. The ideal woman was a guardian
angel, who purified the home so that men might find peace and es-
cape there from the realities of the outside world. Ruskin described
woman's talent as one for "sweet ordering." She was protected from
the hardening process which inevitably sullied men because she did
not venture outside the domestic sphere. Woman's contribution to
society rested in her ability to create a peaceful shelter for the family. "Her great function is Praise: she enters into no contest."[13]

The angelic creature who inhabited Ruskin's "vestal temple," the
home, was prepared for no other function. Since the social organization was built on the assumption that marriage was a woman's
only goal, it made no provision for the single propertyless gentlewoman. There were a number of single women and widows of
means who enjoyed a great deal of independence, but they made up
only a very small minority. Single women generally found themselves in a dependent position in the household of a father or a
brother. Unless their fathers were able to leave them a competence,
the position of these women was pitiable. The only respectable occupational alternatives to marriage for genteel women were authorship or governessing. Jane Austen, with superb wry sarcasm, had
earlier put the case for marriage quite plainly, when she gave Charlotte Lucas's reasons for accepting Mr. Collins: "Marriage had always been her object, it was the only honourable provision for well-

12. Charlotte Bronte, *Shirley* (Harmondsworth, Eng.: Penguin Books, 1974), chap. 22.
13. John Ruskin, *Sesame and Lilies* (Boston: Colonial Press, n.d.), pp. 86–87.

educated young women of small fortune and however uncertain of giving happiness, must be their pleasantest preservative from want."[14] Emily Shirreff restated the point in 1858, when she attempted to expose the need for an improved educational program for middle-class girls. She deplored the system which, because it usually left single women ill-provided for, appeared designed to make them accept any match as preferable to spinsterhood.[15]

The difficulty was that by 1850, the middle-class girl, whose only training was for marriage, faced the probability of "redundancy." Extra women were a serious problem, despite the insistence of prestigious journals that the dilemma of unmarried women was their own fault. The *Saturday Review* stated, "Married life is a woman's profession; and to this life her training—that of dependence—is modelled. Of course by not getting a husband, or by losing him she may find that she is without resources. All that can be said of her is, she has failed in business, and no social reform can prevent such failures."[16]

When W. R. Greg wrote "Why Are Women Redundant?" in 1862, he was dealing with a problem that had concerned the middle classes for many years. In *Shirley* Charlotte Bronte had condemned society for refusing to face the increasing problems of excess women. She asserted that people preferred not to be reminded of their social obligations. "Old maids, like the houseless and unemployed poor, should not ask for a place and an occupation in the world: the demand disturbs the happy and rich: it disturbs parents."[17] But by mid-century the problem was of such proportions that the middle classes could no longer ignore it. There were too many women in England and the excess had to be dealt with. Greg noted the seriousness of this problem in the upper classes. Hundreds of thousands of unmarried women were attempting to earn their own livings. A high proportion of these redundant females were

14. Jane Austen, *Pride and Prejudice* (London: J. M. Dent & Sons, 1906), chap. 22.
15. Shirreff, *Intellectual Education*, p. 410.
16. "Queen Bees or Working Bees," *Saturday Review*, 21 February 1857, p. 172.
17. Bronte, *Shirley*, chap. 22.

scattered throughout the middle and upper levels of society and had little or no chance of finding gainful employment.[18] Many shared Greg's concern that the growing excess of single women was greater in the middle classes than in the working classes, where women were already a part of the industrial workforce.

The Napoleonic wars could be held responsible for only a small part of the disproportion between the sexes. The Empire's need for an ever-growing number of men in the Civil Service was a far more disrupting factor. Canada, Australia, Tasmania, and New Zealand attracted adventurous young men of the middle classes, as well as the criminal and destitute, who were forced to leave England. For many women, discouraged from emigration by the hardship of life in the colonies, this drain on the supply of marriageable men combined with other trends to leave them husbandless.[19] Census figures in 1851 showed that of women between the ages of 25 and 34, out of every 1,000, 329 were single, 643 married, and 28 widowed; of women of all ages (including children too young to be married), out of every 1,000, 598 were single, 330 married, and 72 widowed. An even more interesting figure is that for male marital status. In 1851 of men between the ages of 25 and 34, out of every 1,000, 356 were single, 627 married and 17 widowers; of men between 35 and 44, out of every 1,000, 162 were single, 795 married and 43 widowers; of men of all ages, out of every 1,000, 625 were single, 337 married and 38 widowers.[20] In 1851, there were 365,159 more women than men in England.

Not only were there fewer men, the men that there were often remained bachelors. The expense of maintaining a wife and family discouraged men even of the upper classes from marrying until quite late, if at all. A survey in 1874 reported that the average age of marriage between 1840 and 1870 was 29.93 years for the clergymen, doctors, lawyers, members of the aristocracy, merchants, bankers,

18. W. R. Greg, "Why Are Women Redundant?" *National Review* 14 (April 1862): 186.
19. Neff, *Victorian Working Women*, p. 12.
20. B. R. Mitchell, ed., *Abstract of British Historical Statistics* (Cambridge: Cambridge University Press, 1962), pp. 15–16, 12.

manufacturers and "gentlemen" queried.[21] This meant that many middle-class women could look forward to lengthy periods of court-ship or, in many cases, spinsterhood. A contemporary commenta-tor, politician and educational reformer Sir Thomas Dyke Ackland of Oxford University, condemned the postponement of marriage in the *Western Times* of October 1863. He attributed the practice to foolish ideas about the fashionable requirements of a middle-class establishment and reiterated the assertion that unless the trend ended great numbers of women would be condemned to impover-ished single lives.[22]

Middle-class women, completely unequipped for self-support yet facing that necessity in increasing numbers, could no longer be ig-nored. They began to demand opportunities for employment, "an open field with a fair day's wages for a fair day's work."[23] The bore-dom of idleness was now a real economic problem and many women faced a desperate, albeit genteel, poverty. Daughters of professional men with incomes between £500 and £1,000 realized the burden their support represented. The longer they remained at home un-able to contribute to their own upkeep, the greater the financial difficulties of the family. If they did not marry, they could only con-template the eventual necessity of earning a living.[24]

The fact that governessing offered the only occupational alterna-tive for most of these women made the issue one of increasing con-cern for the middle and upper classes. Governesses' earnings were meager, positions were few, and they faced the probability of an old age of dependency on relatives, friends, or in many cases the work-house. In 1841 the Governesses' Benevolent Institution was founded to relieve the poverty of these women with small sums of

21. Charles Ansell, *On the Rate of Mortality, the Age at Marriage, the Number of Children to a Marriage, the Length of a Generation, and Other Statistics of Families in the Upper and Professional Classes* (London: National Life Assurance Society, 1874), p. 4.

22. Rita McWilliams-Tullberg, *Women at Cambridge, A Men's University—Though of a Mixed Type* (London: Victor Gollancz, 1975), p. 21.

23. D. M. Craik, "A Woman's Thoughts about Women: Female Handicrafts," *Chambers's Journal* 28 (July 1857): 24.

24. Miss Downing, "Work as a Necessity for Women," *Victoria Magazine* 18 (January 1872): 221.

money, annuities where necessary, and both an asylum for elderly governesses and a home for unemployed ones.[25] Because the governess was a familiar figure in middle and upper-class homes, and because most families had a relative or friend in that unenviable position, their difficulties led to concrete action. Indeed, the recognition of the economic plight of the redundant middle-class woman was seen by some early feminists as the most important stimulus for the organization of a women's movement after 1850. In 1866 Bessie Rayner Parkes wrote that, despite individual demands for reform of women's legal and social status, little would have been accomplished without the compelling pressure of economic necessity. The financial distress of the redundant woman made the women's movement a subject of public interest and elicited popular support for reform efforts.[26]

If the Industrial Revolution solidified the image of the idle middle-class woman, it brought working-class women out of their homes and into the mills and factories, as well as into domestic service. The Census of 1841 provided the first collection of occupational data for women and although the information is not completely accurate, it does show that the majority of women were working in five categories: as domestic servants, needlewomen, and factory, agricultural, and domestic industry workers. The factory workers had the shortest hours and the best rates of pay. In other occupations low wages and bad conditions were the inevitable result of an overstocked labor pool.[27] By 1859 Harriet Martineau could report: "Out of 6 millions of women above 20 years of age in Great Britain . . . no less than half are industrial in their mode of life. More than a third, more than two millions, are independent in their industry, are self-supporting like men."[28]

The fact that working-class women acquired economic indepen-

25. Bessie Rayner Parkes, *Essays on Woman's Work*, 2d ed. (London: Alexander Strahan, 1866), pp. 91–93.

26. Ibid., pp. 54–55.

27. Ivy Pinchbeck, *Women Workers and the Industrial Revolution, 1750–1850* (New York: F. S. Crofts, 1930), p. 315.

28. Harriet Martineau, "Female Industry," *Edinburgh Review* (American ed.) 109 (April 1859): 172.

dence because of the Industrial Revolution cannot be overemphasized. It should be noted that the employment of married and single
women long predated the Industrial Revolution and there is little
evidence that industrialization brought a decline and fall for working-class women from a "golden age" in which they did only "suitable" work in the bosom of the family.[29] In the case of single working women the gain in social and economic independence was
striking. In domestic industries like spinning, lace-making, and
weaving, family wages had prevailed and women had had little or
no opportunity to handle their own earnings. Their rates of pay
were low since women's wages were considered supplementary. But
once women who worked outside the home received their own
wages, and in many cases her control over her own wages meant a
girl could leave home at an early age to become "her own mistress."
In 1833 testimony before the Factory Commission revealed that
factory girls usually insisted on their independence at about sixteen
years of age, and by 1840 it was reported that jobs in manufacturing
tended to raise the condition of women by providing independent
earnings for them.[30] Heads of families were often resentful of the
change in method of payment, but single working-class women
were able to claim an economic and socially independent identity.
Contemporaries disagreed about the effects of factory and workshop
on women. Many shared the view expressed in W. E. Hickson's
"Report to the Handloom Weavers Commission." He approved of
the individual wage which provided an opportunity for single young
women to save as much as £100 between the ages of sixteen and
twenty-five. This accumulated capital, he claimed, would enable
them to set up housekeeping when they married.[31] Others, how-

29. Eric Richards, "Women in the British Economy since about 700: An Interpretation,"
History 59 (October 1974): 342. An important discussion of the positive aspects of the eco-
nomic role of women during the Industrial Revolution is contained in Neil McKendrick,
"Home Demand and Economic Growth: A New View of the Role of Women and Children in
the Industrial Revolution," in *Historical Perspectives: Studies in English Thought and Society in
Honour of J. H. Plumb* Neil McKendrick, ed. (London: Europa, 1974), pp. 152–210.

30. Pinchbeck, *Women Workers*, p. 313.

31. W. E. Hickson, "Report to the Handloom Weavers Commission," *Parliamentary Papers*, 649 (1840), p. 44.

ever, were certain that young women would squander the money. They considered the individual wage an evil development, since "each child ceases to view itself as a subordinate agent in the household."[32] It should be remembered that despite the heat of these opposing views, only a few working women held factory jobs.

The increase in domestic service was extraordinary. By mid-century every family that could afford a domestic servant had one, since no claim to true gentility could be substantiated without the preliminary qualification of servantry in the home. Domestic service employed by far the largest number of working women in the mid-Victorian period, and its steady rise was a clear reflection of the increase in the middle class which supported it.[33] The working-class woman in domestic service was a natural complement to the idle woman the middle class had enshrined. Despite the fact that by mid-century working-class women were withdrawing from agricultural labor in substantial numbers, it can be said that their essential work expectations changed very little throughout the mid-Victorian period. It was true in 1850 and remained true for the next twenty-five years that women for whom employment was a necessity made up a large reservoir of cheap labor which was required for a limited variety of employments and was absolutely without organization or bargaining power. Very few working-class women had any choice but to take any means of earning a living offered them.[34]

The bulk of working-class women could neither read nor write. The Return of Marriage Registers for 1851 shows that in that year, out of 154,000 women married in England, nearly 70,000 signed their names with marks.[35] Married women of the working classes were in a somewhat different position from their single counterparts. Long before the factory replaced the home as the center of in-

32. P. Gaskell, *The Manufacturing Population of England* (London: Baldwin & Cradock, 1833), p. 93.
33. Geoffrey Best, *Mid-Victorian Britain, 1851–1875* (London: Weidenfield & Nicolson, 1971), p. 87.
34. Ibid., pp. 109–10.
35. Janet Dunbar, *The Early Victorian Woman* (London: George Harrap, 1953), p. 143.

dustry, married women had served as assistants to their husbands or had worked independently in domestic industries or as day laborers in the fields. Those that assisted their husbands received no wages. Like their single counterparts, when they worked on their own their wages were extremely low, since they were presumed to be supplementary. Not until the home ceased to be the center of activity did the married woman worker become an object of concern. Engels asserted that "when women work in factories, the most important result is the dissolution of family ties."[36] Recent studies have shown that with industrialization women had increasing difficulty in combining their productive and reproductive roles.[37]

Married women who became wage earners outside the home encountered new problems. Their earnings never balanced the loss of the family's domestic center. Children were no longer in the care of mothers, but were farmed out, often badly fed and dosed with laudanum to keep them quiet. The women's low wages evaporated on ready-made foods and other items necessary to women no longer able to cook and care for their own homes. The family suffered, but because of her peculiar legal status the married woman worker suffered even more. Married women working outside the home earned individual wages, but their marital status deprived them of the right to their earnings. The married woman of the working class became an object of concern only when numerous cases came to the public attention in which a drunken husband demanded and squandered the wages that his wife had hoped would keep her children from starvation. By 1859 Harriet Martineau could write about several cases brought before the new Divorce Court and the police magistrates which illustrated the problems of working wives. In every instance the women came seeking legal protection for the earnings by which they supported their households.[38] Publicity led people to question the dual system of law, which left married factory women

36. Harold Perkin, *The Origins of Modern English Society, 1780–1880* (London: Routledge & Kegan Paul, 1969), p. 149.

37. Louise Tilly and Joan W. Scott, *Women, Work and Family* (New York: Holt, Rinehart & Winston, 1978), pp. 144–45. Additionally, disturbances in the family as a result of industrialization are analyzed by Neil J. Smelser in *Social Change in the Industrial Revolution* (Chicago: University of Chicago Press, 1959).

38. Martineau, "Female Industry," p. 172.

without protection for their wages.[39] The problem would not have aroused public attention, however, had it been confined to women of the working classes. The question of married women's wages was only one facet of the married woman's property issue which stirred the middle classes in the fifties.

The legal status of the married woman or *feme covert* differed substantially from that of her unmarried sister, the *feme sole*. If marriage represented safe haven and social status, it also brought with it an amazing set of disabilities. Outside the family married women had the same legal status as children and lunatics; within it they were their husbands' inferiors.

Married women had not laways been in this situation. In Anglo-Saxon times both wife and widow were well protected. To the Anglo-Saxons marriage was a roughly equal partnership, which could be broken by either wife or husband. A law created by King Aethelbert stated, "If a wife wish to depart with her children, she shall have half the goods."[40] The Norman conquest changed women's position. The feudal society of the next several hundred years was an essentially military one in which the superiority of men over women seemed natural. There seems to have been no legal basis for the idea of the perpetual guardianship of women, but the minor was in the guardianship of her father or lord and the wife in the guardianship of her husband. A woman generally passed from father or lord to husband long before she reached the age of twenty-one. Not until she became a widow was an heiress likely to be free from guardianship. The legal records of the period make constant use of phrases implying the absolute subjection of a wife to her husband. A wife could not plead in court without her husband, nor could she make a will without his consent. It was noted in 1202 that during her husband's lifetime a wife had nothing of her own—she could not even make a purchase with money she might be given.[41]

Law and custom put a wife in her husband's guardianship and

39. Margaret Hewitt, *Wives and Mothers in Victorian Industry* (London: Rockliff, 1958), pp. 3–5.

40. Doris Mary Stenton, *The English Woman in History* (London: George Allen & Unwin, 1957), p. 8.

41. Ibid., pp. 30–31.

gave her land, goods, and money to him. This situation prevailed until the late nineteenth century. Sir William Blackstone explained a wife's legal position in his *Commentaries on the Laws of England* (1765–69): "By marriage, the very being or legal existence of a woman is suspended, or at least it is incorporated and consolidated into that of the husband; under whose wing, protection and cover she performs everything; and she is therefore called in our law a 'feme covert.'"[42] Although Blackstone asserted that these measures were primarily for women's protection, "so great a favorite is the female sex of the laws of England,"[43] the fact was that the law put married women at a severe disadvantage. Put in simple terms, under the Common Law, a wife's property, earnings, liberty, and even her children all belonged to her husband. "My wife and I are one and I am he," was one way of expressing the effect of the law.[44] A wife could not sue, nor be sued. She could not be called as a witness. Her children could be taken from her. She could not free herself from her husband, no matter how cruelly she was treated. Until 1857, only a special act of Parliament could grant a divorce. Even after the Divorce and Matrimonial Causes Act of 1857, divorce remained a costly and difficult procedure, almost impossible for a woman to obtain.

A husband had the right under the law to his wife's obedience, to her society, and to her services. If she left him, a writ of habeas corpus directed against the person with whom she was living would force her to return.[45] Public opinion was slow to change. Although as early as 1852, in deciding one such case in favor of the wife, Lord Campbell declared that "a husband has no right at Common Law to the custody of his wife," it was not until the 1891 case of *R. v. Jackson* that it was declared illegal for a man to imprison his wife in his own house.[46] It was even accepted custom, at least among the

---

42. William Blackstone, *Commentaries on the Laws of England*, ed. George Chase, 4th ed. (New York: Banks Law Publishing, 1921), bk. 1., p. 154.

43. Ibid., p. 159.

44. Strachey, *The Cause*, p. 15.

45. Reiss, *Rights and Duties of Englishwomen*, p. 45.

46. Ibid., pp. 47–49.

poor, that in his house a husband could beat his wife as he pleased, so long as the stick with which he beat her was no thicker than his thumb.

In regard to property ownership the feme covert suffered grievously by comparison with the feme sole. The property rights of a feme sole were at Common Law identical with those of a man. She could dispose of her property either during her lifetime or by will. So long as she had some means of income, the single woman was in a gratifying independent position. "A single woman with a narrow income," insisted a gently sarcastic Jane Austen, in *Emma*, "must be a ridiculous old maid, the proper sport of boys and girls, but a single woman of good fortune is always respectable, and may be as sensible and pleasant as anybody else."[47] If a woman were betrothed to be married, however, her rights were immediately curtailed. The doctrine of the union of husband and wife resulted, as far as the Common Law was concerned, in making a gift of a woman's property to her betrothed, while it conveyed no corresponding gift of his property to her. Without the benefit of a marriage settlement and the protection of the Courts of Equity, a wife gave up all she possessed to her husband, even her own earnings. In return for her property, her husband was expected to give her maintenance and protection.

A married woman could own clothing and personal ornaments suitable to her position in society. These were her "paraphernalia," and she was not permitted to dispose of them, either during her life, or by will, without her husband's consent. An allowance, called "pin-money," was generally assigned a middle-class wife, so that she could keep up appearances consistent with her husband's dignity and social position. But her pin-money was not hers to dispose of and any sum she saved out of it was held to be her husband's and not hers. Pin-money and paraphernalia secured a mere nominal independence for middle class married women.[48]

Many women in 1850 cared little about their legal status and

---

47. Jane Austen, *Emma* (Boston: Houghton Mifflin, 1957), vol. 1, chap. 10.
48. Reiss, *Rights and Duties of Englishwomen*, pp. 20–22.

gave no thought to the abstract question of rights. Most echoed the
sentiments expressed by Margaret Oliphant in an article opposing
legislative reform. She considered "injured wives" accidents of nature whom no legal effort could eradicate. Legislation for the few
cases of marital discord seemed irrational to her and to a large portion of her reading public.[49] To the women of the middle and
working classes who had the misfortune to be married to a drunkard
or an extravagant man, the law in 1850 offered little consolation.
Custom and tradition offered powerful support to the legal status
quo and when John Stuart Mill, on the occasion of his marriage in
1851, repudiated the existing legal characteristics of the marital relationship, he was voicing an advanced and unpopular viewpoint.
He rejected the power that the marriage law conferred on the husband. He recorded a formal protest against the law and declared
that in their marriage he and Harriet Taylor intended to retain
complete individual freedom of thought and action.[50]

Marriage might present many difficulties under Common Law,
but for those with sufficient wealth there was an alternative. Legislative change was slow to come because a complex alternative legal
system had evolved to protect the property of the upper classes. The
Courts of Equity, which for some centuries had been trying to restrict the Common Law rights of the husband, had devised the marriage settlement. Equity was a system of law which had grown up
side by side with the Common Law, superseding or supplementing
it, and which was administered, not in the ordinary courts, but in
the Court of Chancery. By 1800 the Court of Chancery had been
successful for two centuries in arranging for upper-class married
women to hold property independent of their husbands and to exert
over this property the same rights which belonged to men or single
women. The aim of Chancery had not been to increase the rights of
married women, but to protect estates, primarily so that wealthy fathers could feel secure in settling property on daughters who might

49. Margaret Oliphant, "Laws Concerning Women," Blackwood's Edinburgh Magazine 79
(April 1856): 381.

50. Friedrich August von Hayek, ed., J. S. Mill and Harriet Taylor (Chicago: University of
Chicago Press, 1951), p. 168.

marry unscrupulous husbands. Marriage settlements were expensive insurance policies and Chancery lawyers traditionally considered husbands as the enemy. The fact that the married woman benefited by the settlement was incidental. The Courts of Equity did not think any more highly of women's capabilities than did the Common Law courts.

Chancery achieved its object by using the principle of trusteeship. A trustee could be appointed to protect the property of a person—a married woman or a child under the age of majority—who legally could not hold property of his or her own. In a marriage settlement, the trustee was appointed to protect the property for the separate use of the married woman. It became apparent that under this system a married woman might be persuaded to give the property to a cajoling husband, although she could not be forced to do so. The trustee was powerless under the law to stop her if she wished to make such a gift. In order to prevent a wife's extravagance, Lord Edward Thurlow refined the trust further. His provision, called "restraint upon anticipation," made it impossible for a married woman either to give away her property or to charge it with her debts.[51] Restraint upon anticipation resembled the strict settlement, which made a property "owner" in reality only a tenant for life, deprived of the freedom to dispose of any part of the property before or after his or her death. Restraint upon anticipation gave a woman an income without endangering the body of the estate.

Equity made it possible for a married woman to contract and to sue, a right limited by the restraint upon anticipation governing a married woman's use of her property. She was even able to sue her husband when she had no other way of protecting herself against him. The right to sue meant that a woman's existence apart from her husband was recognized. Equity entitled a married woman to a (limited) legal status as a person.

The use of marriage settlements to protect the property of married women failed to solve a number of problems. Most marriages were celebrated without benefit of a settlement. Lord Lyndhurst re-

51. Reiss, *Rights and Duties of Englishwomen*, pp. 23–26.

marked in the House of Lords in 1856 that nine out of ten marriages in England were contracted without any settlement at all.[52] Since marriage settlements were extremely complex, they required expert legal advice, the expense of which made it impossible for a poor man to protect his daughter when she married. A wife's property and the income from that property might be protected by Equity, but her earnings (wages) were excluded from such protection. In any case, the Courts of Equity would not interfere where a wife's property was under £200. By the middle of the nineteenth century two separate systems of law affecting married women existed side by side in England, one for the rich and one for the poor. The fact that they often contradicted one another made the situation all the more disturbing.

Why was no attempt made to correct so obviously muddled and unjust a legal system before the 1850s? Albert Dicey attempted to explain the slow course of parliamentary action by suggesting that the law is always sluggish in reacting to changes in public opinion. He noted that the daughters of the wealthy were well protected by Equity and the daughters of working men possessed little property to protect. He also noted that working-class girls were unable to articulate their problems and could not bring them to the public attention. Dicey concluded that though the abstract injustices were no greater, the wrong was far more visible to the public by 1870, when action was finally taken, than it had been in 1832. This he attributed in great part to the Industrial Revolution.[53]

The fact that the Industrial Revolution changed the role of women workers and created the idle women of the middle classes cannot be denied. However, the rebellion that organized itself at mid-century had additional roots outside the industrial upheaval. Elie Halevy insisted that the birth of feminism was due to influences not directly related to the Industrial Revolution. He traced the movement to intellectual, not economic, sources and asserted

---

52. Sir Thomas Erskine Perry, "Rights and Liabilities of Husband and Wife," *Edinburgh Review* (American ed.) 105 (January 1857): 102.

53. Albert Venn Dicey, *Lectures on the Relation between Law and Public Opinion in England during the Nineteenth Century* (London: Macmillan, 1917), pp. 384–86.

that the philosophy of the French Revolution and the eighteenth-century Enlightenment stimulated feminist thought and subsequent activity.[54] But while intellectual sources were significant in the birth of the new movement, no single factor can be credited with its creation. Halevy rejected an exclusively economic interpretation, but Harold Perkin insists that "the emancipation of women was in fact one of the most important and characteristic consequences of industrialism."[55] A brief survey of the early feminist period will demonstrate the inadequacy of so limited an explanation and will illustrate how inextricably economic, intellectual, political, and social developments were bound together. The seemingly isolated individual protests of the first half of the nineteenth century can be viewed as part of a growing pattern, illustrating clearly the complex of forces that merged in mid-Victorian feminism.

The birth of feminism is generally dated at 1792, the year that Mary Wollstonecraft wrote and published *A Vindication of the Rights of Women.* Her book, inspired by the doctrines of human rights and liberty that abounded in the atmosphere of the French Revolution, presented a passionate, if not always reasoned, appeal to end female subjection. She asked for equal educational and professional opportunities for women, full citizenship, and the right of married women to own property and to have a share in the custody of their children in case of marital separation. She also wanted divorce to be made easier for women and wanted men to be legally responsible for their illegitimate children. "Let men take their choice, man and woman were made for each other, though not to become one being; and if they will not improve women, they will deprave them."[56] The book aroused bitter disapproval, and personal insults were heaped upon its author. Horace Walpole called her a "hyena in petticoats,"[57] and Hannah More condemned the book unread.

Hannah More was a member of the famed bluestocking circle.

54. Elie Halevy, *A History of the English People in the Nineteenth Century,* 2d rev. ed., 6 vols. (New York: Peter Smith, 1952), 2:490–91.
55. Perkin, *Origins of Modern English Society,* p. 157.
56. Mary Wollstonecraft, *Vindication of the Rights of Women* (New York: W. W. Norton, 1967), p. 261.
57. Kamm, *Rapiers and Battleaxes,* p. 20.

She had been successful as a school teacher and was praised both as a dramatist and a poet. She wrote to Lord Orford in 1793 that she had been urged to read the *Vindication* but was resisting all such suggestions. She disliked the title and insisted that she had as much liberty as she could presently make use of. She did not feel that women would be capable of public participation. "To be unstable and capricious, I really think, is but too characteristic of our sex; and there is no animal so much indebted to subordination for its good behavior as woman."[58] More was sufficiently intelligent to realize that in writing these words she was betraying her sex, for she admitted in the same letter that if she had still been young she might perhaps have written differently. In any case, her disapproval of Wollstonecraft's work was shared by most influential people and the book was only briefly a source of discussion, as much because of the scandal attached to its author's personal affairs as for its content. The *Vindication* did not become the cornerstone of the women's movement until late in the nineteenth century.

For nearly a generation after the *Vindication* appeared little deliberate propaganda for the liberation of women was published. Not until 1825 did a substantial work appear which set out a coherent argument for the full emancipation of women, even for their admission to the legislature. There were isolated publications of feminist tendencies in the interim, perhaps the most notable being Sydney Smith's "Essay on Female Education," which appeared in 1810. Smith brought humor and irony to his subject and produced a carefully reasoned and witty essay questioning the idea that women were naturally inferior to men. He admitted the difference in understanding between most men and women, but attributed it to the different ways young men and women were trained and educated. If boys and girls were brought up with the same educational and cultural opportunities, he insisted, they would become adults with equal capacities. The same proportion of men and women would prove highly intelligent or deadly dull.[59] The essay, though written

58. William Roberts, ed., *Memoirs of the Life and Correspondence of Mrs. Hannah More*, 3d ed., 4 vols. (London: R. H. Seeley & W. Burnside, 1835), 2:372.

59. Sydney Smith, "Essay on Female Education," *Edinburgh Review* (American ed.) 15 (January 1810): 299.

so early, ranked as a masterpiece of feminist literature for many years and was quoted extensively by Smith's successors. It is an interesting indicator of the progress of thought on women's capabilities at that early date, but reflected no active momentum for change. The sentiments expressed in Smith's essay were not popular in 1810. Although he dealt only with the possibility for better intellectual development in women, his arguments if carried to their logical extreme pointed toward political equality and accompanying social upheaval. Equal education and admission of equal intelligence led to equal public participation for men and women.

In 1825, William Thompson of Cork, a socialist and adherent of Robert Owen's theories of cooperation, wrote and published a book grandly titled *Appeal of One Half of the Human Race, Woman, Against the Pretensions of the Other One Half, Man, to Retain Them in Political and Thence in Civil and Domestic Slavery.* He wrote the book in answer to a passage in James Mill's "Article on Government," which appeared in the *Encyclopaedia Britannica* in 1820. So incensed was Thompson that he printed Mill's offending paragraph on his title page:

> One thing is pretty clear, that all those individuals whose interests are indisputably included in those of other individuals may be struck off from political rights without inconvenience. In this light may be viewed all children up to a certain age, whose interests are involved in those of their parents. In this light also women may be regarded, the interests of almost all of whom is involved either in that of their fathers, or in that of their husbands.

Thompson set out a fervent argument for full legal and political equality of men and women. He advocated educational reform and female suffrage. He absolutely denied the possibility of female inferiority and rejected the assignment of women to a separate sphere. It was unfortunate for his cause that his method of securing women's rights entailed adoption of a cooperative social order, in which, apparently, marriage did not exist. The implied abandonment of English family life overshadowed and discredited in the public mind all arguments for women's emancipation. The new socialism's support of the feminist cause strengthened the people's instinctive fear of the new ideas involved in feminism.

There were other voices raised in support of feminist views in the years immediately preceding the passage of the Reform Act of 1832. The Utilitarians generally dissented from the sentiment against women's suffrage expressed by James Mill in his "Article on Government." In his *Autobiography* John Stuart Mill indicated that he and the circle of younger Utilitarians supported women's suffrage. They were pleased that Jeremy Bentham shared their sentiments.[60] As early as April 1824, in the second number of the *Westminster Review*, John Stuart Mill attacked the *Edinburgh Review* for supporting a code of dual morality and espousing a subordinate role for women. He suggested that men would not agree to the education of women because they enjoyed the sense of power afforded by women's dependence on them.[61]

William Johnson Fox, a noted Unitarian preacher and editor of the *Monthly Repository*, was an ardent political reformer of Benthamite convictions. Harriet Taylor was a member of Fox's circle and it was he who first introduced her to Mill in 1830.[62] In 1834 Fox set up house with his collaborator, Eliza Flower, and this irregular union led to his isolation from a badly split Unitarian community. Fox was an early advocate of women's rights. For him that meant support of educational reform and alteration of the marriage laws. In a discussion of some of Tennyson's poems which appeared in the *Westminster Review* in 1831, he asserted that woman's influence within the family was a strong argument for improving her educational opportunities: "Upon what every woman is, depends what the world is, both in the present and the future."[63]

The Unitarians had long supported the emancipation of women. Mary Wollstonecraft, whom Fox praised highly, was herself a Unitarian, and the *Vindication* received a favorable notice in the short-lived Unitarian journal *The Christian Miscellany*.[64] The *Monthly*

60. John Stuart Mill, *Autobiography* (Indianapolis: Bobbs-Merrill, 1957), pp. 67–68.
61. *Westminster Review* 1 (April 1824): 525.
62. Michael St. John Packe, *Life of John Stuart Mill* (New York: Macmillan, 1954), p. 127.
63. *Westminster Review* 14 (January 1831): 221.
64. Mineka, *Dissidence of Dissent*, p. 79.

Repository continued the Unitarian feminist tradition, and one of Harriet Martineau's first contributions to the magazine was an article on women's education which appeared in 1823.[65] Martineau's feminism was moderate and concentrated on educational reform and the improvement of woman's status under the law. Fox's was a far more radical philosophy. In 1832 he wrote an article entitled "A Political and Social Anomaly." In it he pointed out the absurdity of allowing political power to devolve upon a queen while educated women were denied a vote in the election of representatives: "Woman is vested with the entire power of the State, or not entrusted with its meanest fraction. She is a divinity or a slave."[66] In the same article he outlined the general inadequacies of woman's position. The nurturing of feminine delicacy was depriving women of all but superficial attainments. The trouble was that women were educated only to get married and trained to be dependents rather than companions. The law that deprived married women of legal autonomy guaranteed their social slavery.[67] Fox's *Monthly Repository* was consistent in its support of women's emancipation; it was also far in advance of common opinion. Though its circulation was small, never more than one thousand copies, it reached a select audience and through that audience helped create a climate receptive to change.[68]

In the meantime, however, the advocates of "woman's place in the home" were gathering strength and opposing even the mildest suggestions for improvement of women's education. In 1835 a book entitled *Woman as She Is and as She Should Be,* a strong attack on female education, appeared. The anonymous author noted that women's influence was already excessive and asserted that women must be made to see their inferiority to men and to realize the folly of any independent action. Woman's weakness was her key to power, her strongest attraction. Independence was unfeminine and the more dependent women became the more men would cherish them.[69] In

65. Webb, *Harriet Martineau*, p. 180.

66. William Fox, "A Political and Social Anomaly," *Monthly Repository* 6 (1832): 638.

67. Ibid., p. 641.

68. Mineka, *Dissidence of Dissent*, p. 296.

69. John Killham, *Tennyson and the Princess: Reflections of an Age* (London: Athlone Press, 1958), p. 98.

1839, Sarah Stickney Ellis cautioned women to remember their place in the divine order and to accept their lot with resignation and humility. She glorified self-denial and obligation to duty, which for women were best expressed in dedication to family and subordination to men.[70]

There was as yet no true debate on the reform of women's legal or social status. When Queen Victoria ascended the throne in 1837 the issue remained for the most part on the periphery of the public consciousness. Those women who would lead the first battles for emancipation were the same age as the queen or much younger. Charlotte Bronte was twenty-one, Marian Evans eighteen, and Florence Nightingale was seventeen. Barbara Leigh Smith was ten and Emily Davies only seven. Yet, even at that early date, the first parliamentary debate concerning woman's status was about to burst into public notice. The sensitive question of infant custody precipitated that first legislative action.

The devoted mother rocking a cradle was the ideal image for the Victorian period. The irony in that symbol of home and family was that the mother had no legal right either to the cradle she was rocking or to its occupant. A long series of judicial decisions had recognized the father's right to custody of his children and to complete control over their upbringing and their religion.[71] Caroline Norton, a professed antifeminist but an accomplished author and influential woman, challenged that tradition and helped to change the law in 1839.

One of the three beautiful granddaughters of Richard Brinsley Sheridan, Caroline took London society by storm in 1826. She was married in 1827, at the age of nineteen, to George Chappel Norton, a brother of the third Lord Grantley. It was an unhappy marriage from the beginning. Personal incompatibility was aggravated by opposing political views, since Norton entered Parliament as a Tory, while all the Sheridans were ardent and outspoken Whigs. In 1835, while Caroline was visiting a sister, George took their chil-

---

70. Sarah Stickney Ellis, *The Women of England* (London: Fisher, Son, 1839), p. 469.
71. Reiss, *Rights and Duties of Englishwomen*, p. 16.

dren from the family home. He put them in the care of a cousin of his and refused to allow their mother to see them. The following year he brought an action of criminal conversation with his wife against Lord William Melbourne, who was one of her constant visitors. The jury dismissed the case for lack of evidence, deciding that the action was a result of domestic spite and political bluff. However, Caroline Norton found that in this trial, which concerned the protection of her reputation, she had no standing at all. A married woman, unprotected by a marriage settlement, she could neither sue nor be sued. She could not be represented by counsel at the trial. At the end of the case she was still tied to Norton by the unbreakable marriage bond, unable to gain access to her children, and her name was smeared all over the London papers. Norton refused to support her, then claimed her possessions and earnings as his own. She had begun a literary career in 1829, two years after her marriage. She gained considerable success, contributing to and editing several popular literary annuals, such as *La Belle Assemblée*, *Fisher's Drawing-Room Scrap-Book*, and *The Keepsake*. All these earnings Norton now claimed.

Caroline Norton fought back with words. She did not argue for feminine emancipation; indeed, she repudiated the concept of female equality: "The wild and stupid theories advanced by a few women, of 'equal rights' and 'equal intelligence,' are not the opinions of their sex. I, for one (I, with millions more), believe in the natural superiority of man, as I do in the existence of a God."[72] She argued instead from a sense of personal outrage and campaigned on the basis of a mother's natural right to her children. In a letter to Mary Shelley, the daughter of Mary Wollstonecraft and William Godwin, she explained her willingness to risk further unpleasant publicity. Having no fear of notoriety, she wanted to convince other women that there was no disgrace in claiming justice. If women demanded their natural rights publicly they would be making real progress.[73] She began to write pamphlets, which she had

---

72. Jane G. Perkins, *Life of Mrs. Norton* (New York: Henry Holt, 1909), pp. 149–50.
73. Percy Fitzgerald, *Lives of the Sheridans*, 2 vols. (London: Grolier Society, n.d.), 2:439.

privately printed after the publisher Murray hesitated to take them for fear of prosecution. Five hundred copies of *The Claim of a Mother to the Custody of Her Child as Affected by the Common Law Right of the Father* were published in 1837 and circulated among influential legislators, lawyers, and the like. The pamphlet contained evidence she had collected of cases even worse than her own and she wrote: "I abjure all other writing till I see those laws altered . . . it is the cause of all the women of England. . . . Meanwhile, my husband has a legal lien on the copyright of my works. Let him claim the copyright of this."[74]

In early 1837, Thomas Noon Talfourd, M.P. for Reading, who had appeared as junior counsel for Lord Melbourne in the 1836 trial, introduced an Infant Custody Bill in Parliament. The bill was withdrawn before its second reading, but was brought up again during the next session. The opposition to this bill was similar to that encountered by all future bills affecting woman's position: it was considered a threat to the unity of the family and was resisted violently in Parliament and in the press. Sir Ernest Sugden, one of the bitterest opponents of the Infant Custody Bill, contended in the debates of early 1838 that a woman's rights must be sacrificed. He insisted that conceding her rights against her husband would mean conceding her right to act independently and warned that any encouragement of woman's independent action would cause the dissolution of the family.[75]

During the summer of 1838, while the bill was being debated in the House of Lords, the *British and Foreign Review* published a strong attack on it and Caroline Norton. The *Review*, established in 835, was an offshoot of the Literary Association of the Friends of Poland and was in its early issues primarily concerned with a campaign for the restitution of an independent Poland. In a broader context, it favored free trade and an extension of the franchise but vigorously opposed the ballot, the Charter, rights for women, and the abolition of the House of Lords. The article noted that the fundamental

74. Strachey, *The Cause*, p. 37.
75. Reiss, *Rights and Duties of Englishwomen*, pp. 82–83.

inferiority of women was natural, in accordance with Christian teaching, and basic to English traditions. Recognizing the doctrine of sexual equality would destroy the family and permanently weaken the social fabric.[76] The article associated Norton with feminism and feminism with socialism, and it promised social upheaval if the Infant Custody Bill passed. It condemned the writings of Mary Wollstonecraft and Harriet Martineau as encouraging that revolution, ridiculed the concept of higher education for women, and illustrated clearly the inflammability of the woman's question and the anger that could be generated by any attempt to legislate change in women's status. Norton had no legal redress despite the libel in the article. She retaliated with a letter published in *The Times*. Six months later she wrote *A Plain Letter to the Lord Chancellor on the Infant Custody Bill* under the pseudonym Pierce Stevenson. She had a copy sent to every member of Parliament. After a further brief debate the Infant Custody Act passed into law in the summer of 1839. The act was relatively minor in its scope. It gave power to the Court to grant to a mother the custody of her children under seven and access to her older children at stated intervals, if adultery had not been proven against her.[77] Despite its narrow scope, it was the first legislative action to change woman's status. It recognized the necessity for legal intervention within the marital relationship to protect women's rights, although societal attitudes toward the family and woman's place within it remained virtually unchanged for decades to come.

Despite the heat of opposition to the bill, a women's movement had not yet organized, nor had feminist views coalesced around any program for action. Caroline Norton's crusade was an individual action arising out of personal difficulties. Not until the fifties did legislative change in woman's status become the focus of organized feminist activity.

During the forties humanitarian impulses focused attention on working-class women, among others. In 1842 the *Report on Mines*

76. *British and Foreign Review* 12 (July 1838): 353.
77. Kamm, *Rapiers and Battleaxes*, p. 26.

of the Royal Commission on Children's Employment was published. It was authored by Hugh Seymour Tremenheere, who
served on numerous royal commissions and who was instrumental
in bringing about more than fourteen acts of Parliament, his stated
object being the improvement of the condition of the working
classes. The *Report on Mines* devoted considerable attention to the
woman worker.[78] The testimony of women working in the pits sixteen hours a day horrified the public. On June 7, 1842, Lord Ashley
delivered a speech before Parliament describing the evils suffered by
women and children in the mines. He wrote in his diary: "For two
hours the House listened so attentively that you might have heard a
pin drop, broken only by loud and repeated marks of approbation."[79] Emotions were stirred and Richard Cobden, whose political theories had kept him hostile to Ashley's work, now went over
to his side. A law was quickly passed which removed children under
ten from the mines and forbade women to be employed under-
ground. In 1844 factory women were included in the law prescribing a maximum of twelve hours of work per day, to be performed
only between 5:30 A.M. and 8:30 P.M., for women and young persons above thirteen in the textile trades. The Ten Hours Bill, further limiting working hours for women and children, was passed in
1847. Finally in 1850 a law was passed establishing an eight-hour
working day for women and young persons. It fixed the workday
within the limits of 6 A.M. and 6 P.M., or 7 A.M. and 7 P.M.; allowing an hour and a half for meals, with work ending at 2 P.M. on
Saturday.[80]

   This legislation resulted from humanitarian campaigns and included women in much the same way as children were included, as
entities needing protection. In many cases, the protective legislation hurt women as much as it helped them. In excluding women
from the mines, the law caused great unemployment and provided
no alternative occupations. Starvation condemned these women as
much as pit work had. The public disclosures of abominable work-

78. See Pinchbeck, *Women Workers*, pp. 244–63, for a summary of the *Report*.
79. Neff, *Victorian Working Women*, p. 73.
80. Ibid., pp. 73–75.

ing conditions did provide feminist writers with useful data, however. In a series of articles in 1843, *The Athenaeum* surveyed the *Report on Mines*. In one of those articles Anna Jameson summed up the findings and called them evidence of a dangerous neglect of women's education. In a revised version of that article, published in 1846, she noted that never before had women been considered primarily as laborers. The *Report on Mines* had forced the public to acknowledge the existence of the woman worker.[81] The investigations of working conditions which took place in the forties did highlight the difficulties of the working-class woman in the labor force, but her status and her educational and employment alternatives were little changed as a result of those studies.

The forties also witnessed the establishment of Queen's and Bedford Colleges. In reality little more than secondary schools, these institutions founded at the decade's close were meant to provide an organized educational program for governesses, whose inadequate training was a matter of some concern.[82] The attitude toward education for women was changing. As early as 1844 *The Athenaeum* observed the shift in public opinion, reporting that a member of Parliament had spoken in Liverpool in favor of reforming women's education and had received an enthusiastic public response.[83] Throughout the forties improved education for women was advanced as a way to enhance their true capabilities, but those abilities were still quite clearly defined as different from male abilities and were expected to be exercised within a strictly circumscribed female sphere.

In 1851 two sisters, Maria Grey and Emily Shirreff, later active in the development of secondary schools for girls, wrote *Thoughts on Self-Culture Addressed to Women*, which outlined the need for women's education and intellectual development. They advocated improved educational facilities for women, deplored the lack of librar-

81. Anna Brownell Jameson, *Memoirs and Essays* (London: R. Bentley, 1846), p. 213.
82. See Tuke, *History of Bedford College*, and Rosalie Glynn Grylls, *Queen's College, 1848–1948* (London: George Routledge & Sons, 1948), for the early history of these institutions.
83. *The Athenaeum*, 2 March 1844, p. 189.

ies, colleges, and lectures, and asserted that only a sound and liberal education would prepare women for married or single life. They were quick to point out that education would not alter woman's natural position in relation to man, only enhance that relationship: "When a woman with gentle but dignified acquiescence in the inevitable conditions of her lot, yet evinces by the tone of her character and pursuits, that she bears in mind those higher grounds of equality, it is then that she is truly the helpmate of him whom she obeys without losing her self-respect."[84] Grey and Shirreff defended the education of women, arguing that the family would benefit, not suffer, from it, and they quoted Sydney Smith's 1810 "Essay on Female Education" to ridicule the fear of opponents: "What can be more absurd, than to suppose that the care and perpetual solicitude a mother feels for her children depends on her ignorance of Greek and mathematics, and that she would desert an infant for a quadratic equation."[85] In her own work of 1858, *Intellectual Education and Its Influence on the Character and Happiness of Women*, Shirreff made plain her support for educating women, but forcefully expressed dismay with those who demanded equality between the sexes. She considered the doctrine of equality absurd and deplored radical political theories advocating women's suffrage and full public participation. She felt rivalry between men and women was unnatural and would undermine the social order.[86]

Maria Grey and Emily Shirreff represent one of two distinct styles of effort on women's behalf that formed complementary, if sometimes antagonistic, aspects of the women's movement during the next fifty years. One line, academic and cultural, gave persistent proof of women's worth in the life of the state and pressed for education, facilities for work, and amenities for self-improvement and self-expression. The other, revolutionary, demanded a more basic change of attitude including all that the first group claimed and more—the total equality of woman and man in the home and in

84. Emily Anne Eliza Shirreff and Maria G. Grey, *Thoughts on Self-Culture Addressed to Women* (Boston: William Crosby & H. P. Nichols, 1851), p. 24.

85. Sydney Smith, cited in Ibid., p. 373.

86. Shirreff, *Intellectual Education*, pp. 421–24.

the state. "The Enfranchisement of Women," published in the *Westminster Review* in July 1851, embodied the claims of the second group.[87] Published without attribution, the article, which John Stuart Mill later credited to Harriet Taylor, demanded complete equality of opportunity for women. Although it caused little discussion at its publication, the article became the basis for *The Subjection of Women*, Mill's classic feminist work, published in 1869. Barbara Leigh Smith supported the sentiments expressed in "The Enfranchisement of Women." She belonged to the second group of reformers and worked for the removal of all disabilities affecting women. Her formation in 1855 of the first regular feminist committee began the organized women's movement of the mid-Victorian period. Economic, intellectual, political, and social forces had combined during the first half of the nineteenth century with individual female protests, so that by mid-century the women's question was a matter of public concern.

87. John Stuart Mill, "The Enfranchisement of Women," in his *Dissertations and Discussions*, 4 vols. (New York: Henry Holt, 1874), 3:93–131.

ɷ III ɷ

FIRST ATTEMPTS:
AN EDUCATIONAL EXPERIMENT
AND THE MARRIED WOMEN'S
PROPERTY CAMPAIGN

Barbara Leigh Smith was an unusual leader for the married women's property campaign. Single, wealthy, and independent, she suffered from none of the misfortunes she fought against. A strong Unitarian family tradition of public service in defense of radical causes, mingled with a personality independent almost to eccentricity, produced an indefatigable feminist organizer. She was careless of convention and occasionally an embarrassment to her more respectable allies, but above all she was unquenchably enthusiastic, generous with money, and a catalyst activating feminist campaigns on many fronts. She fully accepted the Unitarian precept that one must strive to create a more perfect world and saw her wealth as an instrument for societal improvement, acknowledging her moral responsibility to contribute both time and money to reform endeavors. She stated her conviction plainly in *Women and Work*, written in 1857: "Money is a power which we have not the right lightly to reject. It is a responsibility which we must accept . . . God sent all human beings into the world for the purpose of forwarding to the utmost of their power, the progress of the world."[1]

Not only did Benjamin Smith provide a generous independent income for his eldest daughter in 1848, he also allowed her great freedom, encouraging her to participate in activities hitherto unusual for women. In 1850, Barbara Smith and her friend Bessie Rayner Parkes traveled through Belgium, Germany, Austria, and

---

1. Barbara Bodichon, *Women and Work* (New York: C. S. Francis, 1859), pp. 13–14.

Switzerland, serving as chaperones for each other. The idea that two young women of twenty-three and twenty-one might travel alone through Europe with no male protection was as yet unacceptable. Smith caused an uproar in the stolid German hamlets by wearing blue-tinted spectacles. In further defiance of convention the two young women abandoned corsets, adopting loose-fitting comfortable clothing for their sketching tours.[2] They both condemned the fashion of tight-lacing and the fetish of the eighteen-inch waist. Smith had once drawn a diagram of the Venus de Milo's bust measurements, comparing them with those of pigeon-chested Victorian women who had, she felt, sacrificed both health and natural grace to support an unnatural ideal.

The two friends were acutely aware of the political ferment around them in Germany and Austria. Barbara Smith was disturbed by the signs of despotism she observed in Austria. She wrote her aunt Julia that she had not previously realized how important political and intellectual freedom were: "I did not think, when I was so glad to go into Austria, how the sight of people ruled by the sword in place of law, would stir up my heart, and make me feel as miserable as those who live under it."[3]

The trip was thus a political awakening for the two young women as well as an opportunity for them to live, for the first time, on their own. Lifelong friends, Barbara Smith and Bessie Parkes shared similar family backgrounds. Parkes became an important member of the Langham Place circle of feminists which Smith led in the late fifties. The Parkes family were also Unitarians, upholding a long tradition of radical politics. Joseph Priestley, Bessie Parkes's great-grandfather, was a Unitarian preacher and scientist. He was a trendsetter in Biblical as well as scientific studies and was credited with the first serious criticism of the doctrine of the virgin birth in England. Priestley wished to be judged as a pioneer of religious reform. In addition, he was an ardent supporter of the French Revo-

2. Marie Belloc Lowndes, *I Too Have Lived in Arcadia* (New York: Dodd, Mead, 1942), p. 3.

3. Barbara Leigh Smith to Julia Smith, May 1850, Bodichon Papers, Fawcett Society Collection, City of London Polytechnic, London.

lution. His home had been burnt by rioting mobs in Birmingham on the night of July 14, 1791.[4] Bessie Parkes's father, Joseph, was one of the leading Radicals in Birmingham, a man who proudly claimed in 1832 that Jeremy Bentham, George Grote, and James Mill were the source "of all the power and moral courage I have brought to bear in favour of the people."[5] He was active in the anti–Corn Law campaign and so devoted to politics that Richard Cobden chided him in 1846 for "going to bed at *two* o'clock with cold feet, all your blood having flowed to that centre of Whiggery, your 'heart!'"[6]

Bessie Parkes once told her daughter that her first memory of Barbara Smith was of seeing Benjamin Smith kneeling down to tie his young daughter's shoestring, an act so extraordinary for an early Victorian father that she remembered it for the rest of her life.[7] The girls met only occasionally until the late forties, when the Parkes family, hoping that sea air would benefit their consumptive son, Priestley, took a house at Hastings next door to the Smiths. Here the two young women developed the ties based on common social and political concerns that linked them through life. Years later Parkes described their early friendship and the excitement of the period. She remembered the years between 1846 and 1851 as a time of promise following on the successful anti–Corn Law effort. Peace and economic plenty coupled with religious toleration and spreading educational opportunities brightened the atmosphere that overwhelmed Parkes and Smith as they stood in the nave of the first Crystal Palace on opening day, May 1, 1851, waiting for Victoria and Albert's procession.[8]

In 1850, when they returned from Europe, the two friends met Dr. Elizabeth Blackwell, the only woman in the English-speaking

4. Holt, *Unitarian Contribution*, p. 111.

5. Joseph Hamburger, *Intellectuals in Politics: John Stuart Mill and the Philosophic Radicals* (New Haven: Yale University Press, 1965), p. 180.

6. Norman McCord, *The Anti–Corn Law League, 1838–1846*, 2d ed. (London: Unwin University Books, 1968), p. 207.

7. Lowndes, *Arcadia*, p. 12.

8. Bessie Parkes Belloc, "Barbara Leigh Smith Bodichon," *Englishwoman's Review of Social and Industrial Questions* 22 (July 1891): 146.

world to have qualified as a doctor. Born in England, Blackwell had been raised in the United States, had studied medicine in Geneva, New York and at the Maternité in Paris, and had come in 1850 to study with Sir James Paget at St. Bartholomew's Hospital in London. She was treated courteously at the hospital, but had no social connections until Parkes and Smith took her in hand. She lived in spartan lodgings, disliked the English climate, and missed her Parisian friends and the joys of study under the trees in the Luxembourg Gardens. Parkes and Smith introduced her to a lively London circle and she remembered their first visit vividly. They sympathized with her medical efforts, filled her rooms with paintings and flowers, and took her into their family circles. They introduced her to Lady Noel Byron and Russell Gurney, Anna Jameson and Michael Faraday. They shared ideas and made enthusiastic plans for increasing employment alternatives to provide "practical work" for women.[9] This was the beginning of Blackwell's lifelong association with the Smith family. Benjamin Smith sent her money to start a hospital in America and during the sixties and seventies she visited Barbara Bodichon for months at a time at Blandford Square in London.

The "practical work" which Barbara Smith chose first to attempt was starting a school. This was not an uncommon venture for wealthy young women of the period. Ordinarily it involved buying uniforms in one's favorite colors for a number of ragged children, giving each of them a bible, and teaching the girls sewing and the boys a trade. Sunday and elementary schools in the first half of the nineteenth century tried to provide rudimentary knowledge to a large number of children, their prime concern being reduction of the per capita expenditure per pupil. Andrew Bell and James Lancaster, early educational reformers, advocated the monitorial system, which allowed one teacher assisted by monitors to control huge classes of between two and three hundred. The curriculum of public elementary schools and of private schools was extremely restricted. The Census of 1851 found that all day schools taught read-

9. Elizabeth Blackwell, *Pioneer Work in Opening the Medical Profession to Women* (London: Longmans, Green, 1895; reprint, New York: Sourcebook Press, 1970), p. 175.

ing, but only 50 percent of private schools taught writing, and only 48 percent of private schools taught arithmetic. Advertisements for elementary schools generally made it quite clear that beneficiaries of this charity could expect no more than the most basic schooling, since the aim was to reach a multitude, not to give intensive education to a few.[10]

Barbara Smith's was not an ordinary private elementary school. Along with £300 a year, her father had given her title to the Westminster Infant School in Vincent Square. The old progressive school which he and James Buchanan had built could not be revived, however, and Smith began a new venture. She was impressed by the Birkbeck schools established by William Ellis, an advanced educationist. She began by searching for a young woman to serve as teacher in her new elementary school, which she conceived as a "people's" school. She planned to send the teacher to a Birkbeck school for special training. In 1853 Elizabeth Whitehead, a young Unitarian woman then giving private lessons, heard of Smith's project from William Johnson Fox. His description of the possibilities of the scheme interested her deeply. Whitehead wrote offering her services to Smith.[11] Benjamin Smith was shown the letter and told his daughter that Whitehead was, in his opinion, the teacher who could make her experiment a success. Barbara Smith arranged for Whitehead to further qualify herself with a six-month course of study, including attendance at the Birkbeck school in Peckham, under the direction of William Shields. Whitehead described the school at Peckham years later in an attempt to convey the special quality of the educational experiment which she and Smith tried to duplicate. Shields taught by a combination of questions and answers, reinforcing knowledge with practical experiments and illustrations. Mental training rather than rote learning was his goal, and he encouraged students to assume that there was always something to be investigated, that neither he nor they had

10. David Wardle, *The Rise of the Schooled Society* (London: Routledge & Kegan Paul, 1974), p. 8.

11. Elizabeth Whitehead Malleson, *Elizabeth Malleson, 1828–1916: Autobiographical Notes and Letters* (London: Printed for private circulation, 1926), p. 45.

reached the limits of knowledge.[12] Shields praised Whitehead's talents, telling Smith that she had grown from a teacher into an "educationist."

While Elizabeth Whitehead studied, Barbara Smith chose a location for the school. Quarters were rented at the Portman Hall, in a poor neighborhood near Smith's London home in Blandford Square. The hall had been used for temperance meetings and remained available for gatherings of this and other societies in the evenings. The room was carefully equipped for the educational experiment. A raised platform was built at one end of the room and fitted with a swing-slate (blackboard) and music board to improve the quality of collective lessons. The sides of the hall were decorated with maps, pictures, and framed slates. A gallery at one end of the room and a small side room served for individual class teaching.[13] The physical surroundings never quite overcame the sober atmosphere created by the temperance meetings held there each evening. All evidence of the children had to be put away when these events occurred and the walls rehung with temperance tracts. Smith insisted, however, that the value of the school depended on the vitality of the work done in it and minimized the inconvenience of its shared quarters.[14]

Spiritually, the school descended from the ideas of James Buchanan, Barbara Smith's childhood tutor. It had no uniform, no punishments, and no creed. The Portman Hall School opened on November 6, 1854, and immediately adopted a coeducational setting. Boys and girls learned side by side, although it was noted at the time that none of the boys were older than eleven and therefore represented no real distraction and did not suffer by learning the same lessons as the girls. Had they been older the coeducational question would have raised more serious objections. Elizabeth Whitehead contended that the balancing of the sexes in the school was a positive good and that boys and girls accepted the situation

12. Elizabeth Whitehead Malleson, "The Portrait of a School," *Journal of Education* 18 (September 1886): 358.
13. Malleson, *Autobiographical Notes*, p. 47.
14. Malleson, "Portrait of a School," p. 358.

with equanimity.[15] Not only were the sexes mixed, but different
social classes were represented as well. Whitehead's sisters and
Smith's nieces attended the school, as did the children of Smith
family friends, including Ricciotti Garibaldi, son of the Italian
democratic leader. The sons and daughters of neighborhood trades-
men and workers made up the majority of the eighty students. The
weekly fee was kept at sixpence, while the actual upkeep of the
school was provided by Smith. It amounted to a considerable expenditure over the years.

The school was secular and nondenominational, numbering
among its pupils Catholics, Jews, freethinkers, and Unitarians. Barbara Smith asserting that "it demonstrated the much disputed fact
that the absence of theological or Biblical instruction need not involve the religious tone of a school."[16] Each morning began with
an inspirational reading, Christian parables interspersed with secular poems or stories intended to teach moral, not sectarian lessons.
The mixed community of children which Smith created at the
Portman Hall School eliminated accepted social and religious
boundaries which caused dismay, even among reforming friends.
Octavia and Miranda Hill were asked to join Smith, her sisters
Isabella and Nanny, and William Johnson Fox's daughter in teaching at the school, but although Octavia Hill joined the project with
no hesitation (she taught a drawing class), Miranda Hill had grave
doubts about the school's lack of religious association. Octavia tried
to persuade her sister that joining the project would not compromise her beliefs. She did not feel that the exclusion of religious
teaching was an important enough reason to ignore the excellent
secular work going on at the institution, and she thought the moral
tone of the school taught as much indirectly as actual religious lessons did at church-affiliated schools.[17] Unconvinced, Miranda
consulted the Rev. Frederick Denison Maurice, the Christian So-

15. Malleson, *Autobiographical Notes*, p. 48.

16. Malleson, "Portrait of a School," p. 358.

17. C. Edmund Maurice, ed., *Life of Octavia Hill as Told in Her Letters* (London: Macmillan, 1913), p. 182.

cialist leader. He warned her not to have anything to do with the project and she did not join her sister in teaching there.

Lessons at the Portman Hall School included English, French, drawing, and music. Physiology and hygiene were also taught, with particular emphasis placed on health habits. Elementary physical science was taught with illustrations, "object lessons" being deemed of primary educational importance. Barbara Smith reluctantly used the monitorial system in subjects which demanded a great deal of individual attention, such as reading and arithmetic, but was aware of the drawbacks of this method and attempted to compensate for it. Elizabeth Whitehead wrote of how carefully the monitors were instructed in their duties, drilled constantly in details such as the correct pronunciation of words in order to achieve a high standard of expressive reading. An effort was made to give meaning to the most routine exercises, so that the practice of penmanship was carefully combined with the copying of extracts of poetry and prose chosen for their literary and moral value.[18] Lessons were tailored for half- and three-quarter-hour sessions, directed at maintaining high levels of attention. Punctuality and consistent attendance were encouraged by the promise of Saturday visits to museums and picture galleries.

The school operated for some ten years with a variety of teachers and volunteers. After one year of teaching Elizabeth Whitehead's health broke down and Julia Smith took her for a rest cure to Konigstein, Germany. She returned to Portman Hall, but ill health forced her to give up teaching within a year, although she retained an inspectorship of the school throughout its existence. Barbara Smith became increasingly involved in feminist issues shortly after she opened Portman Hall and while she continued to support it financially, she became less directly involved in day-to-day activities. In 1864 she decided to close the school in order to concentrate her finances and time on her feminist responsibilities. She donated its equipment to Elizabeth Whitehead, now Malleson, for the

18. Malleson, "Portrait of a School," p. 359.

Working Women's College. The Mallesons had founded the college in 1864 as a complement to the Working Men's College they had earlier established in Great Ormond Street, London.

The Portman Hall School was remembered by one of its pupils as a distinctive experiment, an ideal mixed school, characterized by a lack of corporal punishment and a concentration on the development of intellectual skills rather than on memorization.[19] Barbara Smith's educational and social principles were given their first concrete existence in this elementary school setting. Her interest in education was not confined to young children, however; nor did the closing of Portman Hall mark the end of her contribution to educational theory and experiment. She visited educational institutions of all types in Europe and America and wrote on elementary and secondary education in the years between 1854 and the founding of Girton College in the 1870s. She continued to develop her theories regarding the importance of a nondenominational educational setting aimed at producing a totally developed individual, physically as well as intellectually cultivated.

In 1858, during her honeymoon year in the United States, Barbara Bodichon visited the Englewood School at Perth Amboy, New Jersey. The school was the center of the Raritan Bay Union, a semi-communal community founded by Marcus Spring in 1853. The school pioneered in coeducation and was the first institution in the United States where young women took gymnastics. Bodichon wrote enthusiastically to her father about the school and about Theodore D. Weld, the abolitionist, who ran the school with his wife Angelina Grimke Weld. Bodichon was struck by the successful mixing of races in the classroom. She was impressed by the program of physical education for women and the scientific training available to them. And she was delighted by the talent and enthusiasm of the young women she met there: "Some of these girls will be heard of in the world, I am convinced."[20] The Englewood School embodied Bodichon's ideals in a unique setting. Part of a radical ex-

19. Ibid.
20. Barbara Bodichon to Benjamin Smith, 11 May 1858, *An American Diary*, pp. 142–43.

periment, it had little connection with the routines of ordinary people. However, her educational theories were also demonstrated in more commonplace American settings. In December 1857 she wrote from Cincinnati, expressing admiration for its school system. The school buildings were large and well-equipped, the textbooks of high quality and the teachers well-trained. The students spoke better English than Bodichon had ever heard in ordinary British classrooms. Coeducation appeared successful and the social classes mixed with no apparent ill effects. She was certain that these schools were an important "democratic element" within the society, providing the best mechanism for upward mobility.[21]

Her concern with education reform in England focused, in later years, on higher education for women, but as early as 1859 Barbara Bodichon expressed herself publicly on the deficiencies of education for middle-class women and girls. In written testimony sent to the Education Commission in August 1859, she deplored the lack of competent women teachers for girls' schools, asserting that fathers refused to educate girls for teaching or any other profession, since the investment might be wasted by early marriage. She believed that the laws affecting married women in England were of basic importance in determining the quality of education for women and girls and was certain that no educational reform would occur until the legal status of married women was altered.[22]

At the fourth annual meeting of the National Association for the Promotion of Social Science held in Glasgow in September 1860, Barbara Bodichon contributed a paper, read in her absence by Bessie Parkes. As a pressure group the Social Science Association was not in the same category as the Benthamites who preceded it or the Fabians who followed it. It was larger and lacked the sharp intellectual focus which characterized the other two. However, its subtle influence on social policy was undeniable. One of its most important contributions was in giving middle-class female reformers the

21. Barbara Bodichon, "An American School," *English Woman's Journal* 2 (November 1858): 198–200.

22. "Report of the Commissioners Appointed to Inquire into the State of Popular Education in England," *Parliamentary Papers*, 21 (1861), p. 103.

opportunity to participate as committee members and speakers. Mary Carpenter found a forum for her ideas on juvenile delinquency. Louisa Twining and Frances Power Cobbe worked and spoke on poor law reform. Bessie Parkes and Barbara Bodichon presented papers on women's education and employment. Indeed, the content of Bodichon's *Women and Work* was reflected in a variety of papers presented by both men and women before the Association's Education and Social Economy departments during the first decade of its existence.

The Association began in the autumn of 1856 with an informal meeting at Lord Henry Brougham's home. Social workers, lawyers, educationists, economists, doctors, businessmen, and legislators gathered to discuss the founding of an organization for the collection and dissemination of information in the field of social economics. The Association was formally inaugurated at a second meeting on July 29, 1857. Between 1857 and 1885 this body, modeled on the British Association, achieved nationally what earlier statistical societies had attempted locally. Its annual congresses, held in various major cities throughout Great Britain, were important civic occasions and resulted in volumes of *Transactions*, which provide an invaluable documentary record of middle-class thought on social problems.

Bodichon's paper, "Middle Class Schools for Girls," was reprinted in the November 1860 issue of the *English Woman's Journal*. Observing that most people agreed on the inadequacy of the government-supported Anglican National schools and the Dissenters' schools of the British and Foreign Schools Society, which attempted to provide a practical education for working-class children, Bodichon asserted that schools for girls of the middle class were generally greatly inferior even to these schools. Defining the middle class as that which could afford to pay more than the two pence a week required by Anglican National and Schools Society schools and which attempted to differentiate itself from those immediately below it on the social scale by providing for the education of its own children, she surveyed schools charging from six pence a week to fifteen shillings a quarter, which catered to the children of small shopkeepers and mechanics, too rich or too genteel to attend Anglican National or Schools Society schools. She criticized the National and British schools for failing to teach children to help themselves, thereby creating unthinking individuals incapable of rational independent judgments: "I stopped a child in the midst of a chapter in the Bible as she gabbled 'and His coming was foretold by the prophets.' 'Who were the prophets?' I asked. The girl stared me in the face and said, 'What father makes in his shop.'"[23]

If visits to National and British schools produced interviews of this discouraging if comic character, the cheap private day schools, academies, institutes, and collegiate establishments for young ladies and gentlemen were infinitely worse. Corporal punishment was common, quarters were unsanitary, and teachers were completely untrained. "Mistresses of such schools have often told me they *were not used to work—were ladies, and quite unfit for this sort of thing!*"[24] The poor quality of the education provided by these schools could not be overemphasized. Bodichon was certain that tradespeople would discover that their gardeners' children received a better education than they could provide for their own children at twice the cost. She pointed out the importance of this segment of the middle class as a civilizing agent for the working classes, noting the potential for upward mobility within the social ranks. Just above the working class, these people could influence laborers more than could the upper classes because they were in constant contact with working-class people. If the peripheral middle class had more than the artificial fashionable values given them by the upper classes, they would themselves improve and in the process that improvement would filter down the social scale.

Bodichon dismissed the doctrine that girls' private schools must be self-supporting, noting that while the principle of self-support was admirable, there was no reason why it should apply to girls' schools more than boys'. The endowments that had made magnificent schools and colleges available to generations of boys had not

23. Barbara Bodichon, "Middle Class Schools for Girls," *English Woman's Journal* 6 (November 1860): 169.
24. Ibid., p. 170.

made men less independent, "not a whit pauperised." She hoped that the future would bring endowments for women's schools on the scale of those of Christ Church or Eton: "Giving education, the very means of self-help, is the safest way of being charitable."[25] It would be wiser for charity to flow from the rich to the middle class, rather than to the poorest class. Aid to the poorest would be wasted because the rich failed to understand the true needs of the poor. The poor might be turned into a class of beggars, but the middle class would accept help and maintain its independent spirit. She suggested that wealthy educated women devote themselves to providing education for girls of the middle class. The many rich young English women who were bored, having accomplishments and no outlets for them, might organize and employ their talents in a volunteer effort. The principles earlier applied in the staffing and organization of the Portman Hall School are clearly visible in this plan.

Bodichon advocated raising the standards for mistresses of girls' schools by allowing them to take the examinations designed for students who were not university members. The system followed at Cambridge for non–university members included an examination each year for students under sixteen and another for students not more than eighteen. Students were examined in English (including reading aloud, spelling, and dictation), history, geography, Latin, French, German, arithmetic, mathematics, natural philosophy, and other subjects, and received a certificate after passing these examinations. The extension of these examinations to female teachers would provide some guarantee of their adequate preparation for their positions.

Bodichon had definite ideas about the proper curriculum for the girls' schools. She stressed the necessity of "object lessons," citing William Shields' Birkbeck School at Peckham as a model of this type of teaching. Drawing, singing, French, arithmetic, and bookkeeping were to be taught. Although it was important to consider girls' future responsibilities as wives and mothers, Bodichon insisted

25. Ibid., p. 172.

that it was equally necessary to remember that most of these women would have to work for at least some part of their lives. The advantages and disadvantages of the different types of employment available to women should be explained to older pupils. They needed to understand the principles of social and political economy. Above all, these girls needed knowledge of the colonies and preparation to be emigrants. Many women refused to face the unknown and remained behind when husbands or brothers left for Australia, the Cape, or other distant settlements: "The daughter of a nursery gardener, about thirty years of age, told me tremblingly that she had consented to go with her family to Australia, 'but how she was to get through the earth to the other side, where she understood Australia to be, she did not in the least know.'"[26]

"Middle Class Schools for Girls" is an interesting survey of the deficiencies in education available to that portion of the population just above the working poor. The middle-class girls described are just barely within the boundaries of the class and deprived by their status of the opportunity to gain the rudiments of education available to workers through the Anglican National schools. Basic literacy and training for practical application in the home or for employment are the goals discussed. Bodichon is clearly evaluating a system utilized by a class far below her own and prescribing a voluntary and charitable effort by members of her own upper-class circle to rectify the situation. The Portman Hall School provided a model for the proposal, although mixing sexes or social classes is not suggested. The difficulties faced by this class of women in gaining employment and the questions of emigration and redundancy are central considerations. Public concern regarding surplus women had increased to such an extent by the time "Middle Class Schools for Girls" was written that Bodichon's prescription for female education was echoed in other papers brought before the Social Science Association, as well as in the press. The problems of women, in particular of women needing gainful employment, concerned Bodi-

26. Ibid., p. 176.

chon throughout the fifties, and this article on women's education was only one indication of the focus her work had taken since her first experiment with progressive elementary education.

It is not quite clear what decided Barbara Smith to begin a campaign in 1854 against the existing property laws as they affected married women. She was, as noted, single and wealthy and took her independence and equality as a matter of course within her private circle. By the time she was twenty-one, however, she had met single girls and married women who made her realize how unique her position was. She was acutely aware of the injustice of the laws of marriage and divorce and in her analysis of J. S. Mill's *Political Economy* in 1849 had made clear her belief in the necessity for change in those laws. From that time she continually insisted that the "deconsideration" of women embodied in those laws was at once the cause and result of all female legal disabilities.[27]

Throughout the thirties and forties Caroline Norton's marital difficulties were discussed at the Smith table, since Thomas Noon Talfourd, who introduced the Infant Custody Act in Parliament, was a prominent Unitarian and a friend of Benjamin Smith. The marital problems of Anna Jameson, a friend of Barbara Smith's aunt Julia, were also a matter of concern to the household. Anna and Robert Jameson married in 1825. Throughout their unhappy marriage she was a prolific writer, her literary income serving to support them both. In 1833, after a temporary marital separation, Robert Jameson became a judge in Canada and afterward Chancellor of the Province of Toronto. Anna joined her husband in Canada, but by 1836 they decided on a permanent separation. Jameson agreed to send his wife an allowance of £300 a year, but did not pay it, and when he died in 1854 he left her nothing. She supported herself and her widowed mother and sisters by writing. Generous friends combined to provide her an annuity of £100 a year. Her personal unhappiness and the financial difficulties resulting from her mar-

27. Frances Power Cobbe, *Autobiography*, 2 vols. (Boston: Houghton Mifflin, 1894), 1:154.

riage made her bitter about the laws regulating that relationship: "Any conventional law binding the one party and absolving the other as regards the most sacred of all the obligations incurred by such a contract—mutual truth, in word and act—must of necessity place both parties in a false position and render the whole contract of marriage a standing lie."[28] Jameson was a great influence on Barbara Smith and her friends Bessie Parkes, Adelaide Procter, and Anna Mary Howitt. She became their patroness in many feminist projects and called them her "adopted nieces."[29] She was prominent in the extraparliamentary activities in support of a Married Women's Property Bill in 1856 and 1857. Her personal situation, of concern throughout the years to Julia Smith, could only heighten Barbara's awareness of the injustice of the marriage laws and strengthen her resolve to work for legislative change.

In 1853 John Wharton's *Exposition of the Laws Relating to the Women of England* was published. This 557-page treatise explained the legal status of women in great detail, but made little public impact. Even Barbara Smith's new friend George Eliot remained unsympathetic after reading the book. "Enfranchisement of women only makes creeping progress; and that is best, for woman does not yet deserve a much better lot than man gives her."[30] During 1853 Smith studied the laws affecting women and with advice from a family friend, Matthew Davenport Hill, Recorder of Birmingham, in 1854 she drew up and published a much more concise study than Wharton's legal tome. Her pamphlet *A Brief Summary in Plain Language of the Most Important Laws of England Concerning Women* sold for a few pence and created a sensation. A second edition was published in 1856 and a third, considerably enlarged, in 1869. Concise and clear, the pamphlet was in its way far more effective than previous outbursts of feminist propaganda. It began by explaining the legal conditions of single women—their ability to own property, their position as heirs, their ability to vote on parish questions but

28. Clara Thomas, *Love and Work Enough: The Life of Anna Jameson* (Toronto: University of Toronto Press, 1967), p. 208.
29. Ibid., p. 209.
30. George Eliot to Mrs. P. A. Taylor, 1 February 1853, *George Eliot Letters*, 2:86.

not for members of Parliament, their responsibility as property owners to pay taxes despite disfranchisement. The legal and social restrictions on employment for single women were detailed. Women
could hold no important offices except for that of Sovereign. They
could not serve in government or the church and were excluded in
fact, if not in law, from the professions.[31]

The opening section on single women was followed by a discussion of the laws concerning married women, a long list, including
those concerning a husband's absolute right to his wife's property
and earnings, whether she was living with him or not. "A man and
wife are one person in law; the wife loses all her rights as a single
woman, and her existence is entirely absorbed in that of her husband."[32] Barbara Smith had discovered what many were still un-
aware of—that a man actually had a legal right to the property of
his betrothed wife, who could not dispose of her property without
his knowledge, once she had given him a promise of marriage. She
explained the position of the engaged woman, the complexities of
marriage settlements, and the question of legal custody of infants
and children in cases of separation of husband and wife. The laws of
divorce were reviewed, including the difficulty and expense of the
action, and the impracticability of such a proceeding being undertaken by a woman. It required an act of Parliament to obtain a divorce and cost between £600 and £700. Women could not be plain-
tiffs, defendants, or witnesses during the proceedings. Grounds for
divorce were adultery by the wife and in some cases "aggravated
adultery" by the husband.[33]

The last section of legal explanation, preceding several pages of
"Remarks," concerns illegitimate children and their mothers. The
text is dispassionate, a bland exposition of the legal question which
was so personally important to the five illegitimate children of Benjamin Smith. The illegitimate child could not inherit except by bequest, having no legal claim to family property or surname. Barbara

31. Barbara Bodichon, A Brief Summary in Plain Language of the Most Important Laws of
England Concerning Women (London: Holyoake, 1854), p. 2.
32. Ibid., p. 4.
33. Ibid., p. 6.

Smith's eccentricities were sometimes attributed to a rebellion against the stigma of illegitimacy, but whatever her personal traumas were, the discussion of the issue in *Laws Concerning Women* is trenchant and unemotional.

In the concluding section, the position of married women in England is compared with that of women in France, Hungary, and Germany. In those countries, and in some of the American states, women were able to own and dispose of their property even when married. The basic argument in the "Remarks" is against overlegislation. The remedy for woman's unjust treatment by the law is to be found in a removal of those bad laws; Smith does not envision reform in terms of increased legislative action. The Remarks clearly reflect a strong belief in an individualistic, noninterventionist mode of government. Smith seeks to justify legislation concerning married women's property in the tradition of the free traders who led the anti–Corn Law campaign. Progress is assessed by the ability to dispense with legislation. As society evolves, external restraints should become unnecessary:

> Women, more than any other members of the community, suffer from over-legislation. A woman over 21 . . . if she unites herself to a man, the law immediately steps in, and she finds herself legislated for, and her condition of life suddenly and entirely changed. Whatever age she may be of, she is again considered as an infant—she is again under "reasonable restraint"—she loses her separate existence, and is merged in that of her husband. "In short," says Judge Hurlbut, "a woman is courted and wedded as an angel, and yet denied the dignity of a rational and moral being ever after."[34]

Smith's discussion of the effect of restrictive marriage laws on working women included a repudiation of the principle of protection. Through education, working women could learn to manage their own finances. The power of husbands over the earnings of their wives represented injustice, not protection. The married women of

34. Ibid., pp. 8–9.

the working class suffered most under the law because they faced the possibility of economic privation in addition to the loss of spiritual independence by virtue of their married state. "All who are familiar with the working class know how much suffering and privation is caused by the exercise of this *right* by drunken and bad men."[35] The problem of battered wives was the subject of extensive discussion in the contemporary press.

Asking "why does marriage make so little legal difference to men, and such a mighty legal difference to women?" Barbara Smith concluded that abolition of the current laws regarding property would be a practical and just step toward improving women's legal status: "We do not say that these laws of property are the only unjust laws concerning women to be found in the short summary we have given, but they form a simple, tangible, and not offensive point of attack."[36] She had carefully chosen the property laws because she felt that they could be altered without offending the bulk of British society. It was an interesting choice, reflecting some sophistication. Revolutionary as her personal view of women's equality might be, she suggested first a reform that she estimated would be acceptable to moderates, since extreme opponents of change in woman's status were unlikely to be moved by any appeal. She wrote her pamphlet in unemotional, indeed rather dull prose to emphasize the reasonableness of the case and the solidity of its foundation. For so ebullient and unconventional a personality, *Laws Concerning Women* represented uncharacteristic moderation, giving evidence of Smith's pragmatism and political acumen. This strong practical sense served later when organization of extraparliamentary activity became necessary, and it is important to remember that this quality served Smith and feminism quite as much as, if not more than, the romantic panache for which she is primarily remembered.

It is not surprising that Smith's brief factual account of the law led to a demand for action. The men and women of the upper classes, long protected by the courts of chancery, were often ignorant of

35. Ibid., p. 10.
36. Ibid., p. 11.

the peculiarities of Common Law. Harriet Grote, wife of the historian George Grote, was typical of this ignorance. She was robbed of her watch and purse one day. When she appeared in court to give evidence, she was astonished to hear the watch and purse described as belonging to Mr. Grote. When the legal reason for this was explained to her, she became so indignant that she joined feminist ranks.[37]

Reasoned and unemotional as the pamphlet might be, any suggestion for change in the laws concerning women engendered heated discussions, and adverse reaction to Smith's publication was strong. Margaret Oliphant was sharply critical in an article published in *Blackwood's* in April 1856, when the married women's property campaign was gathering momentum. She dismissed the pamphlet as a well-intentioned but misdirected effort to repudiate the laws of nature. She gave Smith credit for a clear and accurate summary of the law, but could accept no general need for legislative reform. Antagonism between the sexes would be the primary result of such efforts. The marriage laws merely reflected the divine order and it would be foolish to attempt to redress the grievances of a few by legislating for all members of society.[38] Divorce was anathema to Oliphant and the law protected the social fabric by making the dissolution of the marriage bond nearly impossible: "The business of a righteous and rational law is not to provide facilities for escaping, but to rivet and enforce the claims of that relationship upon which all society is founded. . . . The justice which means an equal division of rights has no place between those two persons whom natural policy as well as Divine institution teach us to consider as one."[39] Oliphant considered Smith's pamphlet "one sided and unequal." Natural order and British tradition determined the roles of husband and wife; tampering with the marriage laws would not alleviate the distress of a few aggrieved wives, but merely weaken the foundations of society. She was convinced that the public mind would never accept any dilution of the principle by which the husband

37. Hester Burton, *Barbara Bodichon* (London: Constable, 1949), p. 60.
38. Margaret Oliphant, "Laws Concerning Women," pp. 379–80.
39. Ibid., p. 382.

was "the sole legal and public representative of all the interests of the wife."[40]

Smith's *Laws Concerning Women* stimulated public discussion of the marriage laws. It was followed shortly by the appearance of a pamphlet by Caroline Norton. George Norton had continued since 1839 to claim the proceeds of his estranged wife's literary work, and when in 1854, he subpoenaed her publishers to produce her contracts with them, she wrote *English Laws for Women in the Nineteenth Century*. It was an emotional description of her personal situation, but her grievances were of wide public interest and the publication increased discussion of the marriage laws in the press. Shortly after this pamphlet appeared, Lord Cranworth, the Chancellor in Lord Aberdeen's Ministry, brought forward in the House of Lords a bill to reform the marriage and divorce laws. As early as 1850 the necessity for reform of the divorce law had been officially recognized and a Royal Commission under the chairmanship of Lord Campbell had been appointed to investigate the matter. The commissioners considered the private act procedure which was the only means available for obtaining a divorce and concluded that it was too difficult and too expensive. In their reports published in 1853 they recommended either abolishing the private act procedure or simplifying it and making it less expensive.[41] The commissioners' recommendations were contained in Cranworth's bill for marriage law reform. In early 1855 Caroline Norton published *A Letter to the Queen on Lord Cranworth's Marriage and Divorce Bill*, an indictment of Cranworth's proposal, which she deemed inadequate, expressed in the same violent language as her 1854 pamphlet. She pledged not to write anything but political pamphlets until the laws were altered.[42]

Caroline Norton's two pamphlets were treated sympathetically by the liberal Christian *North British Review*. The *Review*, however, regretted Norton's continual airing of private grievances. Acknowledging the justice of the case, it cautioned that the repeated public

40. Ibid., p. 385.
41. O. R. MacGregor, *Divorce in England* (London: Heinemann, 1957), pp. 16–17.
42. Perkins, *Mrs. Norton*, pp. 246–47.

outbursts injured the woman's cause, asserting that "the case should be auxiliary to the cause; it should not master and overwhelm it."[43] The bulk of the article dealt with the injustices themselves, reflecting in great part the arguments set forth in Smith's *Laws Concerning Women*. Reform of the divorce law, the issue of paramount importance to Norton, was dismissed, except as it affected the "non-existence" of women, which was the article's central consideration. The merging of woman's identity with that of her husband was deplored. The resulting inequities strengthened the case for legislative reform:

> This theory of the non-existence of women pursues its victims from the schoolroom to the grave. Trained from the first to be dependent upon men, they pass through different stages of dependence, and at the last find they cannot bequeath to another man the ring on their finger, which they have worn from their earliest girlhood, or the Bible in which they first learnt to spell. It cannot be said that they are educated for the proper discharge of the duties of wife and mother; but they are educated for the non-existence which the condition involves. . . . They are fit, indeed; only to be absorbed.[44]

The *North British Review* used Norton's case as a springboard for a consideration of the whole issue of the legal status of married women. However, Norton herself was motivated purely by personal circumstances. She had no interest in Smith's work or in the group of feminists coalescing around the married women's property campaign the following year. She confined her interest to the marriage and divorce bills which were presented between 1855 and 1857, simultaneously with several unsuccessful married women's property bills. Despite her own efforts to dissociate herself from the organizing women's movement, Norton's case and pamphlets publicized the issues which Smith's *Laws Concerning Women* had put before the public. Norton was "news," and the notoriety attached to her

---

43. "The 'Non-Existence' of Women," *North British Review* 22 (August 1855): 301.
44. Ibid., p. 290.

name assured a wide audience for articles about the issue, an advantage which far outweighed the negative reactions her name auto-
matically engendered in some quarters.

But pamphlets and articles could not change the law. Women
were excluded from parliamentary participation, so other means
had to be found to affect legislation. Late in 1855 Barbara Smith
decided that petitioning Parliament might result in action. She discussed her plan with Anna Mary Howitt, an intimate friend with
whom she had spent the summer at Hastings, recuperating from a
bout of ill health. The proposal was presented to Mary Howitt,
Anna Mary's mother, in December 1855, and received whole-
hearted approval. William and Mary Howitt thought Smith had an
excellent opportunity to put together an extraparliamentary reform
organization.[45] The "grand scheme" involved setting up a committee of women to obtain signatures in support of a change in the
property laws. In December 1855 Smith brought a small group of
women together in her father's drawing room in Blandford Square
to approve the text of her petition and coordinate its distribution
and the signature campaign. This was the first committee of women
in England to discuss the rights of their own sex, and it brought a
new political force into existence. Unable to vote or speak in favor
of legislative reform, the women members of the first Married
Women's Property Committee represented the first organized feminist group. Some years later Bessie Parkes noted that though the
married women's property issue was important, it was the establishment of that first committee structure which signaled a real beginning for the women's movement. The committee was the beginning of a communication network that linked women throughout
the country and laid the foundation for organized feminist efforts of
the future.[46] Individual women like Mary Wollstonecraft and Caroline Norton had publicly condemned the injustices of society
against women. More reticent persons like Florence Nightingale
wrote of them in private and struggled against personal frustration

45. Howitt, *Autobiography*, 2:114.
46. Parkes, *Essays on Women's Work*, p. 60.

by individual action. Never before had a group of women met to-gether in England to discuss and organize political action to change the status of the sex.

The committee that Barbara Smith led included Mary Howitt, Anna Jameson, Anna Mary Howitt, Bessie Parkes, Maria Rye, and Mrs. Bridell Fox. Mary Howitt's membership and support was particularly important, since she was prominent in literary circles, happily married, and impeccably respectable. Quakers, William and Mary Howitt were well-known poets who enjoyed close ties to the Rossettis and the Pre-Raphaelite brotherhood. They had known the Smiths since 1845 and their daughter Anna Mary was Barbara Smith's close friend. Despite the protests of S. C. Hall, the antifeminist editor of the *New Monthly Magazine,* and her other conservative friends, Mary Howitt joined the "vulgar" feminist campaign. In March 1854 at a gathering at the Smiths' London home she shocked Anne Thackeray, then seventeen years old, when she announced her opinion that women should sit in Parliament.[47]

The members of the committee worked to collect signatures on more than seventy petitions throughout the country. They were anxious to gain the signatures of eminent women whom the public held in high regard. They feared the consequences of having many signers noted for "strong-mindedness." Mary Howitt discussed the problem in a letter to her daughter in January 1856. She had visited Baroness Angela Burdett-Coutts, wealthy benefactress of many charitable projects, and discussed the petition campaign with her. Coutts approved of the proposed changes in the marriage laws, but withheld her own signature pending further consideration. She told Howitt that several of the women supporting the petition would do it no good: "These ladies hold such free opinions with regard to marriage that people would naturally be suspicious of the intentions of the whole thing."[48] Howitt respected that political wisdom and advised her daughter, "I do think it most needful to have an eye to

47. Carl Ray Woodring, *Victorian Samplers: William and Mary Howitt* (Lawrence: University of Kansas Press, 1952), p. 180.
48. Howitt, *Autobiography*, 2:115.

the moral status of the persons supporting this movement; and that in the fields of science and literature signatures such as those of Mrs. Somerville and Mrs. Gaskell should be obtained."[49]

The literary women rallied to this cause. It united women of radical and moderate views in a common effort. Harriet Martineau, Elizabeth Barrett Browning, Elizabeth Gaskell, Anna Jameson, and Marian Evans (George Eliot) all signed the petition. Jameson later wrote that when she had signed the document she had done so as a protest against the general injustice of the laws concerning women, rather than with a view to the particular problem of married women's property: "What matter how much laws act here or there . . . if they permeate and in some sort vitiate the relations of the two sexes. . . . Not even those who plead for their expedience deny the abstract injustice of such laws."[50]

Gaskell, whose signature was deemed so important by Howitt, had quite a different viewpoint. Wife of a Unitarian minister, mother of four daughters, and a successful fiction writer, she accepted a traditional female role. She confided to Eliza Fox in April 1850 that she was "sometimes coward enough to wish that we were back in the darkness where obedience was the only seen duty of women."[51] That same month she wrote again to Fox, placidly happy that her writing was earning monetary recognition: "Do you know that they sent me £200 for Lizzie Leigh . . . William has composedly buttoned it up in his pocket. He has promised I may have some for my Refuge."[52] Gaskell disliked Barbara Smith personally, as she admitted to Charles Norton in 1860, but she conceded that she respected and admired her courage and dedication.[53] Gaskell thought women inferior to men and in October 1856 dismissed the idea of medical training for women: "I would not trust a mouse to a woman if a man's judgment was to be had. Women have no judgment. They've tact and sensitiveness, genius and hundreds of fine

49. Ibid.
50. "Capabilities and Discapabilities of Women," Westminster Review 67 (January 1857): 29.
51. Gaskell, Letters, p. 109.
52. Rubenius, Woman Question in Mrs. Gaskell's Life, p. 33.
53. Gaskell, Letters, pp. 606–07.

and loving qualities, but are at best angelic geese as to matters requiring serious and long scientific consideration. I'm not a friend of female medical education."[54] Despite these misgivings, she signed the married women's property petition, which Eliza Fox had sent her, and returned it with a lukewarm endorsement. She was convinced that even if the law were altered, unscrupulous husbands could avoid its restrictions. But she admitted that women were ill-used under existing statutes and, although without much hope for improvement, she signed the petition.[55]

Harriet Martineau was very much aware of the problems that faced working-class married women. They wrote to her seeking advice on how to ease their situations and offering to send evidence or money if Martineau would lend assistance.[56] But although she signed the 1856 petition, Martineau was not in favor of a radical feminist campaign and clearly subscribed to the doctrine that education and training would improve women's position quite as much as was necessary. She believed that once women entered the professions and proved themselves there and in business, society would accept their contributions without prejudice. She saw no point in passionate demands for voting rights: "I think the better way is for us all to learn and to try to the utmost what we can do, and thus win for ourselves the consideration which alone can secure us rational treatment."[57] She can best be described as a moderate in the feminist ranks, acutely aware of the inequities in woman's position, but sharing Gaskell's reservations about the wisdom of legislative activitism.

Elizabeth Browning was another prominent author and respectable figure who signed the petition and allowed herself to become known as one of its sponsors. She was outspoken in her criticism of the romantic furor Florence Nightingale's nursing efforts had aroused since 1854. She did not consider nursing evidence of the

54. Elizabeth Sanderson Haldane, *Mrs. Gaskell and Her Friends* (New York: D. Appleton, 1931), p. 285.

55. Gaskell, *Letters*, p. 379.

56. Harriet Martineau, *Autobiography*, 3 vols. (London: Smith, 1877), 2:104.

57. Ibid., 1:402.

highest achievement women might attain and wrote Anna Jameson in February 1855 that she saw no new position gained for women by Nightingale's success: "Every man is on his knees before ladies carrying lint, calling them 'angelic she's,' whereas, if they stir an inch as thinkers or artists from the beaten line (involving more good to general humanity than is involved in lint), the very same men would curse the impudence of the very same women and stop there."[58] Browning was not the ardent feminist the preceding passage might suggest—on another occasion she indicated that she believed women intellectually inferior to men.[59] But despite her own happy marriage she was aware of the inequities of the marriage law and signed the petition. She was dismayed by traditional views of marriage, deploring the fact that men seldom looked for companions to share life, but rather selected hostesses and housekeepers in their wives.[60]

Elizabeth Browning's signature on the married women's property petition indicated her willingness to take positive action to correct a legislative injustice. Her publication in 1857 of *Aurora Leigh* illustrated her disgust with women's failure to prove their abilities and condemned the tendency to substitute words for action:

> A woman . . . must prove what she can do
> Before she does it, prate of woman's rights,
> Of woman's mission, woman's function, till
> The men (who are prating too on their side) cry
> "A woman's function plainly is . . . to talk"—
> By speaking we prove only we can speak,
> Which he, the man here, never doubted. What
> He doubts is, whether we can do the thing
> With decent grace we've not yet done at all—
> Who so cures the plague,
> Though twice a woman, shall be called a leech.[61]

58. Elizabeth Barrett Browning, *Letters*, ed. Frederic G. Kenyon (New York: Macmillan, 1898), pp. 188–89.

59. Alethea Hayter, *Mrs. Browning* (London: Faber & Faber, 1962), p. 185.

60. Ibid., p. 188.

61. Elizabeth Barrett Browning, *Aurora Leigh and Other Poems* (London: Women's Press, 1978), bk. 8, lines 814–43.

Ironically, Browning's annoyance with women's seeming predilection for words was shared by Florence Nightingale, whose work Browning had earlier dismissed. Nightingale would have nothing to do with the married women's property campaigns. She admitted to Harriet Martineau in November 1858, "I am brutally indifferent to the wrongs or the rights of my sex."[62] Drawn reluctantly into suffrage issues in the late sixties by John Stuart Mill, she ignored feminism during its early years. While Barbara Smith crusaded for legal remedies and occupational alternatives for women, Nightingale expressed bitter disappointment with her sex. In 1861 she wrote a long disjointed condemnation of women to her close friend Mary Clarke Mohl, who had just written a book on Madame Recamier. She felt that none of her nurses had learned anything of permanent value in the Crimea and condemned women in general for selfishness and incompetence: "It makes me mad, the 'Women's Rights' talk about the 'want of a field' for them—when I know that I would gladly give £500 a year for a Woman Secretary . . . women cannot state a fact accurately to another, nor can that other attend to it accurately enough for it to become information."[63] Nightingale was in ill health in 1861 and very disappointed that her work was not making greater progress. Her letter was slightly hysterical in tone. Basically, however, she remained consistently unsympathetic to women's organized efforts for emancipation and contributed to the movement only by the example of her personal career. This granddaughter of William Smith contrasted sharply in personality and life style with her vivacious first cousin Barbara Smith. Benjamin Smith's illegitimate family was taboo to the Nightingales, so the two families did not mix socially. Only late in life did Barbara Smith communicate at all with Florence Nightingale. Nightingale pursued her nursing and sanitary reform, oblivious of or, if reminded, somewhat contemptuous of the effort being organized by her cousin.

Another noted woman, quite as consumed by her personal artistic efforts as Florence Nightingale was by her crusade, saw the femi-

---

62. Woodham-Smith, *Florence Nightingale*, p. 316.
63. Ibid., pp. 384–86.

nist campaign somewhat differently. George Eliot did not join the organized women's movement, and she refused to speak publicly on behalf of feminist issues. A close friend of Barbara Smith from 1852, she was, however, quite willing to sign the married women's property petition and to urge her friends to join that effort. Eliot was convinced that her function was that of artist not activist.[64] Individual artistic contribution was for her a primary responsibility, representing the only legitimate occupation for potentially talented men or women. In August 1857 she wrote to Sara Hennell after viewing an exhibit of Rosa Bonheur's paintings: "What power! That is the way women should assert their rights."[65] Whatever her convictions regarding the creative artist's public responsibility towards societal reform, Eliot did lend personal and financial support to Smith's feminist projects throughout the years. On January 6, 1856, she received a letter from Smith and a copy of the petition.[66] Two days later she urged Hennell to support the campaign: "The petition is well and soberly drawn up and has been signed by Mrs. Gaskell, Harriet Martineau and the et ceteras. So you will be in good company, if you care about that."[67] Hennell answered enthusiastically and Eliot forwarded Smith's instructions for obtaining signatures, writing, "I am glad you have taken up the cause, for I do think that, with proper provisos and safeguards, the proposed law would help to raise the position and character of women. It is one round of a long ladder stretching far beyond our lives."[68]

The fact that George Eliot was living with George Henry Lewes and was not recognized in polite circles meant nothing to Barbara Smith, but Eliot's signature on the married women's property petition did not add to its respectability, nor was it publicized. Indeed, Smith's own illegitimacy, her friendship with Eliot and Lewes, and her generally unconventional attitude made her own leadership something of a liability for the committee. Her name was not men-

64. *George Eliot Letters*, 7:44.
65. Ibid., 2:376.
66. John W. Cross, *George Eliot's Life*, 3 vols. (London: William Blackwood & Sons, 1884), 1:315.
67. *George Eliot Letters*, 2:225.
68. Ibid., 2:226.

tioned when the petition was presented, nor was her role publicly emphasized. On March 13, 1856, Anna Mary Howitt wrote her sister Margaret that the petition had been announced in Parliament. The petitions, which had gained over twenty-four thousand signatures, were presented the following day and were mentioned favorably by the *Daily News*. The paper congratulated Sir Erskine Perry on the "remarkable" document and praised the women organizers for their work gathering signatures.[69] On March 17, 1856, Anna Howitt wrote jubilantly about the petition's respectful reception by the Commons. Brougham had presented the petition to the Lords and even there his speech was received favorably.[70] Respectability was the key to acceptance and every effort was made by Smith in the next several months to present the case for reform with consistently impeccable credentials; hence, her leadership remained private, except for the publication of a second edition of *Laws Concerning Women* in 1856.

In February 1856, before the petitions were presented to Parliament, Matthew Davenport Hill presented Barbara Smith's *Laws Concerning Women* to the Personal Laws Committee of the Law Amendment Society, which agreed to take up the issue of married women's property reform, resolving to report to the general body shortly. The Law Amendment Society had been founded in 1844 and numbered among its founders many of Benjamin Smith's friends. Hill, a prominent Unitarian, was one of its founding members and others included Lord Brougham and George Hastings, leaders of the Social Science Association, founded shortly afterward in 1857. On February 23, 1856, Sir Stafford Northcote, M.P., spoke in favor of legislative reform of the laws concerning women at the Law Amendment Society's general meeting. He was particularly concerned by the problems of working-class married women, whose civil disabilities often encouraged physical abuse: "If law was meant to be the substitution of order for brute force, no persons more require the protection of law than women."[71] Others sup-

69. Reiss, *Rights and Duties of Englishwomen*, p. 125.
70. Howitt, *Autobiography*, 2:116–17.
71. *Law Amendment Journal* 1 (1856): 11.

ported Northcote's expressions of concern and members were reminded that the Personal Laws Committee was preparing a report
on the issue. In March 1856 the *Law Amendment Journal* applauded
the presentation of the married women's property petitions, noting
that the signatures had been obtained through the work of a small
group of women and expressing the Society's determination to pursue reform.[72] On April 28, the issue of married women's property
reform again came before the Society's general meeting, and
Brougham suggested that the Society sponsor a public meeting to
discuss the issue.[73]

The meeting took place on May 31 in the rooms of the Horticul-
tural Society at 21 Regent Street, London. The Report of the Personal Laws Committee on the Property of Married Women, largely
the work of Sir Erskine Perry, had been presented to the Society's
general meeting on May 26 and adopted after a brief discussion.[74]
The public meeting was heavily attended and, after lengthy discussion, resolutions were adopted reasserting the need for legislative
reform on married women's property and indicating the Society's
resolve to carry the issue forward in Parliament. The *Law Amendment Journal* noted the high caliber of those attending and the fact
that "a large number of ladies were also present, including Mrs.
Jameson, Mrs. Howitt, and many other lady authors."[75] The
women, including Barbara Smith, whose name was not mentioned
by the *Journal*, were silent participants in the meeting. It was not
yet common for women to attend public meetings and unheard of
for them to speak out in public. Indeed, sixteen years earlier, in
1840, when the American delegation to the World Anti-Slavery
Convention held in London arrived with four female members,
scandal rocked the conference. The women were forced to sit in a
curtained gallery and the British public was outraged when the
leader of the American delegation, William Lloyd Garrison, arrived and stated that he preferred to join the ladies and refused to

72. Ibid., p. 33.
73. Ibid., p. 64.
74. Ibid., p. 89.
75. Ibid., p. 92.

participate in the discussions which followed.[76] The idea that women might enter public discussion was still unacceptable in 1856. The same women who sat quietly by at that May 31st meeting were provided a forum shortly thereafter, for when Brougham established the Social Science Association in 1857, he welcomed women to its membership and encouraged them to address its meetings. But their participation at those meetings met with resistance and ridicule, and as late as 1862 the *Saturday Review* remarked: "There are decided advantages in this Universal Palaver Association. It must be remembered to Lord Brougham's credit that he is the first person who has dealt upon this plan with the problem of female loquacity. . . . It is a great idea to tire out the hitherto unflagging vigour of their tongues by encouraging a taste for stump oratory among them."[77] The "Universal Palaver Association" was as yet unformed in 1856 and public speaking by women was out of the question. The Law Amendment Society meeting was graced therefore, by a properly silent and ladylike feminine contingent.

The Report on Married Women's Property discussed and affirmed at the public meeting, proposed seven alterations to the common law to remove the contradiction of two sets of courts operating under diametrically opposed rules. One law would be established, applicable to all classes:

1. The common law rules, which made a gift of all a woman's personal property to her husband at marriage, would be repealed.
2. A married woman would have the right to hold separate property by law, as she now could in equity.
3. A woman marrying without any ante-nuptial contract would retain her property, acquisitions, and earnings as if she were a feme sole.
4. A married woman having separate property would be liable on her separate contracts, whether made before or after marriage.

76. Kamm, *Rapiers and Battleaxes*, p. 28.
77. "The Universal Palaver Association," *Saturday Review*, 19 November 1862, p. 272.

5. A husband would not be liable for the ante-nuptial debts of his wife any further than any property brought to him by his wife under settlement extended.
6. A married woman would have the power to make a will. If she died without making one, her property would be distributed under the same statue that applied to her husband's property.
7. The rights of succession between husband and wife, whether as to real or personal estate, to curtesy or dower, would be framed on principles of equal justice to each party.[78]

The Report of the Law Amendment Society and the petition campaign were considered and applauded by Caroline F. Cornwallis in the October 1856 *Westminster Review*. She noted that Great Britain was not the first to consider a proposed alteration of the laws of property. This experiment had already begun successfully in the United States. The article dismissed charges that "the Law Amendment Society is grown 'gallant,' that the 'insurrection of the women' will arrest the business of the nation," asserting that approaching so serious a topic in flippant tones "cannot merit a serious answer in this journal."[79] Its closing paragraphs echoed Barbara Smith's *Laws Concerning Women*, noting the harmful effect of over-legislation and describing attempts to reform the marriage laws as part of a continuing campaign to eliminate antiquated or ill-conceived legislation. Opponents of marriage law reform were dismissed as alarmists who opposed all innovation or improvement in legal and social structures.[80]

The opposition was becoming more vocal, however, and their arguments against destruction of the family dominated the married women's property campaign and finally defeated the reform attempts of 1856 and 1857. When in June 1856, Sir Erskine Perry introduced a motion in Commons stating, "the rules of Common Law which give all the personal property of a woman in marriage, and

78. Caroline Frances Cornwallis, "The Property of Married Women," *Westminster Review* 66 (October 1856): 192.
79. Ibid., p. 196.
80. Ibid.

subsequently acquired property and earnings, to the husband, are unjust in principle and injurious in their operation,"[81] the *Saturday Review* responded with stinging satire:

> There is a perfect rage for Acts of Parliament to redress all the little social and domestic miseries of human life. . . . There is a Bill for controlling the sale of dirty books, a Bill for dealing with adulteration . . . and the Bill introduced by Lord Raynham to prevent cruelty to animals, which will put a stop to live-bait fishing and galloping a horse to a railway station. And finally there is Sir Erskine Perry's Bill for redressing all the hitches which occur about money matters between married people.[82]

Having reduced the issue to a ridiculous triviality, the magazine attempted to show how dangerous any change in the laws of property would be for societal stability, portraying the family and the sanctity of the marriage vows as under siege. The women reformers were characterized as unnatural members of their sex. During the brief debate in Commons, the Attorney General, Sir Alexander Cockburn, concurred with Perry's opinion that common law and equity should be made less contradictory. However, he urged Perry to withdraw his abstract resolution, so that the Government might prepare a more concrete proposal for introduction during the next session. The opposition expressed in the *Saturday Review* was duplicated during the debates in Commons. A Mr. T. Chambers reflected the general fear when he cautioned: "No doubt the evils which now existed required remedy and ought to be attended to, but to introduce into every house in England the principle of separate rights, separate interests, and a separate legal existence between man and wife, was to nullify and destroy the law of marriage altogether, as far as regarded its sacredness and sanctity."[83] Perry agreed to withdraw his motion, urging that the government not delay too long before introducing the promised legislation.

81. *Hansard's Parliamentary Debates* (Commons), 3d ser., 142 (1856): 1277.
82. *Saturday Review*, 15 June 1856, p. 135.
83. *Hansard's Parliamentary Debates* (Commons), 3d ser., 142 (1856): 1283.

As early as this first parliamentary debate on married women's property, the specter of another bill rose to haunt its advocates. The Marriage and Divorce Bill was already being considered in Parliament and seemed from the beginning to undercut the concept of a separate Married Women's Property Bill. Several of the debaters on Perry's motion mentioned the need for divorce reform, and their statements reflected the general feeling that such reform would solve all of the difficulties associated with the property rights of married women. Mr. J. G. Phillimore noted during the debate that there was a need for some reform of the divorce law, but warned against weakening the "ideality of interest" between husband and wife. "Nothing could be more frightful than to teach wives that their interests were on one side and those of their husband on the other."[84] The Solicitor General, Sir Richard Bethell, made it clear that he considered a Married Women's Property Bill a secondary issue. He dismissed the concept of a separate act and suggested instead that when the Marriage and Divorce Bill finally came to the House of Commons it might be possible to insert a provision concerning the property of married women who had been deserted by their husbands.[85]

Despite its brevity, this first tentative parliamentary consideration of the laws concerning the property of married women stimulated public discussion. An article supporting reform of the property laws appeared in the *Westminster Review* in January 1857. The author asserted that the laws governing married women's property influenced the position of all women, married or single, since fathers educated all daughters with marriage in mind and, because of the laws, saw no reason to waste time teaching them practical or independent thinking. The "deconsideration" of women was carefully detailed in this article, which concluded with a warning that the obvious injustice in the property laws weakened the entire legal foundation upon which the nation operated.[86] In that same month

84. Ibid., p. 1281.
85. Ibid., p. 1282.
86. "Capabilities and Discapabilities of Women," pp. 23–40.

Sir Erskine Perry, anxious to keep the issue before the public, published "Rights and Liabilities of Husband and Wife" in the *Edinburgh Review*. Perry recalled Lord Lyndhurst's remark in the House of Lords that nine out of ten marriages celebrated in England were contracted without marriage settlements. He emphasized in print, as he had in debate, the harshness of the Common Law to all married women unprotected by marriage settlements, dramatizing his point with several case histories. He concluded with a strongly worded plea for immediate change of the law, perhaps as a reminder to the Government of its promise to introduce a motion in the coming parliamentary session.[87]

The Government motion never came, and on May 14, 1857, Perry stood in Commons to voice his regret at the delay and to state that he could wait no longer. He then introduced another bill to amend the law of property as it affected married women. The bill was a detailed program for reform incorporating the proposals put forward in the Report of the Law Amendment Society, published in 1856. Public reaction was the same as it had been in the previous year. *Punch* reported the day's events: "The proceedings in the Lords were strictly uninteresting and had only the merit of being short, in the other House Women's Wrongs came up, and of course there was a good deal of laughter."[88] Perry's bill got no further than its second reading, primarily because of the simultaneous passage through the House of the Marriage and Divorce Bill, which succeeded in gaining greater public interest and support. Caroline Norton, who had refused to join Barbara Smith's efforts, had chosen instead to work for the passage of a Marriage and Divorce Bill incorporating amendments designed to alleviate the situation of women living apart from their husbands.

The divorce bill, whose primary purpose was to make divorce possible without a special act of Parliament, was much more palatable than any suggested change in the legal status of women. The

87. Perry, "Rights and Liabilities of Husband and Wife," pp. 94–106.
88. "Essence of Punch," *Punch* 32 (May 1857): 201.

"Norton Amendments" were incorporated into the bill, which passed into law in 1857. Clause 25 of the Divorce and Matrimonial Causes Act of 1857 read as follows:

> In every case of a judicial separation the wife shall, from the date of the sentence and whilst the separation shall continue, be considered as a 'feme sole' with respect to her property of every description which she may acquire or which may come to devolve upon her.[89]

In the following year, 1858, the Divorce and Matrimonial Causes Amendment Act was passed, according to which "every wife deserted by her husband may apply to the judge ordinary for an order to protect any money or property in England she may have acquired or may acquire by her own lawful industry."[90] By relieving the worst hardships concerning the property of married women, the divorce act effectively eliminated Sir Erskine Perry's Married Women's Property Bill.

The passage of the Divorce and Matrimonial Causes Act in 1857 was a decisive break with the past. The main object of the act was the creation of a new Court for Divorce and Matrimonial Causes to which was transferred all jurisdiction then exercised in matrimonial matters by the ecclesiastical courts in England. The primary purpose of the act was to make the civil system of divorce established by the House of Lords in 1697 (the Private Act Procedure) more widely available. The act made the divorce procedure more easily affordable and less cumbersome but did not change the grounds for the action or introduce any new principles.[91] Thus the cases which aroused the greatest public sympathy were dealt with, while more radical change in the law continued to be viewed with suspicion. The *Saturday Review*, a confirmed opponent of any change in the legal status of women, voiced the general opinion: "In the presence of the Divorce Bill which embodies the only parts of Sir Erskine Perry's Bill which are at all reasonable—those which deal with the

89. Rubenius, *Woman Question in Mrs. Gaskell's Life*, p. 11.
90. Ibid.
91. MacGregor, *Divorce in England*, pp. 17–19.

property of women legally separated—it would be absurd to consider the absurd and abortive proposal."[92]

The social conscience was not ready to accept any real change in women's legal status and, having to its satisfaction insured protection of injured wives, considered the problem solved. The married women's property campaign was over, and the issue remained hidden for the next ten years. But Barbara Smith's committee was only getting started. The newly organized women's movement turned from this parliamentary defeat to the issues of women's occupational and educational opportunities. The most important and lasting contribution of the committee was its continued existence. The group constituted the nucleus of mid-Victorian feminism. The petition campaign created an informal network throughout the country, which passed information to the provinces and drew sympathetic women to London to join reform projects after 1858. In the second edition of *Laws Concerning Women*, published late in 1856, Smith showed that she was aware that numbers and organization were vital if women were to affect change in their situation. By no means a call to arms, the concluding remarks in the pamphlet clearly indicate that its author felt that the responsibility for changing their lives lay with women themselves; indeed, in the particular instance of property reform Smith asserted that change depended upon the will of working women, a concept never previously articulated: "It only remains for the working women who earn money to say—'This law is a great injustice to us, we wish to have our own money earnings in our own power,' and the law will be abolished."[93] The realization that women's own organizing efforts could affect legal and social structures had led Smith to plan the petition campaign in 1855, bringing together her closest friends in the first feminist committee in Great Britain. The abortive effort on behalf of married women's property reform represented a decisive break from the attitude expressed by Charlotte Bronte in *Shirley* in 1849. Bronte's despair at female uselessness, echoed less dramatic-

---

92. Reiss, *Rights and Duties of Englishwomen*, p. 127.

93. Barbara Bodichon, *A Brief Summary in Plain Language of the Most Important Laws of England Concerning Women*, 2d ed. (London: Holyoake, 1856), p. 12.

ally by Maria Grey and Emily Shirreff in *Thoughts on Self-Culture* in 1851, was directed at men in a plea that they change women's role, the assumption being that only men had the power to reform society and that they bore total responsibility for woman's place within it. The married women's property campaign was a cooperative effort between men of reform tendencies and women who had made the first active step toward self-emancipation. All feminist activity for the next half century was an extension of that first cooperative effort, while every effort by women on their own behalf stemmed from Barbara Smith's expressed conviction that women, when organized and active, could affect their own destiny.

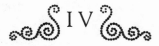

IV

FRIENDSHIPS, MARRIAGE,
AND AN AMERICAN JOURNEY

The years between 1850 and 1857 were turbulent for Barbara
Smith's personal life. The fervor which characterized her feminist
commitment extended to emotional attachments and a wide variety of friendships. During the establishment of Portman Hall
School, throughout the married women's property campaign, and
when she was writing *Women and Work,* Smith was deeply involved
in her painting and in the Pre-Raphaelite circle. It was during this
period that she met Marian Evans (George Eliot), with whom she
shared a lifelong friendship, as extraordinary for the depth of their
rapport as for the contrasting natures of the two women. There was
a painful interlude in the mid-fifties, a poignant if peculiar love affair with John Chapman, which ended in complete mental and
physical collapse for Smith. This was followed by a period of recuperation in Algiers and marriage to Eugène Bodichon. The scenario
had melodramatic overtones; the characters were all drawn slightly
larger than life. But there can be no understanding of Smith, the
feminist activist and educational reformer, without some compre-
hension of the vibrant yet curiously vulnerable woman whose complex temperament made her a strikingly effective catalyst for the
women's movement.

With Anna Mary Howitt and Bessie Parkes, Barbara Smith
formed a circle of Pre-Raphaelite women. Elizabeth Siddal also
shared a place in that circle. Siddal, whom they called a "stunner,"
served first as a model for Walter Deverell and soon became Dante
Gabriel Rossetti's model, personal protégée, and obsession.

The original aim of the Pre-Raphaelite brotherhood, to paint realistically from observed objects, had drawn William and Mary Howitt toward the circle as early as 1848.[1] It was because of their association with Rossetti, Holman Hunt, and the Irish poet William
Allingham that their daughter Anna Mary and her friend Barbara
Smith joined the circle. On a painting trip in 1855 the two young
women wrote with pride that they had inadvertently chosen the
very site on Benjamin Smith's Clive Dale farm where Holman
Hunt had painted his sheep for *Our English Coasts* in 1852. They
were overjoyed at finding traces of his paint and turpentine on the
table where they were working.[2]

Painting, poetry and spirit-rapping occupied them during 1853
and 1854. With her sisters Nanny and Bella, Anna Mary Howitt,
Bessie Parkes, and Christina Rossetti, Barbara Smith formed the
Portfolio Club, which met periodically to exhibit sketches and lis-
ten to poetry on prescribed themes. The club continued meeting for
several years and as late as 1862 Smith, now Madame Bodichon, arrived from Algiers and wrote happily to William Allingham of her
affectionate attachment to its members. She had brought a drawing
from Algiers to present at a club meeting and confided that she and
her sister Nanny always looked on the organization with possessive
pride.[3]

Dabbling in watercolors or poetry were common pastimes for
young women of the period, but it would be inaccurate to dismiss
Smith's work as the product of a Victorian dilettante. Rossetti admired her paintings, while Ruskin sent encouraging comments. She
had two shows at the French gallery in London in 1859 and 1861.
George Eliot was pleased during the first show when an artist
friend, F. W. Burton, expressed admiration for Smith's work. He
thought the landscapes showed talent and had many fine qualities
despite their "want of finish."[4] Evaluating the 1861 show, *The Ath-*

1. Woodring, *Victorian Samplers*, pp. 166–70.
2. Howitt, *Autobiography*, 2:111–12.
3. Barbara Bodichon to William Allingham, July 1862, in William Allingham, *Letters*,
ed. H. Allingham and E. Baumer Williams (London: Longmans, Green, 1911; reprint, New
York: AMS, 1971), pp. 77–78.
4. George Eliot to Barbara Bodichon, August 1859, *George Eliot Letters*, 3:128.

enaeum, which often wrote scathingly of polite ladies' art, complimented the quality and style of Smith's Algerian landscapes.[5] A
French critic described her as the Rosa Bonheur of landscape painting.[6] Painting was extremely important to Smith's spiritual well-
being, but she had difficulty reconciling her artistic commitment
with her social activism. Struggling to meet all the demands on her
time, she complained to Elizabeth Malleson of her inner turmoil
shortly after her marriage. She felt a duty to her artistic talent: "I
should like to give all I had to schools, and earn my own living by
painting. . . . I do wish I had three immortal lives. I would spend
one only with my Eugène, and the other two for art and social
work."[7] Many years later in 1869, she still felt guilty about how
much she enjoyed painting and how much time it took from social
projects. She admitted to William Allingham that she enjoyed the
praise of the critics. It soothed her conscience and allowed her to
spend time painting while neglecting reform efforts.[8]

However, in 1853 life was only beginning, promising adventure
and good fellowship in every new experience. That spring and summer Smith joined Rossetti, Siddal, Parkes, and the Howitts,
mother and daughter, in a series of séances at the Hermitage, the
Howitt residence. Night after night Rossetti regaled them with
ghost stories, while Smith filled their ears with anecdotes told her
by Lady Byron about the ability of that noblewoman's mother, Lady
Milbanke, to discover water by means of a divining rod.[9] Spiritualism was the latest fad. All over England strange rappings and bump-
ings were heard in the night. Pictures fell off walls, objects began to
float about drawing rooms, and voices came calling from the dead.
In May 1853 Mary Howitt wrote her husband, away on an extended
Australian visit, describing the new phenomenon: "The great talk
now is Mrs. Stowe and spirit-rapping, both of which have arrived in
England."[10] The phenomenon was popular among all classes and

5. *The Athenaeum,* 13 April 1861, p. 5.
6. Belloc, "Barbara Leigh Smith Bodichon," p. 147.
7. Malleson, *Autobiographical Notes,* pp. 51–52.
8. Barbara Bodichon to William Allingham, 1869, Allingham, *Letters,* p. 88.
9. Howitt, *Autobiography,* 2:100.
10. Ibid., p. 99.

sects. Members of the Church of England, Unitarians, and free-thinkers of Howitt's acquaintance had all become infected by the mystic spirit. Even Robert Owen had made a public statement of his belief in the spirits. Mary wrote that Anna's friend Barbara was deep in an investigation of the power of the occult.[11]

The Howitts came to spiritualism on the road from Unitarian rationalism to Roman Catholicism. They were typical of many who had been rationalistically inclined during the Chartist forties and were reacting to the ascendancy of science with a retreat into Christian faith. Smith's involvement with the occult was short-lived. Spiritualism was amusing and piqued her imagination, but she was not overwhelmed by the fad. While Anna Howitt remained a believer at least until 1862, science in the person of their old family friend Professor Michael Faraday prevented any of the Smiths from succumbing entirely to spiritual speculation. Years later Eugène Bodichon became completely caught up by spiritualism, but his wife remained immune, cured by her early experience. William Rossetti reported in March 1870 that she rejected spiritualism and had no definite belief in or opinion about the existence of the disembodied soul.[12]

Studies of the occult provided diversion, but the life of art, in painting, building, and furniture design, absorbed and fired Smith's imagination. She devoted a considerable sum to the building of a country house. A forerunner of William Morris's protest against Victorian fussiness, Scalands cottage in Robertsbridge, near the Hastings homes of other Smiths, was simple and uncluttered. It was built in the style of a Sussex manor house of the period of the Norman Conquest. The front door opened straight into the living room, which was heated and dominated by an open brick fireplace. It became traditional for weekend guests to sign the sides of the fireplace before they left. The cottage defied Victorian taste. Smith called it a protest against "Victorian worship of smugness and pre-

11. Ibid., pp. 99–100.
12. William Michael Rossetti, *Rossetti Papers, 1862–1870* (New York: Charles Scribner's Sons, 1903), pp. 499–500.

tentious comfort."[13] The walls were lined with plain white book-shelves and the floors covered with plain matting. Tables were ornamented with bowls of wildflowers and palettes and brushes. In later years every shelf and cabinet was filled with Smith's famous collection of blue and white Algerian pottery or stocked with embroidered Arab vests and burnooses. Scalands sat on a hill in a pinewood clearing and its environs hypnotized William and Mary Howitt, who visited in April 1864. They described the woods and flowers and the surrounding homes of Smith's father and brothers in idyllic terms.[14] Nearly twenty years later Mary Howitt remembered the beauty of the place and wrote with nostalgic pleasure of the spring she and her husband had spent there.[15]

Simple comfort in a country setting, Scalands provided a place to retreat and restore one's health or spirit. Wealth allowed Smith to indulge herself in Scalands. At a time when most young women rarely spent a moment unchaperoned, the concept of a single young woman planning for and spending her income on a weekend home was frowned upon. Her family supported Smith's project. They permitted her privacy and independence despite the criticism of respectable friends. Simplicity was the hallmark of her life there. Indeed, Rossetti gently mocked her spartan habits during his visit in March 1870: "Barbara does not indulge in bell-pulls, hardly in servants to summon thereby—so I have brought my own. What she does affect is any amount of thorough draught."[16]

Smith, herself accustomed to the comfort of a wealthy home, indulged her sense of humor and social justice by entertaining rich and poor guests quite differently. Since she enjoyed plain living and was untroubled by physical inconvenience, she refused to pamper the pompous and followed the rigorous traditions of Scalands in London and later in Algiers. She enjoyed her guests' amazement.

13. Violet Hunt, *The Wife of Rossetti* (London: John Lane, 1932), p. 110.
14. Howitt, *Autobiography*, 2:156–57.
15. Ibid., p. 310.
16. Dante Gabriel Rossetti to William Allingham, 17 March 1870, Rossetti, *Letters*, 2:819.

She practiced a ruthless household economy and was delighted when lunch with Dean and Lady Augusta Stanley and Gladstone was graced by a cut gooseberry pie, doing double duty after dinner the night before. Whenever wealthy guests dined with her she gave them mutton and plain food. But when poor civil servants and starving artists were invited she made certain they were served a sumptuous repast.[17] The tradition was not always accepted with equanimity, particularly her practice, on her final check of table arrangements, of carrying a bottle of water with her and heavily diluting the half-filled decanters of sherry and claret.[18]

The early fifties demonstrated more than Smith's artistic ability or household economies. Her friendship for Rossetti and interest in the health of Siddal was spontaneous and whole-hearted. She was to champion society's strays of every class and religion throughout her life. She was tolerant, in the best sense of the word, in the same manner as her father and grandfather before her.

Siddal was chronically ill most of her life. She modeled for Rossetti, was engaged to him for several years, finally married him, and died shortly afterward of an overdose of laudanum. In 1854 she was seriously ill. Smith made many and varied arrangements for trips to the country, even attempting to convince the impractical couple that Siddal should enter a nursing home run by her cousin Florence Nightingale. In April 1854 she arranged for Siddal to stay in Hastings.[19] She wrote to Bessie Parkes to work out the details of lodgings, cautioning Parkes about the necessity of keeping Siddal's modeling career a secret: "She is of course under a ban having been a model (tho' only to two PRB's [Pre-Raphaelite Brothers]) ergo do not mention it to any one."[20] Smith herself cared nothing for conventional morality. She wished to make Siddal comfortable and to avoid talk about the girl in the village that might force her to give up her country retreat.

17. Betham-Edwards, *Mid-Victorian Memoirs*, pp. 71–72.
18. Ibid., p. 72.
19. Dante Gabriel Rossetti to Ford Madox Brown, 19 April 1854, Rossetti, *Letters*, 1:186.
20. Barbara Smith to Bessie Parkes, April 1854, Troxall Collection, Princeton University Library, Princeton, N.J.

Rossetti borrowed money from Allingham for train tickets, deposited Siddal in Hastings and returned to London. He assumed that Smith would take full responsibility for the invalid. Siddal gradually gained strength and by the end of May after several short stays at Scalands she and Rossetti became engaged. "The indefatigable and invaluable"[21] Smith made numerous plans for her recuperation, but the couple ignored her advice and returned to London a short time later.

The brief interlude absorbed Smith's energies as fully as any project she would later undertake. Although feminist concerns and marriage weakened her ties to the Pre-Raphaelites, in 1870 she provided similar support and a haven at Scalands for Rossetti, who was by that time broken in health and spirits by drugs and alcohol.

Siddal's young benefactress was herself about to undergo the first in a series of bouts of ill-health. Glowing good looks and the titianesque appearance so often remarked upon by contemporaries masked her tendency to sudden serious collapses. In the midst of success with Portman Hall School, as the married women's property campaign was germinating in her mind, she became ill and was forced to leave for Rome to recuperate. Rossetti wrote Allingham in January 1855 of the shocking news. Smith had been declared a victim of weak lungs and was only then showing signs of recovery.[22] This first illness may have been lung disease or could have been a forerunner of the nervous collapse that prostrated Smith in 1856. Immersed in art and numerous social projects, Smith was driving herself unmercifully. Her optimism and emotional strength had seemed unbounded and these first signs of weakness startled her friends. She continued to suffer periodic depression throughout her life.

The Pre-Raphaelite women, Smith, Parkes, and Howitt, spent the early fifties attempting to clarify personal as well as political credos. The issues of freedom, personal liberty, and social responsibility consumed them even more than their pursuit of artistic or liter-

21. Dante Gabriel Rossetti to William Rossetti, 14 May 1854, Rossetti, Letters, 1:195–96.
22. Dante Gabriel Rossetti to William Allingham, 23 January 1854, ibid., 1:239.

ary excellence. If spiritualism tempted Howitt, Catholicism convinced her, and it became Parkes' personal solution as well. By 1854, Howitt, brought up a Quaker, was "as good as a Catholic," and her room at Scalands was full of fonts for holy water and china Christs hanging on ebony crosses.[23] Parkes and Smith spent long hours discussing religion, but Catholicism did not satisfy Smith's needs. In 1860, worried about the depression her younger sister Nanny was suffering following their father's death, she wrote George Eliot about the possible solace offered by Catholicism and explained her own rejection of that alternative. She understood her sister's need for the comfort that Catholic ceremony and ritual could provide. The routine of daily matins and vespers appeared to her a healing source. But she rejected Parkes's argument that the Catholic Church was the best agent for providing the world with order, justice, and aid for the poor and sick. Even if the church were fulfilling those objects (and Smith did not feel it was), she saw no reason that some other social organization might not do so in the future.[24]

Smith's personal credo was a combination of paganism and deep religious belief. When questioned about her religious affiliation, she dismissed the issue by declaring that she was a "Sanitarian."[25] A rationalist and a believer in individual liberty and equality, brought up in the Unitarian tradition, Smith saw no simple solutions for the world's injustices. The clearest expression of her bittersweet philosophy is found in a letter she wrote to comfort her cousin at the beginning of what neither woman realized would be Hilary Bonham-Carter's fatal illness. Bonham-Carter was suffering a loss of religious faith and was profoundly depressed. Smith tried to comfort her with the formula she herself had come to depend on:

> As I do not know how best to answer with the *great consolation* which I believe in as existing somewhere, you must take the second best, on which I live myself, always feeling that there is

23. Hunt, *Wife of Rossetti*, p. 110.

24. Barbara Bodichon to George Eliot, 22 December 1860, George Eliot Letters, Beinecke Library, Yale University, New Haven, Conn.

25. Barbara Stephen, *Emily Davies and Girton College* (London: Constable, 1927), p. 37.

some way of solving the riddle of the suffering world which I cannot see. I have faith, but I am ignorant, and do not live religiously. If I bear troubles and get on in life at all, it is on very second-best expedients which I do not much respect myself —a sort of rough wooden scaffold bridge of life where some day I hope to see a perfect arch. I do not understand God's ways at all in this world.[26]

Planning each day so that no time was left to think of oneself was helpful. The discipline of routine activities coupled with the support of good friends had often buoyed her spirits. Despite the difficulty of finding some way of "harmonizing the world," she refused to surrender to chronic melancholy. The sense of public obligation engrained in the Smiths for more than three generations sustained her and provided an outlet for her zeal. She agreed with George Eliot that "the highest calling and election is to *do without opium* and live through all our pain with conscious clear-eyed endurance."[27] She and Eliot spent long hours discussing questions of faith and sharing personal doubts.

Eliot and Smith were close friends for nearly thirty years. They enjoyed a rare intuitive understanding of one another. When in 1859 the novel *Adam Bede* created a literary sensation, all London speculated about the identity of its mysterious author. Barbara Bodichon wrote Eliot from Algiers after reading only brief extracts. She was overjoyed and certain that her friend must be the author: "Very few things could have given me so much pleasure. 1st That a woman should write a wise and *humorous* book which should take a place by Thackeray. 2nd That you *that you* whom they spit at should do it! I am so enchanted so glad with the good and bad of me! both glad—angel and devil both triumph!"[28]

No one else guessed, none had supported Eliot with such open encouragement during her years of social censure, and she responded warmly. She thanked Bodichon for her friendship, which

26. Barbara Bodichon to Hilary Bonham-Carter, 30 January 1865, Bonham-Carter Family Papers.
27. George Eliot to Barbara Bodichon, 26 December 1860, *George Eliot Letters*, 3:365–66.
28. Barbara Bodichon to George Eliot, 26 April 1859, ibid., 3:56.

meant more than all the letters of praise or fine reviews.[29] George
Henry Lewes told Bodichon of their delight that she had known in-
stinctively of Eliot's authorship: "You are *the* person on whose sympathy we both counted, and only just escaped having the secret
confided to you before you went, but we are glad you found it out
for yourself!"[30]

In June 1859 Bodichon returned to England, where speculation
about *Adam Bede* continued. She was revolted by the savage reaction to rumors that Marian Evans was George Eliot. She agonized
after a reception where she was told that if the fact had been known
when the book was published, every newspaper critic would have
condemned it. Lewes's and Eliot's extramarital living arrangement
remained a social stigma stronger than the force of talent. She
wrote Eliot that all respectable people were cowards. She was bitter
at societal hypocrisy and convinced that most women were jealous
of Eliot's ability.[31]

Eliot, accustomed to her "excommunication," dismissed hollow
social acceptance and thanked Bodichon for her unselfish friendship: "I will not call you a friend—I rather call you by some name
that I am not obliged to associate with evaporated professions and
petty egoism. I will call you only Barbara, the name I must always
associate with a true large heart."[32] Clearly the strength of their
friendship over a lifetime was based upon shared convictions and
emotional empathy overriding the seeming contrast in their natures. As late as 1869 Charles Norton wrote of Eliot as an object of
interest and curiosity to society, something of a social pariah: "She
is not received in general society, and the women who visit her are
either so emancipée as not to mind what the world says about them,
or have no social position to maintain."[33] Bodichon had wealth
and position, but absolute contempt for convention and deep loy-
alty to those she cared for.

29. George Eliot to Barbara Bodichon, 5 May 1859, ibid., 3:64.
30. Ibid., 3:64–65.
31. Barbara Bodichon to George Eliot, 28 June 1859, ibid., 3:103.
32. George Eliot to Barbara Bodichon, 23 July 1859, ibid., 3:119.
33. Charles Eliot Norton to George William Curtis, 29 January 1869, ibid., 5:7.

Yet Bodichon and Eliot could hardly have been more different on the surface. The writer was stormy and introspective, the feminist, ebullient and unceasingly crusading. These are the images that have survived the years, but they are stock descriptions that do nothing to enlighten or explain. The physical differences seemed to mirror the inner contrast: Eliot, dark and plain, a brooding presence; Bodichon, golden-haired, a sunlit beauty, whose face Browning termed a benediction. The surface contrast belied the similarities beneath. The two unconventional women were both feminists in the most basic sense, the one an active reformer, the other expressing conviction through her novels. The artist and the writer spent endless hours discussing the nature of talent, the responsibility it brought, and the fact of its possible existence in every human being.

Eliot supported Bodichon's feminist campaigns with signatures or contributions. She made no public appearances and wrote no tracts for the movement, insisting that her contribution was through her novels. She appreciated Bodichon's dedication and action: "The part of the Epicurean gods is always an easy one; but because I prefer it so strongly myself, I the more highly venerate those who are struggling in the thick of the contest."[34] Bodichon agreed that Eliot was, through her fiction, making the greatest contribution the world could expect. She believed that Eliot was one of the women who would influence humanity most deeply.[35]

Their friendship had begun in June 1852 at an evening party which Barbara Smith and Bessie Parkes attended at John Chapman's home. In 1851 the handsome editor of the *Westminster Review* had invited Eliot to share his home with wife Susannah and mistress Elizabeth Tilley. Tilley's jealousy of Eliot caused an uproar which sent the latter back to Coventry. She needed an outlet for her literary talent, however, and Chapman needed writers, so a few months later she was back in his volatile household in the Strand. Here Bessie Parkes's mother called, wishing to meet Eliot because

34. George Eliot to Charles Bray, 30 October 1857, ibid., 2:396.
35. Barbara Bodichon to George Eliot, 10 August 1859, ibid., 3:128.

she was translating Strauss's *Leben Jesu* under Joseph Parkes's sponsorship. Bessie Parkes became friendly with Eliot and on June 29,
1852, brought Smith to meet her. Eliot was impressed by Parkes's
noble-looking friend who seemed so anxious to make an "indelible
impression."[36] Shortly after that Eliot began to dine at Blandford
Square and in July 1853 she went with Sara Hennell and Susannah
Chapman to spend a weekend with Smith and her aunt Julia in
Surrey.[37]

Smith and Eliot became such close friends that when Eliot and
Lewes considered setting up household in the summer of 1854 they
asked for her advice. Lewes, already married, could not afford the
expense of petitioning for the act of Parliament necessary for a divorce. His wife, Agnes, was openly conducting an affair with
Thornton Hunt, but Lewes did not have the resources to sue for a
separation and bring an action against Hunt, as the law required.
Smith held strong views on the injustice of the law which made divorce possible only for the rich and, having recently deplored the
situation in *Laws Concerning Women*, found her friends facing the
practical consequences of the legal inequity she had written about.
The human dilemma was not easily solved. Years later Smith recalled the moment and her own feelings: "What earthly right had I
to advise her in such a case? . . . I replied that her own heart must
decide, and that no matter what her decision or its consequences
should be, I would stand by her so long as I lived."[38] Smith's
staunch support was expressed in a letter, which survives only
through Eliot's comment to Sara Hennell: "I send you a letter
which I have had from Barbara Smith. I think you will like to see
such a manifestation of her strong noble nature. Burn it when you
have read it."[39]

The summer of 1854 was the beginning of an emotional crisis for
Barbara Smith. She appeared to be duplicating George Eliot's expe-

36. George Eliot to Bessie Parkes, 30 October 1852, ibid., 2:65.

37. George Eliot to Sarah Hennell, 29 June 1853, ibid., 2:107–08.

38. Matilda Betham-Edwards, *Reminiscences*, rev. ed. (London: Unit Library, 1903),
p. 141.

39. George Eliot to Sarah Hennell, 21 July 1855, *George Eliot Letters*, 2:211.

rience. She began an affair with John Chapman, whose liaisons were renowned and everchanging. The Chapmans, with Elizabeth Tilley, moved to Blandford Square in July 1854. On July 14 Eliot reported to Bessie Parkes that Barbara's aunt Julia Smith was to be their lodger.[40] Chapman and Barbara Smith saw one another constantly until their affair reached its extraordinary finale about a year later. A series of letters which he wrote to her in August and September 1855 reveal their plan to form an extramarital union. Not yet a doctor, Chapman had no hesitation in prescribing for Smith, who suffered from irregular menstrual cycles and other "female complaints." His letters are filled with intricate schemes to prevent their meetings being discovered. Indeed, his plans tend toward the overelaborate precaution reminiscent of French farce. He insisted that Smith mail her letters in envelopes addressed by a third party (Anna Mary Howitt) so that suspicion might be avoided.

In the winter of 1855, Smith suffered the collapse which necessitated a trip to Rome. It was apparently a psychological as much as physical breakdown, caused primarily by the difficulties of her relationship with Chapman. His letters are clearly the products of an egomaniac and, while we have none of her replies, the affair is vividly portrayed in what Gordon Haight has aptly characterized as a "singular melange of love-making, petty economies and quite unprintable clinical details."[41] In a singularly un-Victorian discussion of feminine hygiene, the letters prescribe a course of hip baths and horsehair socks to establish a regular "flow," followed in the next paragraph by sublime professions of love. On August 22, 1855 Chapman began a letter in tones of selfless spiritual renunciation: "Never let me encumber your spirit or violate your soul's freedom for one hour . . . above all things do not cleave to me for a day for the sake of shielding me from suffering."[42] He turned immediately to the earthly plane, ending with an unromantic admonition: "I

40. Ibid., 2:165.
41. Gordon Sherman Haight, *George Eliot and John Chapman* (New Haven: Yale University Press, 1940), p. 88.
42. John Chapman to Barbara Leigh Smith, 22 August 1855, Chapman Papers, Beinecke Library, Yale University, New Haven, Conn.

urged you to pay especial attention to your bowels, but did not tell you what to take; I now enclose a prescription for some aperient pills which will also help the iron and the bath."[43] He went so far on one occasion as to write to a physician using his wife Susannah's name, describing Smith's symptoms and asking for medical advice.

By the end of August 1855 the couple was considering plans for establishing their life together. Chapman suggested that it would be wisest for him to maintain a "nominal" home with Susannah, where he would spend time with her and the children. He insisted that Smith should announce her plan to live with him to her family: "You would then maintain your right and equal relation towards them, and would be able without fear and undue anxiety and without the knowledge of the world to be really united with me and to look forward with joyous anticipation to becoming a Mother."[44] How this last was to be achieved without the world knowing was not explained. Chapman discussed this plan with his wife and told Smith that Susannah felt "unsettled" by the proposal. He assured Smith, however, that Susannah did not object so much to their relationship as to its becoming public knowledge.[45]

Mingled with love and medicine, remarks in Chapman's letters indicate that Smith's wealth was no small stimulus to his devotion. Having undergone bankruptcy, he was in chronic financial difficulties. His questions about Smith's finances were as detailed as those about her physical symptoms. He made careful inquiries about her income and prospects. On September 4 he could not refrain from exhibiting some disappointment over the size of her resources: "You have at present *less* money and expect finally to have *more* than I had been led to suppose. I thought you had now £250 and would ultimately have £500 a year. I am sorry for your sake that I am mistaken."[46] His estimate of Smith's resources was incorrect, since she had at this time an income of at least £300. It is an open question whether she deliberately understated her wealth to test his motives.

43. Ibid.
44. John Chapman to Barbara Leigh Smith, 29 August 1855, Chapman Papers.
45. John Chapman to Barbara Leigh Smith, 4 and 8 September, 1855, Chapman Papers.
46. Ibid.

In any case her fortune was a prime consideration since, once Susannah and the children were provided for, Chapman would only have about £100 of his own and the *Westminster Review,* whose increasing popularity he depended upon to make him independent.[47]

Chapman continued to urge Smith to announce their plan to her father. However, when she indirectly espoused the cause of free love, Benjamin Smith told her she might go to America if she wished to practice her principles. In this instance the elder Smith reacted precisely as any Victorian father might, his own early irregular union notwithstanding. Undaunted by parental disapproval of the experimental way of life, Chapman pressed Smith to continue discussions with her father. She was to argue the issue of free love and once her father was persuaded of the value of the abstract principle she was to inform him of their specific intention.[48] He assured the disheartened Smith that, once he had enlightened her father, the latter would prove their staunchest ally and supporter.[49] A few days later he promised that they would soon be as happy as Lewes and Eliot.[50] Smith finally told her father everything. He was horrified by their plan and forbade them to meet again. Chapman consoled Smith with assurances that her father would ultimately change his mind and that his reaction arose from love of his daughter. He was piqued and could not refrain from questioning the purity of Benjamin Smith's parental feelings: "He ought to be thankful that across all the difficulties and untoward changes of this strange world his favorite daughter has the love and devotion of a man the very elect of her own soul, and who, reason as well as feeling assures he will ever be her real mate."[51] Smith's continued discussion of the issue had no effect on her father or brother Ben and despite Chapman's "yours until death," the September 22 letter ended the connection. Chapman never mentioned the affair again except for a note in his diary of 1860 describing an evening party at which

47. Haight, *George Eliot and John Chapman,* p. 90.
48. John Chapman to Barbara Leigh Smith, 14 September 1855, Chapman Papers.
49. Ibid.
50. John Chapman to Barbara Leigh Smith, 17 September 1855, Chapman Papers.
51. John Chapman to Barbara Leigh Smith, 22 September 1855, Chapman Papers.

Smith's brother Ben was a guest. He carefully avoided speaking to Ben Smith, whom he held at least partially responsible for ending the affair.[52]

Barbara Smith spent the fall of 1855 and winter of 1856 immersed in the married women's property campaign. She was under great emotional strain. In June 1856 Eliot and Lewes invited her to join them for a few days at Tenby near Ilfracombe. They hoped that a country holiday would help her to overcome the depression following her disappointment over Chapman. Eliot congratulated her on Ruskin's praise of her painting and added, "I shall say nothing of sorrows and renunciations, but I understand and feel what you must have to do and bear."[53] Smith stayed at Tenby for four days, sketching and painting and in lengthy conversation with Eliot, who was struck by the change that had occurred in her friend: "We enjoyed her society very much, but were deeply touched to see that three years had made her so much older and sadder."[54]

Smith was fighting depression with ceaseless exertion. She devoted herself to social reform and never spoke of her disappointment.[55] By the autumn of 1856 she broke down. The family decided to travel, her brother Ben accompanying Barbara, Nanny, and Bella to Algiers. The trip was ostensibly for Bella's health. She was exhibiting symptoms of tuberculosis and Algiers was just becoming fashionable with Victorians as a winter retreat for sufferers from that disease. Ships between Marseille and Algiers carried great numbers of French and English invalids to what, despite malaria and cholera, was considered a health-giving climate. But Barbara's physical and emotional collapse was the real reason for the family's sudden decision to winter in Algiers. They called her illness a general "weakness" and never mentioned Chapman or the emotional depression which precipitated the journey.[56]

52. John Chapman, Diary, 5 March 1860, Chapman Papers.
53. George Eliot to Barbara Smith, 13 June 1856, *George Eliot Letters*, 2:255.
54. Gordon Sherman Haight, *George Eliot, A Biography* (Oxford: Oxford University Press, 1968), p. 205.
55. Ibid.
56. Hester Burton, author of an early popular account of Bodichon's life, wrote me on 29 September 1978 that she was prevented by the Smith family as late as the 1940s from men-

Algiers appealed to the artist as well as the tourist in Smith. Its exotic landscapes and human variety piqued her interest and re-awakened her enthusiasm for life. She wrote later that the country had a strong effect on all visitors: "The newness of everything, the strange intoxicating effect of the exhilerating air, . . . seems to make all who breathe it forget home, country, friends, troubles, and annoyances for a time, and give themselves up to the pure enjoyment of living."[57]

In Algiers Smith met Eugène Bodichon, a French physician born in 1810, who had settled in the colony in 1836. His father's family, from Brittany, were old bourgeois stock and Bonapartists. His mother, Antoinette Le Grand de la Pommeraye, was descended from a noble Breton family of royalist and Catholic sympathies. As a medical student in Paris he had become a Republican and a friend of Louis Blanc. He practiced among the varied races of the Algerian colony, wrote on their cultural anthropology, and developed theories about the effect of climate on behavior.[58] He studied malaria, which was one of the colony's major problems, and developed a theory on the benefit of planting forests of Australian eucalyptus trees in the area to eliminate the disease.[59] In later years he and his wife spent large sums to put this agricultural theory into practice.

Eugène Bodichon became a corresponding member of the Algerian Chamber of Deputies in 1848 and was one of the leaders of the movement to abolish slavery in the colony. His election address expressed some of his idealism: "These are my hopes for the future —that mankind will become a single united family."[60] His lengthy work, De l'Humanité, published in Paris in 1866 and carefully re-

---

tioning the illegitimacy of the Smith children, the Chapman affair, or the mental instability which troubled Julia Smith as well as her niece Barbara Bodichon.

57. Barbara Bodichon, "Algiers: First Impressions," English Woman's Journal 6 (September 1860): 32.

58. Bodichon's anthropological theories are fully stated in his Etudes sur l'Agerie et l'Afrique (Algiers: Privately printed by the author, 1847), and his "Society in Algiers," English Woman's Journal 6 (October 1860): 95–106.

59. Barbara Bodichon described this theory in "Australian Forests and African Deserts," Pall Mall Gazette (1868).

60. Burton, Barbara Bodichon, p. 90.

viewed in *The Athenaeum*, echoed Benjamin Smith's sentiments regarding the worth of labor in the service of mankind: "Consider the
universe as your country and mankind as your family. Forget services you render to others; remember those you receive. Honour
the living more than the dead."[61] A strange man, who became
more eccentric with age, Bodichon appealed to Barbara Smith as
much because of his bizarre foreign qualities as for his social and political idealism. When Elizabeth Whitehead asked why she had
married him, she answered that he matched her image of Caracta-
cus. "He is in fact an ancient Briton. . . . I think him the handsom-
est man ever created." She realized that others did not share her
feelings. Many of her friends found the doctor "ugly and terrific."[62]
The couple became engaged in April 1857 and were married at the
Unitarian Little Portland Street Chapel in London on July 2, 1857.

Smith's family was not enthusiastic about the match; her friends
were apprehensive. George Eliot and George Lewes were "not quite
satisfied" with the engagement announcement. They had been trying to help Smith find a publisher for a series of articles about Algerian life. Her sudden engagement to a man who spoke little English, was seventeen years her senior, and whose life seemed
permanently attached to the exotic colonial society troubled them.
They wondered at what appeared an extreme reaction to the end of
the Chapman affair.[63]

It would be tempting to dismiss Eugène Bodichon as a wild-eyed
eccentric, calling upon Smith family anecdotes about his predilec-
tions for meditating in the pine woods in an Arab burnoose, doing
his own laundry, wandering about Scalands in French peasant
blouses, or appearing at London parties accompanied by groups of
desert sheiks in full Arab dress. He certainly never felt comfortable
in London, spending most of his time in England at Scalands. However, his socialism and advocacy of the simple life were in the style
which William Morris worked to create some years later. He was a
respected physician and leader within Algerian social and political

---

61. Review of *De l'Humanité* by Eugène Bodichon, in *The Athenaeum*, 8 September 1866,
pp. 301–02.
62. Malleson, *Autobiographical Notes*, p. 77.
63. *George Eliot Letters*, 2:320.

circles. The very unorthodoxy which distressed her friends attracted Smith and made them a compatible couple.

Smith's view of marriage made any more conventional union unlikely to bring success. Her belief that marriage led women into legal slavery had made Chapman's extramarital proposition especially attractive. The legal loss of identity which she had condemned in *Laws Concerning Women* made conventional marital arrangements difficult for her to contemplate. Her relationship with Eugène Bodichon revolved around their mutual agreement not to interfere in one another's lives. They spent half each year in England, half in Algiers. In Algiers she painted and was a busy hostess. In England she devoted herself to feminist activities. In later years they did not always accompany one another because of ill health, but the freedom of the arrangement derived, not from lack of interest, but from Eugène's recognition that they could have no life together unless Barbara felt confident in the maintenance of her separate identity. Nowhere is this more clearly illustrated than in the journal she kept of her honeymoon trip to America. In March 1858 she wrote a strong statement explaining her intention to retain the name Smith and couple it with Bodichon. It is a clear indication of her firm belief that marriage involved the partnership of equals and her rejection of the concept of the married woman's absorption within coverture, a submersion symbolized by the disappearance of the maiden name:

> First let me say a word about Barbara Smith, particularly for
> John Thomas who has said three or four times in his letter that
> it is not correct to call myself Barbara Smith Bodichon. I believe he is wrong as a matter of law. I do not think there is any
> law to oblige a woman to bear the name of her husband at all,
> and probably none to prevent keeping the old name. To use it
> is very useful, for I have earned a right to Barbara Smith. . . .
> Dr. says he should think it folly for me to use his name except
> as a convenience in society, and if we have a line of English
> descendants they will be Bodichon-Smiths.[64]

64. Bodichon, *An American Diary*, p. 134.

The Smith family found the couple's arrangements for split lives disturbing. Barbara wrote with injured astonishment to George Eliot that her father felt their willingness to separate indicated a lack of depth to their affection.[65] The couple seemed well-suited, however, and Eliot was reassured when they visited with her and Lewes in England shortly after their marriage: "We think the *essential* is there—that he is a genuine right-feeling man. They are wisely going to America for a year, and I hope that in time he will learn to speak English so as to be an 'organ' better fitted to this 'medium' of English life than he is at present."[66]

The couple shared marital responsibilities during their year in America in a manner absolutely unheard of in well-regulated Victorian households. They spent most of that year traveling, but settled for a month in New Orleans, renting two rooms and setting up housekeeping. Housekeeping for them did not mean maids and cooks. Barbara made careful note in her diary of the cost of foodstuffs and calmly reported that she was concentrating on painting, while her husband attended to domestic arrangements. He did the housekeeping and marketing and she noted with pride that he cooked beautifully.[67]

While Eugène Bodichon wrote no formal renunciation of the marriage laws, as John Stuart Mill had in 1851 on the occasion of his own marriage, it was apparent that the couple approached marriage as equals, legal questions notwithstanding. It should be noted nonetheless that this most modern of unions was firmly rooted in an absolutely traditional formal marriage settlement. Benjamin Smith, advanced and radical as he might be in other matters, exhibited a father's deep concern for the protection of his daughter's estate. Smith had put a swift close to his daughter's flirtation with the practice of free love. It is perfectly possible that he did so as much out of dislike and distrust of bankrupt John Chapman as to protect her reputation and societal position. When Barbara Smith contemplated marriage, however, Benjamin's Victorian paternalism and fi-

65. *George Eliot Letters*, 3:267.
66. George Eliot to Sara Hennell, 19 August 1857, ibid., 2:377.
67. 21 December 1857, Bodichon, *An American Diary*, p. 67.

nancial acumen surfaced. He chose to rely for security on legal documents rather than on the good intentions or high principles of his daughter and her future husband. On July 1, 1857, a marriage settlement was filed in St. Marylebone and Westminster between Barbara Leigh Smith, spinster and Eugène Bodichon, physician. It set aside an income for Barbara Bodichon during her life to be paid "notwithstanding coverture" and "for her separate use, independently and exclusive of the said Eugène Bodichon and of his debts, control, interference and engagements."[68] The document protected her property, rent, and stocks from Eugène Bodichon during her life and guaranteed it to the children of her marriage after her death or, if there were no children, to the Leigh Smith family that survived her.

The married women's property campaign was over, and significant reform of the legal status of married women would not come for more than twenty years. Benjamin Smith was a member of that wealthy segment of society able to take advantage of the protection the Courts of Equity provided. Therefore, in a somewhat ironic twist of fate, the woman who had begun the marriage law reform campaign and who considered the marital state a legal and social inequity against women, entered coverture in the most conventional manner, draped in the respectability of legal verbiage, passed from father to husband with family property and finances intact, protected through the very system she was dedicated to reform.

Marriage provided Bodichon an unequivocal social position. In France and Algiers there was no knowledge of her questionable birth. She was welcomed as "ma cousine" by everyone at the family home in Brittany. That this mattered a great deal to her is obvious from the way she cherished Eugène Bodichon's family tree and coat-of-arms along with her marriage lines and artist's medals, the most precious of her personal possessions.[69]

The mingling of flamboyant unorthodoxy with a streak of pragmatism and occasional conservative tendencies was characteristic

68. Marriage Settlement, Bodichon Estate Documents, Record no. E/LS/#1, London County Hall, London, Eng.
69. These memorabilia have been acquired by Girton College, Cambridge.

of both Barbara and Benjamin Smith. The peculiar contradiction in both their natures kept them from becoming stock Victorian "oddities." Instead, they represent vividly that segment of the upper middle class most active in mid-Victorian reform movements and most successful in changing law and public opinion gradually, however radical their initial proposals or personal preferences.

The Bodichons decided to travel immediately after their marriage. They left for a honeymoon year in America early in the autumn of 1857. Travel in the United States was popular among the English upper classes in the nineteenth century. Radical thinkers turned to it as a utopia in much the same way they streamed to visit Soviet Russia in the 1920s and 1930s. They came to look at an unpolished, supposedly classless society, to see savages and slave auctions, and make their own observations on the experiment of a written constitution and a majoritarian democracy. They came to mingle with their American counterparts, to share ideas and comments on the social issues that consumed the period.

Boston was more than a convenient terminus for transatlantic crossings. The city represented the strongest link between England and America, providing an intellectual exchange for abolitionists, transcendentalists, Unitarians and feminists. Letters traveled slowly across the ocean. Books and pamphlets laboriously carried reform from England to America or from the New World to the Old. Harriet Martineau and Charles Dickens made their celebrated ways across the United States and Henry Ward Beecher brought his preaching to England, but the most satisfying communication network was built during lengthy sojourns by travelers like the Bodichons, who kept the transatlantic traffic in ideas flowing.

During the thirties and forties interest revolved around the success of American democracy. The publication of Henry Reeve's translation of Tocqueville's *Democracy in America* (1836 and 1840) had a strong impact on British intellectuals. Tocqueville's work was said by some to lean to radicalism at the very moment it was heralded by others as a pillar of conservatism.[70] Mill wrote in 1840

70. Webb, *Harriet Martineau*, p. 137.

that every book by a returned traveler became a party pamphlet.[71] Visitors to the new world brought with them hopes and fears about their own society and their descriptions often mirrored those beliefs more than they captured the reality of American life. Journals published after careful editing upon the traveler's return lost spontaneity, but, more than that, published accounts were often unconsciously molded to fit the author's political and social intentions. Barbara Bodichon's journal of her American journey was never published during her life. Consisting of a series of letters and diary entries, it gives the modern reader an uninhibited picture of America through the eyes of an artist, feminist activist, and above all, an energetic and inquiring mind.

When Harriet Martineau admired Cincinnati on her American trip in 1835 someone said to her: "Yes we have a new creation going on here: won't you come and dabble in the mud?"[72] Twenty-seven years later Barbara Bodichon accepted that invitation, insisting as she traveled on mixing with all classes and races. She visited the required salons and tourist sites, describing all in vivid detail. But most important and to the consternation of many hosts and hostesses, she sought out the schools and churches of the lowly, prayed and talked with free blacks and slaves throughout the South, asked incessant undiplomatic questions, and filtered all replies through an uncompromising intellect before producing her written record.

Bodichon's interest in America centered on the women's movement. She wished to study the methods of American feminists, to compare the domestic and economic positions of American and English women, and to share experiences and create a closer connection with leading American activists. But just as strong as her concern with feminism in the United States was her desire to learn first-hand about slavery. To Barbara, the granddaughter of William Smith, and to Eugène, who had been instrumental in abolishing slavery in Algiers, the survival of the institution in America was difficult to understand. They were carefully prepared for their expe-

71. *Edinburgh Review* 22 (October 1840): 2–3.
72. Webb, *Harriet Martineau*, p. 174.

rience. The usual guidebooks and travel accounts were supplemented by the personal recollections of Elizabeth Blackwell, who welcomed them to New York.

Bodichon told her sister Nanny that Blackwell was an extraordinary human being, "with more power of judgment and more concentrated purpose than any man I ever knew," adding that Blackwell's observations were of invaluable importance: "I always want to know what she thinks of great questions in my life, and in the lives of those near to me. She is sagacious."[73] Blackwell had lived in America from the age of eleven, visiting France for a short period around 1850 to pursue her medical education. She returned to New York to practice medicine and open a women's hospital. When she was growing up her family had close ties to abolitionist leader William Lloyd Garrison. In 1855 her brother Henry married Lucy Stone, a leading American women's rights advocate, who had been educated at Oberlin, where blacks and whites attended classes together.[74]

Blackwell took teaching posts in the South, in Kentucky, North Carolina, and South Carolina, in order to earn money for her medical studies. She had vivid memories of the injustices she had witnessed in those slave-holding communities. In Kentucky she saw no outright brutality, but reported that a solicitous host had once placed a small Negro girl as a screen between her and the fire.[75] In North Carolina the degradation of slavery overwhelmed her and she deplored the injustice of trying to teach slaves a religion which their owners professed to follow while violating its fundamental principles: "I longed to jump up, and taking the chains from those injured, unmanned men, fasten them on their tyrants till they learned in dismal wretchedness the bitterness of that bondage they inflict on their brethren." But she reserved these emotions for her family correspondence, and, asserting that "one person can do

73. Barbara Bodichon to Nannie Leigh Smith, n.d., Fawcett Society Collection.

74. Bodichon describes the Oberlin experiment in a discussion with several Southern women on a Mississippi riverboat in her journal, 11 December 1857, *American Diary*, p. 61.

75. Extract from a letter to her family, 4 April 1844, Blackwell, *Opening the Medical Profession*, p. 20.

nothing," she reassured her anxious relatives that she had not made herself conspicuous or gained the hated name abolitionist.[76]

Primed by Blackwell's remembrances, the Bodichons journeyed overland by train to Ohio before boarding a steamboat for the trip down the Ohio and Mississippi rivers. They made an extended visit to New Orleans, then proceeded by boat and train north through Alabama, Georgia, North Carolina, Pennsylvania, Washington, D.C., and New Jersey, then to Niagara Falls and Canada before the last leg of the journey to Boston and New York before returning to England in June 1858.

The Bodichons visited all of the slave states except Texas.[77] They did not attempt to preach abolition, which would have been as dangerous as it was futile. Instead Barbara tried to reconcile the conversations she had with whites about slavery with the harsh realities testified to by Negroes she encountered. When planters and businessmen along the way assured her that slavery was benevolent and that owners avoided separation of slave families, she returned to her cabin to talk with Polly, "the real black." Having ascertained that Polly had been sold twice, she asked about the woman's children and learned that all three had been sold and never seen again. Bodichon promised to publicize the story of Polly's suffering and to do everything in her power to alter the situation.[78] When in December she first visited the slave auction rooms in New Orleans, she was too late to see a sale, but was told by the auctioneer that slave families were never separated. He insisted that ill-treated slaves could demand sale to a different master. He answered her stream of questions politely and deliberately, but lied continuously: "How our Yankee landlady laughed when I came home and told her. She is no humbug."[79]

In February 1858 Bodichon went alone to a slave auction in New Orleans, arriving early so that she was taken around and shown all

76. Elizabeth Blackwell to her mother, 27 July 1845, ibid., p. 43.
77. Barbara Bodichon and Eugène Bodichon, "Slavery in America," *English Woman's Journal* 2 (October 1858): 94–100.
78. 12 December 1857, Bodichon, *An American Diary*, pp. 65–66.
79. Ibid., p. 70.

the "articles" for sale—about thirty women, twenty men, and twelve or fourteen babies. Three sales were conducted simultaneously. She watched a lot of women and children being sold:

> A girl with two little children was on the block: 'Likely girl, Amy and her two children, a good cook, healthy girl Amy— what! only seven hundred dollars for the three? that is giving 'em away! 720! 730! 735! 740! why gentlemen they are worth a thousand dollars—healthy family, good washer, house servant, etc. 750!' . . . Then a girl with a little baby got up and the same sort of harangue went on until eight hundred dollars, I think, was bid and a blackguard-looking gentleman came up, opened her mouth, examined her teeth, felt her all over and said she was dear or something to that effect.[80]

She moved to another part of the room where women waited to mount the auction stage. She noticed several in conversation with the men nearby, laughing and talking, "in a quiet sad sort of way, not merrily." With the sensitivity that characterized her observations throughout her travels she wrote simply: "The negroes laugh very often when they are not merry."[81] She spoke with another girl of about twenty-five and while they were in conversation two men approached and questioned the girl about her health. They spoke kindly, but examined her exactly as a farmer might examine a cow he wished to purchase.[82] Bodichon felt sick and was angered at the false reports about slavery that she had read in journals and books such as Amelia Murray's respected work.[83] Murray was a firm convert to the benefits of slavery. Bodichon raged at Murray's characterization of sales as merely "disagreeable" and asserted that a just punishment for Murray would be enforced attendance at all auctions held in New Orleans for a two month period.[84] She had read Murray's book as well as Frederika Bremer's popular 1853 travel ac-

80. Ibid., p. 104.
81. Ibid.
82. Ibid., p. 105.
83. Amelia Murray, *Letters from the United States, Cuba and Canada* (New York: G. P. Putnam, 1856).
84. Bodichon, *An American Diary*, p. 105.

count *Homes of the New World* and dismissed both as very poor books on the subject. Both authors had lived in polite society during their travels and seen nothing of the life of the lowly that Bodichon had during her nine weeks in New Orleans. She was convinced that blacks would not reveal their true feelings unless they were away from the confines of white society. To find out what they really thought she visited free blacks and slave churches. She did not care that her calls on black households were an unpardonable offense against the social code.[85]

In Savannah Bodichon attended services at the African Baptist church and became despondent at the thought that nothing could bring solace to blacks but prayer: "Sometimes when I hear them sing, the thought of slavery—what it really is—makes me so utterly miserable. —One can do nothing—nothing—and I see little hope. It makes me wring my hands with anguish sometimes."[86]

The Bodichons stayed in a boarding house in Savannah, where Barbara made friends with a slave named Clara. They had no opportunity to explore plantation slavery during their tour, and their experience among house slaves in city situations meant that they rarely witnessed physical abuse. But Bodichon was horrified when her host had Clara beaten with a cowhide whip for some minor infraction. Only the certainty that her interference would make the situation worse for the slave prevented her active opposition during the incident.[87]

In March 1858 she wrote from Augusta that she had been warned not to express critical views of slavery, since a Unitarian minister had escaped tar and feathers only by fleeing Mobile after allusions to abolitionist doctrines from his pulpit. Bodichon insisted that she was not an abolitionist but desired only gradual freedom. She deplored the tendency of law throughout the world to stifle freedom. She condemned Southern whites for failing to try to educate and elevate blacks and criticized all Americans for denying blacks the opportunities that freedom made available to all others in the nation.

85. Ibid., p. 99.
86. Barbara Bodichon to Benjamin Leigh Smith, 23 February 1858, ibid., pp. 119–20.
87. Ibid., p. 123.

Blunt as always, she ended by admitting that she and her husband had harbored doubts about blacks' innate abilities, but had been convinced of their error: "The race is not so low in the human scale as I supposed before I came here."[88] There was no embarrassment in her observation. She had posed a question for herself and considered her conclusion with dispassionate objectivity. It was characteristic of her approach to life and she might have phrased a similar appraisal of women as a sex. She had no fear of offending by forthrightness. Stating a premise baldly helped her achieve a kind of scientific clarification of ideas. She was, however, more subtle in political situations and quite astute about the effect of rhetoric on public opinion.

Bodichon had come to see slavery in situ and would brook no interference. With brushes and palette she wandered about, unfashionably dressed by Southern standards, forever wanting to visit the wrong people and incessantly asking questions. When they returned to England, the Bodichons published a careful denunciation of slavery, warning of an impending revolution and cautioning right-minded English people to fight the battle of the oppressed and the poor. They condemned Northerners and English people who betrayed their principles once they traveled South, accepting without question the arguments of hospitable Southerners that slavery was benevolent and economically necessary. In particular, they dismissed the reports of travelers as inaccurate and naive, and censured those authors for the damage they had caused in England by fostering public complacency with regard to slavery.[89]

The pages of Bodichon's American journal are a far more eloquent statement of the antislavery position than the couple's published article. Only occasionally lapsing into pedantic statements of political or social positions, the journal's value lies in its unaffected narrative, in the simplicity with which ordinary people are allowed to bear witness in plain words to their own agony.

Bodichon's fact-finding Southern tour brought unavoidable if

88. Ibid., p. 131.
89. Bodichon and Bodichon, "Slavery in America," pp. 94–100.

unpleasant truths about slavery to her correspondents in England. She carried her observations to the North as well, adding to the communication network of the abolitionists. Lucretia Mott asked her many questions about the South and slavery. She told Mott of the eloquence of black preachers, described the slave auctions and secret schools, and assured her that there was widespread knowledge among the slaves of emancipation efforts.[90]

In April 1858 on the train to Philadelphia to visit Lucretia Mott, the Bodichons passed a stick bearing a white flag marking the boundary between slave states and free, Mason and Dixon's line between Maryland and Pennsylvania. Bodichon recorded that though there was no perceptible change in scenery or air, her feelings changed, "so much that it seemed to me as if everything was better, brighter, truer, at once."[91]

The end of their Southern tour marks the end of the most exciting descriptions in the journal. Bodichon pursued women's rights activities in Philadelphia, Boston, and New York. She exchanged information with Lucretia Mott, who showed her a mass of literature from which she made selections to take back to England. They discussed the American suffrage campaign and agreed that Massachusetts would probably make the first step along the road to the vote. Bodichon met women physicians in New Orleans, New York, and Boston and discussed the question of female education and professionalism. She demonstrated a good sense of perspective about what girls "ought" to do. Amused by one woman physician's distress that her young daughter disliked anatomy and cared only for "trifling things," Bodichon complained: "These Women's Rights women are all on the same tack, longing to make facsimiles of themselves. I tell them all they are wrong and absurd—have the children grow up as they will, to be cooks and milliners, soldiers or sailors if they wish it."[92]

Religious services fascinated Bodichon throughout her journey. She was often moved by slave preaching and singing. She visited a

90. Bodichon, *An American Diary*, pp. 140–41.
91. Ibid., p. 137.
92. Ibid., p. 100.

number of Unitarian congregations, but did not hesitate to sample
other services, whatever the denomination. After attending a particularly affecting Presbyterian service in Philadelphia in April
1858, she commented on the fervor of American religion and on
the respect with which American ministers were treated. She found
American churches superior to those of England and the continent.
She was surprised at the respect and affection ministers received in
a country with no state support of the religious establishment.[93]

In Boston the Bodichons made the usual circuit of reform society, meeting abolitionist preacher Theodore Parker, poet James
Russell Lowell, Ralph Waldo Emerson, and a variety of other celeb-
rities. Barbara Bodichon met several women's rights activists including Carolina Maria Seymour Severance, whom she characterized as "one of the best of the WRW."[94] She talked with Maria
Weston Chapman, who was at the center of the Boston Female
Antislavery Society. Chapman was on the executive committee of
the Antislavery Society and had been a delegate to the 1840 World
Convention in London.

Bodichon hated the Boston weather and complained of the heat
and dust, but she was exhilarated by the intellectual and social
challenges she encountered there. She expressed the hope that all
the young men and women of England might spend a year visiting
Boston. Indeed, she wrote her father that many such visitors might
remain because of the wider professional opportunities available.[95]
Boston remained the city where English travelers converged to
compare experiences and argue their significance.

In June 1858 the Bodichons left the circle of Bostonian upper-
middle-class reformers, so similar to that which awaited them in
London, ending a year of observation and travel and bringing the
diary entries to a close.

93. Ibid., pp. 138–39.
94. Ibid., p. 157.
95. Ibid., p. 161.

WORK FOR WOMEN

There was no hiatus in Barbara Bodichon's feminist activities during the years 1857–1858. Her nervous collapse meant that she was in Algiers during the autumn of 1856 and winter of 1857 when the married women's property campaign was grinding to its unsuccessful end. Despite Bodichon's absence, her feminist committee continued its London meetings throughout the period. She did not remain idle in Algiers, but used her period of recuperation to complete a revision of *Laws Concerning Women* and to write *Women and Work*.

Women and Work marked a new direction for the reformers of the Married Women's Property Committee. Abandoning their first campaign directed at legislative change, they launched an effort to expand employment opportunities for women. The pernicious psychological and physical consequences of the cult of female idleness, reinforced by the real poverty of many redundant gentlewomen, were becoming topics of public concern. Bodichon's pamphlet was the first feminist articulation of the issue, igniting the public controversy which raged over the next two decades.

Women and Work appeared first as an article in the February 7, 1857, issue of the *Waverly Journal,* an obscure Scottish periodical. In October 1856, Bessie Parkes had been intrigued by an issue of this journal, which advertised that it was edited by women. She made inquiries, convinced that the magazine, if altered to emphasize women's issues and moved from Edinburgh to London, could provide a permanent forum for the budding feminist cause. The proprietor invited her to contribute articles, hoping to increase the circulation of his journal, which had until then consisted primarily of stories, poems, and occasional articles on charity efforts. Parkes and Isa Craig, a Scottish recruit to the feminist circle, submitted several pieces, while Bodichon contributed "Women and Work." In April 1857, Parkes, traveling in Rome, received an offer of full control of the periodical. Anna Jameson urged her to accept the editorship and by June Parkes had returned to England to undertake the project. Bodichon placed a large sum of money in the hands of solicitor George Hastings for the improvement and, if it became desirable, the eventual purchase of the magazine.[1] The magazine did not attract much public attention during this period.

George Eliot wrote encouraging notes of advice to Parkes. She applauded the articles that dealt with philanthropy and social progress, but tried to discourage a tendency toward "second rate literature." She urged that women's achievement be demonstrated by the content of the magazine and that it not be labeled the product of exclusively feminine efforts.[2] Negotiations for the purchase of the *Waverly Journal* continued throughout 1857, but there were financial difficulties with the proprietor and Hastings advised Bodichon and Parkes that the property was not worth the money and effort already expended. They accepted his advice, ended their association with the magazine at the end of 1857, and, in March 1858 in London, published the first issue of a new periodical, the *English Woman's Journal*.[3]

Women and Work survived its initial appearance in the unsuccessful *Waverly Journal.* It was reprinted as a pamphlet in April 1857 and caught the public attention. It was not well written, lacking the concise objectivity characteristic of *Laws Concerning Women*. The editorial hand of Matthew Davenport Hill was missing and Bodichon's indignation was indulged in passionate prose that diminished rather than heightened the effect. The issues were

1. Bessie Rayner Parkes, "A Review of the Last Six Years," *English Woman's Journal* 12 (October 1864): 364.

2. George Eliot to Bessie Parkes, 1 September 1857, *George Eliot Letters*, 2:379.

3. Parkes, "Review of the Last Six Years," p. 364.

straightforward, however, and the basic themes plainly stated, so that the pamphlet's thrust was not totally obscured.

The value of work for every human being, regardless of sex, is the pamphlet's central premise. The fact that middle-class females are prepared for no occupation except marriage is condemned. Bodichon begins by pointing out that women may face long years before marriage with no productive activity to occupy them. The idleness which society decrees for tens of thousands of its young women causes psychosomatic illnesses, "hysteria in its multiform aspects incapacitates thousands."[4] Worse than that, the surplus of middle-class women insures that a significant number will never marry, and without work they will exist in pointless idleness, whether comfortable or impoverished. Job training for all girls is the only solution. They could learn to work as accountants, nurses, operators of electric telegraph machinery, teachers, managers of washing machines and sewing machines, or similar occupations. The middle-class glorification of the frivolous, weak, ignorant, and sickly woman has resulted in the waste of enormous female potential. Training must be for occupations which utilize woman's intellect and uplift her spirit. "Work—not drudgery, but work—is the great beautifier."[5]

Bodichon goes even further than proposing work to give single women dignity or sustenance. Work, she contends, would be a positive good for married women as well. She does not differentiate between working-class and middle-class women. The fact that sixty thousand signatures were gained for the married women's property petitions indicates the depth of married women's desire and need to work. Many married women want work because they must feed and support children and other dependents. However, married women without financial need should work if they can make a societal contribution. Marriage may not fully challenge the abilities of every woman. Bodichon's statement on work and marriage, from the point of view of Victorian worship of family and motherhood, can only be regarded as blasphemy: "To bring a family of 12 children

4. Barbara Bodichon, *Women and Work* (London: Bosworth & Harrison, 1857), p. 9.
5. Ibid., p. 18.

into the world is not in itself a noble vocation, or always a certain benefit to humanity. To be a noble woman is better than being mother to a noble man."[6] The charge that children or family will suffer if women enter the professions is dismissed. If women fulfill their responsibilities as full citizens they will take better care of their households. Queen Victoria proves this point by fulfilling her responsibilities as monarch and active mother to a large family.

Those middle-class married women who choose not to enter professional life, but devote themselves to household management, "are far from idle." In an extraordinarily modern appraisal Bodichon places a value on the work of the housewife: "Women who act as housekeepers, nurses, and instructors of their children, often do as much for the support of the household as their husbands; and it is very unfair for men to speak of supporting a wife and children when such is the case."[7] By recognizing the monetary value of the duties of wife and mother, she redefines their status as nonworkers, making the first written declaration that woman's traditional role is work with a quantifiable market value of economic significance within the family financial unit.

Women and Work rambles; important points are mixed with anecdotes or long tangential discussions of female fashions. But it concludes with a reassertion of the need for vocational training. Productive application of talent—that is, work—is as necessary for women as it is for men. The final paragraph reminds us that Bodichon is, despite her modernity, a product of the nineteenth century and has not relinquished the belief that there is in fact some moral quality which distinguishes women from men. In dismissing charges regarding the absurdity of the idea of women in the army or at sea, or for that matter in politics, she asserts that the problem is not likely to arise. "Women will rather prefer those nobler works which have in them something congenial to their moral natures."[8] The arts, the sciences, commerce, and education are "perpetual" professions, which will attract women because of their consistency with

6. Ibid., p. 14.
7. Ibid., p. 12.
8. Ibid., p. 51.

humanity's highest moral development. There is a clear differentiation between the sexes in regard to moral qualities and some factor inherent in gender attracts or repels individuals as they choose military or even political careers. The statement is brief, but enlightening because it demonstrates that even this most ardent feminist unconsciously accepted the contemporary image of the feminine nature, attributing special moral qualities to women even though she rejected any inherent intellectual inequality. Her attitude toward political activity was later to change dramatically, but she retained throughout her life her belief in woman's special moral responsibility for civilizing society.

Critics quickly ridiculed *Women and Work* for its lack of organization and emotional excesses. The *Saturday Review* dismissed both the pamphlet and the sex succinctly: "If this is a fair example of what a lady who boasts to have made the subject her own is likely to publish, we are afraid that the sex is not really so developed as we had supposed."[9] Bessie Parkes had published a second edition of *Remarks on the Education of Girls* at about the same time that *Women and Work* appeared.[10] The *Saturday Review* could not resist the opportunity to condemn the two authors and the "strong-minded women" of their circle in one stinging article. Bodichon's arguments were dismissed with the contemptuous assertion: "Women are fatally deficient in the power of close consecutive thought," and the reminder, "Men have too much experience of the sex's charming ways ever to trust them with government or political economy or moral philosophy." Parkes's tract evoked similar sharp censure. Since she had insisted that girls be allowed to read freely in Chaucer, Dryden, Fielding, and Ben Johnson, her purity was questioned. The writer took comfort in the conviction that the "species of vermin" Parkes represented would never infest English drawing-rooms.[11]

The strength of reaction against Bodichon and Parkes indicated the threat that was perceived in their work. The emotional clamor

9. "Bloomeriana," *Saturday Review*, 19 July 1857, p. 224.
10. The first edition was published anonymously by John Chapman in 1854.
11. "Bloomeriana," p. 224.

that had surrounded the married women's property campaign was diverted to arguments regarding the dangers of employment and education for women. Yet initial response to the ideas advocated in *Women and Work* was not totally negative. Indeed, Bodichon's pamphlet found fertile ground among reformers outside her immediate feminist circle. She had the support of the recently established National Association for the Promotion of Social Science, support which proved invaluable when the idea of a Society for the Promotion of the Employment of Women evolved in 1859.

The Social Science Association was proving a formidable extraparliamentary pressure group. Evaluating its first five years, the Association's General Secretary George Hastings analyzed its inception. He denied that there was no such thing as a "science of society," refuting the contention that every community is a mere haphazard aggregation of human beings. Hastings explained that the Association sprang from the belief that many political economists had illogically narrowed their investigations by ignoring questions of moral duty: "A union was needed between the moral and economical sciences, in order to constitute a philosophy which should embrace in its inquiries alike the conditions of social prosperity and the rights and obligations of citizenship."[12] In action, such a conception involved a study of those subjects conducive to social reform. As a speaker at a later Association conference explained the organization's potential: "New ideas originate very rarely in Parliament. They are generally started outside, propagated by agitation and ultimately forced upon Parliament by external pressures."[13]

The original body was the result of the combination of a number of middle-class groups, each concerned with a particular social issue. These issues determined the Association's structure, and its activities revolved around five main departments: Jurisprudence and

12. National Association for the Promotion of Social Science, *Transactions, 1861* (London: Victoria Press, 1862), pp. xvii–xviii.
13. National Association for the Promotion of Social Science, *Transactions, 1879* (London: Victoria Press, 1880), p. xxxi.

the Amendment of the Law, Education, Punishment and Reformation, Public Health, and Social Economy.

These issues brought a substantial body of influential people together with the Association. The General Committee alone had 139 members, including 9 peers or their sons (among them Lord Shaftesbury and Lord John Russell), 27 members of Parliament, 10 fellows of the Royal Society, and several eminent social theorists such as Edwin Chadwick, Charles Kingsley, John Stuart Mill, John Ruskin, James Kay Shuttleworth, and John Simon.[14] The departmental committees contained other noted figures in the fields of social service. Thus, the Jurisprudence department was guided, not only by many practicing members of the Bar, but also by men like Leone Levi, who served as a consultant for the founders of the Charity Organization Society. The Public Health department included Chadwick, Simon, and Southwood Smith among its contributors. Practical workers predominated in the Punishment and Reformation department. Mary Carpenter was a leading speaker in this section.

The true nature of the Association becomes clear when the names of its committee members and speakers are noted. A careful analysis of the twenty-nine volumes of its *Transactions* reinforces the initial impression of a coalition between the wealth of the manufacturing middle class and the evolving professionalism which reached its pinnacle in a highly trained civil service. Amateur reformers and the new professionals mingled in the infant Association in an attempt to create the science of society, which was their solution to the problems of industrialization and overpopulation. Results were uneven, and the *Transactions* contain as many platitudes as hard facts and statistical evidence. It cannot be denied, however, that the Association created a new approach to social reform and mirrored the evolution combining the moral and scientific worlds at mid-century.

14. National Association for the Promotion of Social Science, *Transactions, 1857* (London: John W. Parker, 1858), pp. xv–xvii.

Social policy between 1857 and 1885 was significantly influenced by the activities of the Association, in its role as a forum for ideas, through its extraparliamentary campaigns for legislative change, and through the contributions of individual Association members. Middle-class reform movements during the mid-Victorian period were invariably connected with the Association or influenced by the work of one of its departments. The Association took the existing societal framework as a given, ruling out all political groups supporting radical reforms, such as socialism. An attempt was made to include the working classes by arranging a special meeting for them at each congress. However, working men and women with radical tendencies became disillusioned with the Association. The summons to the first Trades Union Congress of 1868 censured the organization for excluding the "artisan class" from its meetings and *Transactions*.[15]

The Association was not without critics. In 1858 *The Athenaeum* accused it of being "crotchety" and of demonstrating a "craving for further legislative interference, and a desire to enlarge the limits of the functions of government."[16] In 1861 Thomas Love Peacock made the Association the target for satire. In *Gryll Grange* the Association is the Pantopragmatic Society, Brougham is lampooned as Lord Michin Malicho, and Russell as Lord Facing-both-ways. Peacock ridicules the new science of Pantopragmatics, which yields no practical results and consists of endless lectures and a stream of irrelevant statistics.[17]

Criticism was a natural harvest for an organization willing to break down social barriers. In 1857 Isa Craig, a young Scotswoman who was a member of Bodichon's feminist circle, was appointed assistant secretary to the Association by George Hastings. The nomination of a woman to a responsible position within a national organization of the Association's size and influence was a revolutionary gesture. It was the first major step toward women's participation in

15. Sidney Webb and Beatrice Webb, *The History of Trade Unionism*, rev. ed. (New York: Longmans, 1920), p. 738.

16. *The Athenaeum* (1858): 687.

17. Thomas Love Peacock, *Gryll Grange*, 2 vols. (London: J. M. Dent, 1891), 1:71.

public policy. The *Saturday Review* naturally condemned the presence of women at meetings of the "Universal Palaver Association," characterized them as "Lord Brougham's little corps of lady orators," and predicted that the only result of their alliance with the Association would be to affirm the conviction that they were "unladylike."[18] Despite such condemnation, Emily Davies noted shortly afterward, "The Association was of immense use to the women's movement in giving us a platform from which we could bring our views before the sort of people who were likely to be disposed to help in carrying them out."[19]

Barbara Bodichon's conclusion to *Women and Work* had stressed the special moral quality which the female nature could bring to humanizing civilization. Lord Shaftesbury echoed her sentiments as he thanked women for their contribution to the Association's early efforts. He stressed the "peculiar nature" of the female contribution. Men might advance social reform through large scale projects, he claimed, but women could be relied on for the personal and homely touches. Their talent was for issues requiring tact and delicacy, primarily in the domestic sphere. Men would write the social treatises and draft reform legislation, while women would exercise moral influence to assist in correcting social injustice.[20] Shaftesbury was essentially conservative in regard to women, while Bodichon was radical in her insistence on full participation by women as citizens. His speech clearly circumscribed woman's proper sphere of action. However, they represent two ends of a continuum, not diametrically opposing views. It must be noted that Bodichon and Shaftesbury shared the belief that women's contribution to society would be essentially different from that of men. Although expressed more forcefully by Shaftesbury, the concept of moral attributes inherent in gender is similar to that in *Women and Work*. Although the Association rejected the concept of women's inferiority, their

18. "The Universal Palaver Association," p. 272.

19. Emily Davies, "Family Chronicle," p. 259, Girton College Archives, Cambridge, England.

20. National Association for the Promotion of Social Science, *Transactions, 1859* (London: Victoria Press, 1860), p. 10.

definition of the female character determined the limited goals pursued by groups like the Social Science Association, goals acceptable to even the most radical mid-Victorian feminists like Bodichon.

Bodichon's ideas about employment alternatives for women found another platform in the pages of the *English Woman's Journal.* The *Journal,* established in March 1858, and the women's club and employment register which grew up around it were instrumental in providing opportunities for women to enter new professions. The activities of the group of feminists which had begun as the Married Women's Property Committee coalesced around the office of the *Journal,* and the "ladies of Langham Place," led by Bodichon, not only spoke and wrote about reform, but also created agencies for change during the early sixties.

In February 1858 Bessie Parkes had written George Eliot of the limited liability company that had been set up to finance the *Journal*: "We are beginning with £1,000 and a great social interest."[21] In actuality Bodichon provided most of the money; others in the feminist circle were unable to afford more than token contributions. The first issue of the magazine declared that the new monthly was interested in existing industrial employment for women, both intellectual and manual, the best methods for cautiously expanding the sphere of that employment, and the reform of laws affecting the property and condition of the sexes.[22] The objectives Bodichon had set for women between 1854 and 1857 were the basis of that declaration, and during the six years of its existence the *Journal* was the core of the communication network linking the London feminists with women throughout the country.

The *Journal* collected and reprinted speeches on women's issues and eagerly followed the reports of the law courts concerning the working of the new divorce law. The Annual Report of the Governesses' Benevolent Institution was the basis of an article in the first issue describing the wretched situation of that ill-paid group of working women. In future issues campaigns were waged for im-

---

21. *George Eliot Letters,* 2:430.
22. *English Woman's Journal* 1 (March 1858): 75.

proved physical education for girls and for the adoption of simpler styles of clothing for women.

Parkes asked Eliot to contribute to the new periodical, but beyond letters of advice got only a polite refusal. She discussed the work of the magazine with Parkes and Bodichon, but never contributed to it.[23] The *Journal* depended for contributions upon the nucleus of feminists who had made up the original Married Women's Property Committee. Parkes was primarily responsible for day-to-day operations since Bodichon spent each winter in Algiers after her marriage in July 1857. However, Bodichon sent articles from Algiers and the time she spent in England was consumed by the *Journal* and its affiliated services.

Bodichon displayed political pragmatism during various feminist campaigns. She could become emotional and overexuberant about issues, but a strong sense of proportion usually saved her from indulging in sentimental fantasies. Thus, she evaluated the potential influence of the *Journal* realistically and was disturbed that Parkes overestimated the impact. She expected the magazine to serve the reform movement, but worried that the tool might be destroyed by an insular self-righteousness and a lack of literary discipline. From Algiers she confided to George Eliot her concern over Parkes's ecstatic appraisals of the *Journal's* success.[24] Eliot agreed that the magazine had serious flaws and that Bodichon would have to make unpopular criticisms on her next English visit. Succeeding correspondence indicates that Eliot had some doubt about the quality of the *Journal*, but by December 1859 she reassured Bodichon (back in Algiers for another winter) of her belief in its success: "The *Englishwoman's Journal must* be doing good substantially—stimulating woman to useful work and rousing people generally to some consideration of women's needs."[25]

One of the most important columns in the magazine was "Open Council," which asked for readers' opinions on women's issues. Letters came from women in the provinces describing their own situa-

23. George Eliot to Bessie Parkes, 3 February 1858, *George Eliot Letters*, 2:431.
24. Barbara Bodichon to George Eliot, 26 April 1859, ibid., 3:57.
25. George Eliot to Barbara Bodichon, 5 December 1859, ibid., 3:225–26.

tions. Eventually the women themselves began coming to the *Journal* offices in Cavendish Square. They wanted work. Scores of unemployed governesses and needlewomen, widows and orphans suddenly thrown into the labor market, untrained and impoverished, looked to the *Journal* for help. Confronted with the poignant reality Bodichon and Parkes turned from writing articles to keeping an employment register. It was an inadequate beginning. On any given day twenty requests for employment might be received from women who only knew that they did not want to be governesses.[26] The list of women seeking work grew, but few positions opened to them.

The difficulty of placement through the *Journal* register was compounded by the fact that two distinct groups of women were applying for assistance. It became clear that two problems existed. The first involved the professional employment of "born and bred ladies." There was no question that simple trades would not suffice for women of breeding.[27] The second group of women might be sustained through entry into the semimechanical occupations such as printing or law copying or telegraphy, but even that seemed an unattainable goal. Men went on strike when women entered their workshops. The *Saturday Review* echoed general fears, insisting: "Employment is a fixed quantity and therefore, if women come into men's occupations the result must be a lowering of men's wages."[28]

The effect of competition by women had been noted much earlier in the 1840 *Report* to the Handloom Weavers Commission. The commissioners had concluded that women workers had overstocked the trade and brought wages down.[29] The threat of low-paid female competition frightened working men, who then resisted women's entry into the labor market. Middle-class reformers were troubled by the seemingly inescapable underemployment of men threatened when women entered the industrial workforce.

26. Parkes, "A Year's Experience in Women's Work," *English Woman's Journal* 6 (October 1860): 113–14.

27. Ibid., pp. 115–16.

28. "The *Saturday Review* and the *English Woman's Journal*," *English Woman's Journal* 1 (May 1858): 202.

29. Pinchbeck, *Women Workers*, pp. 177–80.

Even so sympathetic a forum as the Social Science Association reflected concern regarding the entrance of women into industrial employment. Charles Bray read a paper at its first congress in 1857 expressing his disagreement with Bodichon's *Women and Work.* Bray was convinced that women must restrict their industrial activities to specialized female occupations. If they competed with men in an already overstocked labor market the results would be disastrous.[30] He was genuinely concerned about reforming women's employment in industry, but disagreed as to the alternatives available. He had corresponded with Bodichon about *Women and Work,* but remained so strongly disturbed that he published his own pamphlet. Charles Bray was the brother-in-law of Sara Hennell, George Eliot's close friend and steady correspondent. Eliot noted the controversy between her two friends in a letter in September 1857: "Mr. Bray, I suppose is going to take the field against the 'working woman,' if I am right in my inference from the letter he wrote to Mrs. Bodichon. Something will come out of the battle, whoever is right."[31]

The controversy grew and in April 1859 Harriet Martineau's "Female Industry," appeared in the *Edinburgh Review.* She insisted that the issue could not be overstated. Taking the themes of *Women and Work* for her own and echoing recent issues of the *Journal,* Martineau explored the problem of female employment alternatives, assured of a wider audience that those other forums could not attract. Apart from employment in agriculture, mills, or factories, women who needed to work for subsistence had only two choices, plying the needle or becoming teachers.[32]

Martineau noted the prejudices of men and women against female employment. The resistance of workers to the introduction of female labor expressed itself in the Staffordshire potteries in an absurdity. Women employed painting porcelain aroused such ill-will that workmen refused to permit supervisors to allow the women

30. National Association for the Promotion of Social Sciences, *Transactions, 1857,* pp. 544–48.
31. George Eliot to Sara Hennell, 21 September 1857, *George Eliot Letters,* 2:383.
32. Martineau, "Female Industry," p. 170.

hand-rests while painting. The prejudice of women was as much of a problem as men's resistance. In a large draper's and mercer's shop the owner's experiment in employing saleswomen failed. Business dwindled—but when the frustrated proprietor hired some shopmen they were deluged with customers, while their female counterparts were left standing idle. The shoppers, nearly all women, simply had no confidence in the ability of women to measure ribbons and fabrics or perform the simplest tasks behind the counter.

Martineau advocated training, as Bodichon had in 1857: "We must improve and extend education to the utmost; and then open a fair field to the powers and energies we have educed."[33] Her article was a clear, well-organized statement of the case first argued in Bodichon's *Women and Work.* It focused national attention on practical possibilities rather than abstract injustice. To strengthen the arguments Martineau described successful experiments in Switzerland and the United States.

In the area of professional education Martineau cited Elizabeth Blackwell's medical pioneering. Blackwell was visiting England at the time the article appeared. In March 1859, at Marylebone Hall, London, Blackwell began a series of lectures on women and the medical profession. Barbara Bodichon, Benjamin Smith, and Bessie Parkes organized and supported the talks, which she gave in London, Manchester, Birmingham, and Liverpool. Blackwell's London lecture inspired Elizabeth Garrett, a member of Bodichon's feminist circle, to become a physician, and she later led the female medical movement in England.[34]

Bodichon took Blackwell to visit George Eliot and George Lewes in June 1859. The couple was impressed by Blackwell's intelligence and dedication, but found her "schoolmistress-like in manner."[35] The humorless and didactic qualities which disappointed Lewes and Eliot were a marked contrast to Bodichon's effervescence, but did not prevent Bodichon and Blackwell from maintaining close ties across the Atlantic for more than thirty years.

33. Ibid., p. 173.
34. Blackwell, *Opening the Medical Profession*, pp. 218–19.
35. Journal of George Henry Lewes, 26 June 1859, *George Eliot Letters*, 3:103.

The spring and summer of 1859 were active for Bodichon. Returning to England from Algiers meant renewing her ties with feminism and art. She arranged an exhibition of her paintings at the French Gallery and went daily to the offices of the *Journal*. The feminists looked to Bodichon for direction, and she found herself overwhelmed by meetings, social obligations, and constant calls for advice. She wrote George Eliot that she was tempted to announce that she and Eugène Bodichon were not actually married. That would insure her peace by making her a social outcast. "You are right to get rid of the world. Sometimes here I get so sick that I think I must run away."[36] Social reform was a compelling obligation, but a yearning for the private world of painting and solitude haunted her. She was never completely able to resolve that personal conflict. The problem was aggravated by the disparity between the Algerian world of her husband and England, which she always considered home.

Even as Elizabeth Blackwell toured England and Harriet Martineau praised American efforts in "Female Industry," Bodichon's *Women and Work* was making its way across the Atlantic. In 1859 the pamphlet was published in New York with a preface, by Catherine M. Sedgwick, which analyzed the difference between English and American society. Sedgwick asserted that America was "plastic and fusible," while England suffered from "inexorable prejudices" which had to be overcome before progress was possible.[37] The basic theme of *Women and Work* regarding the inherent right and responsibility of every individual to work productively was extolled and underlined in Sedgwick's preface.

If American women read *Women and Work* for inspiration, British reformers made more concrete use of its proposals. Bessie Parkes read a paper entitled "The Market for Educated Female Labour" at the October 1859 conference of the Social Science Association. Acknowledging Bodichon's assistance in the preparation of her paper, Parkes went on to discuss proposals for upgrading the teaching

36. Barbara Bodichon to George Eliot, 1 July 1859, ibid., 3:107.
37. Catherine Sedgwick, Preface to *Women and Work*, by Barbara Bodichon (New York: C. S. Francis, 1859), p. 3.

profession. She concluded that women might serve as school inspectors and advocated the opening of the examinations at Oxford to women.[38] To augment Parkes's presentation, which dealt only with the educated woman, Jessie Boucherett, a recent arrival to the London feminist circle, delivered "The Industrial Employments of Women," describing work she had begun in Lincolnshire.

Jessie Boucherett (1825–1905), the youngest daughter of a Lincolnshire landowner, came to London inspired by Martineau's "Female Industry."[39] She had read the *English Woman's Journal* and arrived at its offices eager to join the staff. She wished to found a society which might directly address the problems of women seeking employment. Boucherett was surprised at the elegance and youth of the reformers, among them Bodichon, who struck her as "beautifully dressed, of radiant beauty with masses of golden hair."[40]

The ebullient company at Cavendish Square welcomed Boucherett and by July 1859 a Society for the Promotion of the Employment of Women had been established.[41] Membership required a five-pound donation. The honorary secretaries were Jessie Boucherett and Adelaide Proctor. Sarah Lewin and Emily Crow served as executive secretaries, while an advisory committee included Barbara Bodichon, Bessie Parkes, and Emily Faithfull. In October 1859 the Society was officially affiliated with the Social Science Association at that organization's annual conference in Bradford. The *Journal* moved from Cavendish Square to 19 Langham Place at the end of 1859 and the Society established its headquarters there. Rooms were designated in that building for a ladies' club, which included a dining room and a library.[42]

The work of the Society represented the first practical effort to

38. National Association for the Promotion of Social Science, *Transactions, 1859* (London: Victoria Press, 1860), p. 728.

39. Jessie Boucherett, "The Industrial Movement," in Theodore Stanton, ed., *The Woman Question in Europe* (London: Sampson, Low, Marston, Searle & Rivington, 1884), p. 96.

40. Ibid., p. 97.

41. National Association for the Promotion of Social Science, *Transactions, 1860* 2 vols (London: Victoria Press, 1861), 1:xviii.

42. *English Woman's Journal* 6 (September 1860): 54–60.

prepare women of the lower middle classes for new occupations. The reformers chose to work first with lower-middle-class women after careful study of the social scale. Parkes explained: "For highly educated women we could for a time do nothing; women of no education could do nothing for us, that is to say we could open no new channels for the labour of the former and our experiments would have failed owing to the inefficiency of the latter."[43] Reformers were convinced, however, that they could turn the lowest class of governess into successful tradeswomen and that the most intelligent seamstresses might be trained for a variety of other jobs.

Printing was the first trade considered. Despite the heavy labor involved in presswork, it was determined that women could easily work as compositors. In March 1860 the Victoria Press was opened by Emily Faithfull in Great Coram Street, Russell Square. The Society began by choosing five girls to serve apprenticeships. These were so successful that by October 1860 the number of trainees was increased to sixteen. The Victoria Press became printer for the *Journal* and produced the yearly *Transactions* of the Social Science Association.[44] Law copying was another area that could employ women. The Society opened a law stationer's office in Portugal Street, Lincoln's Inn, which began by employing and training female clerks.[45]

The Society wanted to place female bookkeepers and cashiers in shops. This proved nearly impossible because of the widespread lack of mathematical skills among women. Bodichon had cited this problem in *Women and Work*. When she asked two young women who ran a shop how much profit they earned annually, they were only able to estimate that generally they did not pay more for their goods than they sold them for. When the question of other expenses was raised, the two women indicated that they let lodgings to supplement their income. They had no idea of how much profit

43. *English Woman's Journal* 6 (November 1860): 147.
44. Emily Faithfull, "The Victoria Press," National Association for the Promotion of Social Science, *Transactions*, 1860, 1:819–22.
45. "Annual Report of the Society for the Promotion of the Employment of Women," ibid., p. xix.

or loss was involved in their business, nor of how to keep an accurate accounting of transactions.[46] To rectify this situation, in 1860 the Society opened a business school for girls, where they were taught to write letters, to calculate without a slate, and to keep accounts by single and double entry. Jessie Boucherett ran the school, which charged a shilling per week for instruction.[47] Since many girls came from outside London and had no place to live while being trained, a Ladies' Institute was opened which accommodated fifty residents.

When the Society affiliated with the Social Science Association in 1859, its exclusively female leadership was changed. Lord Shaftesbury became its president and its general committee was composed of twelve men and twelve women. By June 1860 Shaftesbury was able to chair a meeting and reception to survey the Society's accomplishments and to congratulate its feminist originators on the success of their training programs. It is noteworthy that the papers contributed by Bessie Parkes, Jessie Boucherett, and Emily Faithfull were read by male members of the Society. Women had come quite far under the protection of the Social Science Association, but although they occasionally spoke publicly, it was clear on that particular evening that the male members of the central committee were the Society's spokesmen. They did not consciously patronize; they tipped their hats in public resolutions of congratulations. Nevertheless, the tone was clear. Male and female members of the committee did not operate as colleagues yet. The women demonstrated what could be done, the men approved and gave the work credibility by their presence.

Initial Society projects made only small inroads on the enormous pool of unemployed women. The idea of female emigration became increasingly attractive to reformers. As early as 1860 Barbara Bodichon had recognized the necessity for equipping girls for life in the colonies.[48] By 1862 when the controversy over what to do with re-

46. Bodichon, *Women and Work*, 1857 ed., p. 15.
47. "The Society for the Promotion of the Employment of Women," *English Woman's Journal* 5 (August 1860): 394.
48. Bodichon, "Middle Class Schools for Girls," p. 176.

dundant women was raging in the national press, W. R. Greg concluded that female emigration was a major part of the solution.[49]
By that time the Female Middle Class Emigration Society had been established by Maria Rye as a subsidiary of the Women's Employment Society. Rye (1829–1903) had been a member of Bodichon's original Married Women's Property Committee and had organized the Women's Employment Society law-copying operation. Assisted by Jane Lewin, she organized emigration to Australia and New Zealand for numbers of middle-class women. In the summer of 1862 she decided to travel to Australia to spend two years organizing a women's committee to receive and place new arrivals more efficiently. Bodichon headed the fund-raising effort for the trip. In a letter thanking Lord Shaftesbury for a pledge of twenty-five pounds, Bodichon indicated that she planned to continue raising money throughout the two years so that the project would not be a drain on the Women's Employment Society.[50] In October 1863 Bodichon was still actively raising funds and attempting to convince *Journal* readers that this part of the emigration effort was useful. She stressed the need for planning and organizing so that women could make successful transitions to life in the colonies. Direct contributions to young emigrants might be immediately gratifying, but support services for emigrants were costly. Planning and organizing were not glamorous, but they were more permanently useful than direct personal gifts.[51]

Female emigration was primarily a London-based effort. But the Women's Employment Society began to create a network of provincial chapters during its second year of operation. Emily Davies started a branch for the districts of Northumberland and Durham in October 1860. In March 1862 she began a bookkeeping class for ten pupils and by May she had begun a registry for governesses.[52]

Emily Davies (1830–1921), the secretary for almost every wom-

49. Greg, "Why Are Women Redundant?" p. 446.

50. Barbara Bodichon to Lord Shaftesbury, 26 July 1862, Fawcett Society Collection.

51. Barbara Bodichon, "Open Council," *English Woman's Journal* 12 (October 1863): 141–42.

52. Emily Davies, *Thoughts on Some Questions Relating to Women, 1860–1908* (Cambridge: Bowes & Bowes, 1910: reprint, New York: AMS, 1973), pp. 28–33.

en's committee during the early days of organized feminism, eventually directed her efforts exclusively toward improved higher education for women. The daughter of a clergyman from Gateshead, she spent her girlhood in parish work, self-improvement schemes, and religious devotions. She experienced a growing sense of injustice at being denied the university education her brothers enjoyed. Her brother Llewellyn was appointed to a London parish in 1856 and purchased a home in Blandford Square. In the spring of 1857 she traveled with her invalid brother, Henry, to Algiers, and en route she met Barbara Bodichon's sisters Nanny and Bella. Nanny, she wrote later, was the first person she had ever met who shared her feeling of resentment at the subjection of women.[53] After the Smiths introduced her to Barbara Bodichon, she became an active member of their feminist circle. Llewellyn Davies's Blandford Square residence gave his sister easy access to the Smith–Bodichon London home. Initially she worked to organize a northern branch of the Women's Employment Society, but by January 1862 she and her widowed mother had moved permanently to Cunningham Place in London.

On July 18, 1862 Davies agreed to take on the editorship of the *English Woman's Journal,* beginning with the September issue.[54] Throughout 1862 and 1863 she corresponded with Bodichon frequently about the troubled finances of the magazine. It was steadily losing money, quality contributors were refusing to write without payment, and the circulation remained limited. In January 1863 Bodichon sent a check to cover rent and expenses and it was agreed that serious consideration should be given to ending the publication when she arrived in England for the summer.[55] By 1864 the *Journal* had ceased publication and Davies took on editorship of the new *Victoria Magazine,* published by Emily Faithfull at the Victoria Press.[56]

53. Davies, "Family Chronicle," p. 159.
54. Ibid., p. 263a.
55. Emily Davies to Barbara Bodichon, 2 letters, January 1863, Girton College Archives, Cambridge, England.
56. Davies, "Family Chronicle," pp. 288–91.

The work of the Women's Employment Society progressed at
Langham Place even after the cessation of the *Journal.* The feminist
circle continued to function, with Bodichon lending focus and direction each spring when she returned to London. As late as 1872
the Victoria Discussion Society, which Faithfull chaired, held
meetings on the question of employment for women. A paper delivered at its December 4, 1872, meeting restated the theories first articulated in *Women and Work* in 1857. "Work as a Necessity for
Women" contributed no new justifications and suggested no inno-
vative training programs.[57] It illustrated by its similarity with papers of the late fifties that the progress of women in employment
had been limited, that societal resistance to an expanding female
sphere was still strong, and that feminist arguments needed constant repetition to produce any discernible impact.

Special interests were beginning to divide feminists, however.
Separate campaigns needed to be waged if progress toward improved education or increased political participation was to be
achieved. Many reformers believed that only by opening these areas
to women could employment opportunities be expanded. The legal
and social status of women was becoming recognized as a complex
combination of factors, each inextricably bound to the others, yet
each demanding separate action if ultimate modification of the to-
tality was to occur. The Langhamites remained a loosely connected
circle for decades thereafter, meeting one another in a variety of
new feminist committees, each with roots in Bodichon's Married
Women's Property Committee of 1856.

Bodichon was herself in a period of transition. In 1860 she had
suffered a deep personal loss at the death of her father. Benjamin
Smith died on April 12, 1860, and Bodichon wrote to George Eliot
two months later that her tie to him had been much greater than
that of "kith and kin."[58] Together they had championed a variety
of causes; indeed, Benjamin's energy often surpassed Barbara's. His
support for Elizabeth Blackwell's medical work was spirited. He not

57. Miss Downing, "Work as a Necessity for Women," pp. 213–34.
58. Barbara Bodichon to George Eliot, 13 June 1860, George Eliot Letters, Beinecke Library, Yale.

only welcomed Blackwell to his family circle, but proved a generous sponsor, pledging money for her American hospital and willing her a substantial bequest.[59] He had made each of his daughters financially independent and by this gesture created an enduring family unity which owed nothing to economic dependence. Despite their disagreement over John Chapman, Benjamin and Barbara were strongly attached. His death made Blandford Square unusually inactive. The house was left to Barbara and became the Bodichon's London home, but it was shut for a good part of each year.

It was some time before Bodichon recovered her customary animation and for a few years her feminism lacked inspiration or a sense of urgency. In April 1861 George Eliot wrote with concern: "I think of you a good deal, dear Barbara—sometimes with a mingling of sadness at some things that touch you nearly. But there are so many chords in your life, that some joy and consolation lies by the side of every grief."[60] During 1861 and 1862 Eliot tried continually, but unsuccessfully, to find words of solace. Bodichon continued to mourn her father and was increasingly concerned that her marriage was childless. By July 1862 she was forcing herself to go on with routine activities, but was feeling mentally exhausted, attributing her malaise to middle age. She wrote William Allingham that enthusiasm for life was ebbing: "If it were not that at thirty-five one has acquired habits which happily cannot be broken I should not go on as I do; I could not *begin* as I used ten years ago at any of these dusty dirty attempts to help one's poor fellow creatures."[61]

Private sorrows mingled with public ones. Bodichon was deeply troubled by the American Civil War. Her family's antislavery tradition had been strengthened in her by her American experiences. Elizabeth Blackwell sent her constant reminders of the conflict that agonized America. In 1863 and 1864 Bodichon published two articles in the *English Woman's Journal* expressing her horror at English sympathy for the South. The first of these described conditions she

59. Elizabeth Blackwell to Barbara Bodichon, 23 December 1865, Fawcett Society Collection.

60. George Eliot to Barbara Bodichon, 9 April 1861, *George Eliot Letters*, 3:402.

61. Barbara Bodichon to William Allingham, 5 July 1862, Allingham, *Letters*, pp. 78–79.

had witnessed during her Southern tour in 1857–58.[62] It concluded with a strong moral denunciation of the South and a plea that English citizens remember that the cause of the war was slavery, a moral evil which must be recognized. "Accomplices," published in 1864, advocated an English boycott of goods containing Southern-grown cotton. Bodichon drew a parallel between the goods produced by match girls and other abused female workers and slave-produced products. Englishwomen, she claimed, clearly recognized the misery of working girls, just as they understood the evils of slavery. Women must consider themselves accomplices to those injustices so long as they supported the economics of both systems. Slavery was "stolen labour," a far more serious crime than simple theft of goods.[63]

The depression that Bodichon experienced as a result of her personal unhappiness and her sensitive reaction to the horrors of the Civil War was not as severe as her breakdown of 1856. She was determined to continue routine activities and that tenacity was rewarded by a gradual recovery. Throughout her life Bodichon became dissatisfied once a feminist project had moved beyond its initial stages. The detail work required to complete a campaign was invariably left to others. The fact that the Women's Employment Society was well established by 1861 contributed more than a little to her sense of ennui. Beginnings were her talent and it was fortunate that a new challenge presented itself in 1865. By 1869 she could confidently report to Allingham: "I do not think there is much danger of getting utilitarian! I may get sometimes bitter and disappointed and have moods of sadness, but not hardness and for believing less in what the poets believe, no never less. At middle life I have a deeper belief than I had at twenty."[64] She had expressed strong optimism in 1867, even after a debilitating attack of Algerian fever. She chided Allingham for complaining of the deterioration of English society: "I do think England is 'unsatisfactory,'

62. Barbara Bodichon, "Of Those Who Are the Property of Others, and of the Great Power that Holds Others as Property," *English Woman's Journal* 10 (February 1863): 370–81.

63. Barbara Bodichon, "Accomplices," *English Woman's Journal* 12 (February 1864): 400.

64. Barbara Bodichon to William Allingham, 1869, Allingham, *Letters*, p. 87.

and so is France, and so are you and so am I, and I feel *sometimes* as
Carlyle does *always*—but I know well enough—'unsatisfactory' as
it all is, it is—ie. England and its people—better now than it was
at any one time you like to fix upon."[65] The world was improving.
In 1865 Bodichon had renewed her commitment to perfecting it. In
that year she joined forces with John Stuart Mill and women turned
toward the political arena to demand the vote.

65. Barbara Bodichon to William Allingham, 10 September 1867, ibid., pp. 83–84.

~ VI ~
WOMEN'S SUFFRAGE: THE FIRST CAMPAIGN

On July 12, 1865, John Stuart Mill was elected to Parliament by the voters of Westminster. His election address reiterated his conviction that the franchise should be extended to women. Although he had completed but not yet published *The Subjection of Women* at the time of his election, his opinion on women's suffrage had been clearly articulated in *Representative Government*, published in 1860. In arguing for universal but graduated suffrage he dismissed the differences of sex: "I consider it to be as entirely irrelevant to political rights, as difference in height, or in the colour of the hair."[1] As early as July 1851 the publication of "The Enfranchisement of Women" in the *Westminster Review* had expressed Mill's commitment to women's suffrage. Reprinted in Mill's *Dissertations and Discussions,* the original article was inspired by the meeting of a women's rights convention at Worcester, Massachusetts in October 1850. Although Mill attributed the article to Harriet Taylor, the essay reflects his views as much as hers. It contained a strong claim for equal rights in property, in occupational choice, in political participation, and in family status. The essay clearly states the basis on which women might claim the suffrage among other rights: "We deny the right of any portion of the species to decide for another portion, or any individual for another individual, what is or is not their 'proper sphere.' The proper sphere for all human beings is the

1. John Stuart Mill, *Representative Government.* (London: Oxford University Press, 1963), p. 290.

largest and the highest which they are able to attain to. What this is, cannot be ascertained without complete liberty of choice."[2]

The feminist circle at Langham Place supported Mill's candidacy enthusiastically during the spring of 1865. Barbara Bodichon, who had participated in her father's parliamentary campaigns as a child, rejoiced in the opportunity to reenter the political arena. She hired a carriage and had it covered with placards supporting Mill. Joined by Isa Craig, Emily Davies, and Bessie Parkes, Bodichon rode through Westminster in her campaign buggy. As Davies remembered, they had called it giving Mill moral support, but were struck by the suspicion they were doing his cause more harm than good. This fear was heightened when friends reported to the feminists that Mill had been derided as "the man who wants to have girls in Parliament."[3] In any case, Mill was successful and Davies recalled that Bodichon uttered a prophecy about women's suffrage at the time of his election. "You will go up and vote upon crutches, and I shall come out of my grave and vote in my winding sheet."[4] She could not have predicted with greater accuracy. Davies was eighty-eight when she went to the poll in 1919 and Bodichon had been dead for nearly thirty years.

Bodichon's estimate of the time that would elapse before women gained the vote demonstrated her awareness of political realities. Although she threw herself into the suffrage campaign with fervor and pushed hard to organize immediate action during the mid-sixties, she had few illusions about the depth of opposition the proposal would encounter. Many suffragists, because they traveled in radical circles where encouragement and support were automatic, lost perspective about the feasibility of rapid legislative change. Bodichon, however, was a sower of seeds, approaching the suffrage issue as she had the married women's property campaign. She presented the early papers arguing the case for women's votes, established the first major suffrage committee, and organized a petition

2. John Stuart Mill, "Enfranchisement of Women," 3:104–05.
3. Davies, "Family Chronicle," p. 424.
4. Ibid.

campaign in support of legislative reform. She brought the feminist focus back to Parliament, establishing patterns suffragists were to follow during the next fifty years.

Bodichon's first efforts on behalf of women's suffrage coincided with Mill's election to Parliament. On May 23, 1865, the first meeting of a women's discussion society was held at the Kensington home of Charlotte Manning. An outgrowth of efforts to open local education examinations to girls, the Kensington Society attracted about fifty members and served as a forum for the consideration of women's issues. Bodichon was one of its founders and was joined by other Langhamites including Emily Davies and Jessie Boucherett. The organization attracted many feminists from outside the Women's Employment Society such as the founder of the Cheltenham Ladies' College, Dorothea Beale, and of the North London Collegiate School, Frances Mary Buss. Elizabeth Garrett, in the midst of medical studies, joined the society, and perhaps most significant for Bodichon's suffrage work was the membership of Helen Taylor, Mill's stepdaughter.

The Kensington Society gave its first meeting over to a discussion of a paper by Garrett, "What is the Basis and What the Limits of Parental Authority." The topic was still a cause for heated debate and many of the women present rebelled against parental restriction merely by appearing at the meeting.[5] The discussion provided an emotional outlet for many of the women, but to Bodichon that kind of debate was useless because no practical end was served.

When Emily Davies suggested that the papers for the second Kensington Society meeting might deal with the desirability of women's participation in public affairs, Bodichon found her opportunity. Electoral reform was the political question of the moment. Both Bodichon and Helen Taylor mailed in papers advocating the extension of the franchise to women. Bodichon was wintering in Algiers and Taylor was in Avignon when the papers were read on November 21, 1865. Davies had written Bodichon a week earlier to

5. Ibid., pp. 422–24.

praise her paper and expressed disappointment at Taylor's overly radical contribution. She told Bodichon that three other papers had been submitted opposing female suffrage.[6]

Davies's approval of Bodichon's sentiments was not unqualified. During the suffrage campaign and throughout later efforts to establish Girton College, Davies's conservative instincts were alarmed by Bodichon's natural exuberance and strong language. Davies was primarily concerned with higher education for women and throughout the sixties and seventies evaluated all feminist activities in terms of their effect on educational projects. Thus, she was extremely cautious in regard to the suffrage and eventually withdrew from the campaign for fear of jeopardizing her experiment in higher education. Davies was single-minded in her feminism, in sharp contrast to Bodichon.

In November 1865, however, Davies was still willing to work with Bodichon for the vote and advised her to temper the language of her paper in order to make it more palatable. Calling antisuffrage articles "foolish" might be true, she said, but did not seem quite "polite." It would be politic to characterize the disabilities imposed by men on women a "mistake" rather than a "crime," since men were sensitive to indignation. She wrote Bodichon that she did not mind indignant speeches at Kensington discussions, but she worried since the papers would be circulated throughout the country and would probably be read by men already prejudiced against the issue.[7] Her caution reflects a major theme that eventually divided the feminists. Davies feared the risk of talking about the franchise before "first principles" had made more progress. She found the idea of women asserting their rights revolting and unladylike.[8] Many feminists shared her reluctance and worried that an aggressive suffrage campaign would fail and in the process alienate the public mind and associate all women's activities with an unfeminine radicalism. There was certainly strong reaction to Bodichon's appearance at a meeting on the suffrage a short while later. A Mrs.

6. Emily Davies to Barbara Bodichon, 14 November 1865, Girton College Archives.
7. Ibid.
8. Emily Davies to H. R. Tomkinson, November 1865, Girton College Archives.

Schunck wrote to Henry Crabb Robinson in horror at the "Doctor-esses." She objected to their dress and forthright speeches. Bodi-chon disturbed her by appearing with her hair flowing over her shoulders bound only by a velvet ribbon: "What would our great-grandmothers say to such doings?"[9] This was the kind of revulsion Davies wished to avoid. In light of this attitude, it is interesting that these same suffragists were dismissed for their timidity by the suffragettes of the violent pre–World War I movement. Bodichon's petitions and committees were in their time quite as alarming as the rocks and hunger strikes of the Pankhurst family.

Emily Davies's fears notwithstanding, after the papers were read at the November 21 Kensington Society meeting, a resolution in favor of women's suffrage was carried by a large majority. Bodichon immediately proposed the formation of a suffrage committee, but Davies hesitated. Bodichon was anxious to put the suffrage issue be-fore as many women as possible to build a base of support for an extraparliamentary campaign. Davies, acknowledging Bodichon's good intentions, argued that while a perfect committee might prove effective, she doubted their ability to prevent "wild people" from joining and destroying the committee. She opted for encouraging women to use the political rights they already had, to "accustom men's imagination to the spectacle of women taking part in public affairs."[10]

Bodichon was not easily dissuaded. While she admitted the risks attached to a vigorous public campaign, she decided to begin organ-izing quietly. She spent the winter of 1866 in Algiers planning. Im-mediately upon her arrival in London in May she wrote to Helen Taylor to solicit John Stuart Mill's advice and support. Bodichon expressed her desire to do something immediately on behalf of votes for women. Noting that she did not wish to start a petition or begin any public agitation without knowing what Mill and Taylor thought was "expedient," she informed Taylor that she had inform-ally contacted several women willing to work for the cause and had

9. Henry Crabb Robinson, Diary, *Reminiscences and Correspondence*, 3d ed., edited by Thomas Sadler (London: Macmillan, 1872), 2:144.

10. Emily Davies to Barbara Bodichon, November 1865, Girton College Archives.

solicited pledges of financial support. She asked Taylor to write a simple draft petition which the two might discuss when they met, and ended the letter with her personal appraisal that it would be best to try simply for what might be possible to attain, rather than to harbor false hopes of a sweeping reform.[11]

Taylor replied the same day and she was encouraging. She indicated that since a Reform Bill was under discussion in Parliament this was an excellent time for women to begin petitioning. Cautioning that immediate success was unlikely, she agreed with Bodichon: "The most important thing is to make a demand and commence the first humble beginning of an agitation." Giving practical consideration to what could be demanded, she reminded Bodichon of the connection in the English mind between taxation and representation, suggesting that the public would find most palatable the assertion that single women and widows with property had been unjustly denied the privileges their property entitled them to. She advised against asserting the proposition that sex was an improper consideration in regard to political rights. Therefore she proposed a petition asking simply for "the admission to the franchise of all women holding the requisite property qualification," which would mean "petitioning for the omission of the word *male* or *man* from *the present act.*" Taylor spoke for Mill and indicated that if Bodichon could obtain at least one hundred signatures he would consider it a respectable showing: "If a tolerably numerously signed petition can be got up, my father will gladly undertake to present it and will consider whether it might be made the occasion for anything further."[12]

Bodichon was hard at work by the time she reported back to Taylor on May 11. She had formed a committee to gather signatures. Among the members were Davies, Parkes, Boucherett, Garret, and Craig.[13] A few days later the committee received Taylor's draft petition and met at Garrett's home to modify it. Bodichon

---

11. Barbara Bodichon to Helen Taylor, 9 May 1866, Mill–Taylor Correspondence, London School of Economics, London, England.

12. Helen Taylor to Barbara Bodichon, 9 May 1866, Mill–Taylor Correspondence.

13. Barbara Bodichon to Helen Taylor, 11 May 1866, Mill–Taylor Correspondence.

sent Taylor the shortened text, explaining the committee decision: "It would be better to make it as short as possible and to state
as few reasons as possible for what we want, everyone has something to say against the reasons. . . . The fact that we do petition
is the great matter."[14]

The small committee which was working feverishly to gather signatures was composed entirely of women from Bodichon's Langham
Place feminist circle. Once the work began, however, Bodichon
called on Clementia Taylor, who joined the committee and later
led the more radical portion of its members when the group split in
1867. Clementia Doughty Taylor was the wife of the Radical M.P.,
Peter A. Taylor. They were Unitarians, cousins of the Mallesons,
and friends of William J. Fox and Giuseppe Mazzini. Aubrey House
in Kensington, the Taylors' home, was a center of advanced causes
similar to Benjamin Smith's Blandford Square residence. Like the
Smith family, the Taylors were advocates of black emancipation
and adopted and educated a young black woman who eventually
became a physician. Bodichon and Clementia Taylor shared family
and social connections and it was natural for Bodichon to enlist
Taylor in the suffrage effort in 1866. Taylor took over suffragist
leadership when Bodichon turned her attention to reform of wom-
en's higher education. Taylor directed the campaign for the wom-
en's franchise until Millicent Garrett Fawcett, the youngest of
the Garrett sisters, was old enough to preside over the national
movement.

In May 1866, however, Bodichon was totally immersed in the
challenge of this new endeavor. After only a few days' work she reported to Helen Taylor that nearly seven hundred signatures had
been collected. Bodichon was concerned about who would present
the petition. She had talked with Russell Gurney, Conservative
Recorder of London, who was willing to do so if Mill thought it advisable, but her personal preference was for Mill himself: "I told Mr.
Russell Gurney that I myself would rather Mr. Mill presented it but
mine is not a reason only a sentimental feeling! and as all the ladies

14. Barbara Bodichon to Helen Taylor, May 1866, Mill–Taylor Correspondence.

are more conservative than I perhaps Mr. Gurney is best."[15] The rumor that Gurney would present the petition surfaced in the *Spectator*, but however expedient his Conservatism and legal eminence might seem for the cause, it was decided that Mill would make the presentation.

On June 7, 1866, after little more than two weeks work, the petition containing 1,499 signatures was taken to Mill at the House of Commons. Bodichon was ill and could not go, but Davies and Garrett carried the enormous package to Westminster. Nervous about the event, the women were relieved to meet Henry Fawcett, who offered to find Mill and bring him to them. Left with their burden, they realized that they were the only women in the building except for an elderly apple-seller. Rather shy, the two respectable rebels sheltered near the apple-woman's stall and hid the petition under the counter to avoid notice. Mill was heartily amused by their timidity when he arrived, but he was pleased with the bulk of the petition, assuring them, "Ah, this I can brandish with effect."[16] Among the signers were a host of notable women. The fact that the more traditional Florence Nightingale, Harriet Martineau, Maria Grey, and Emily Shirreff joined their signatures to those of ardent radicals Clementia Taylor and Lady Amberley demonstrated the restricted and respectable nature of the demand for which Bodichon's committee had decided to petition.

Neither Bodichon nor Mill was surprised that the petition, reasonable though it might be, made little impact. It was, after all, the first attempt to bring the issue forward for serious consideration. The first suffrage petition, presented to the House of Lords by the Seventh Earl of Carlisle on behalf of the women of Sheffield fifteen years earlier in February 1851, had aroused little comment and left no lasting impression. Two days after he presented Bodichon's petition Mill wrote a parliamentary colleague that he had gone as far as he thought it prudent to go on the subject in that session. He agreed with colleagues in the House that it was enough to open the

15. Barbara Bodichon to Helen Taylor, May 1866, Mill–Taylor Correspondence.
16. Helen Blackburn, *Women's Suffrage* (London: Williams and Norgate, 1902; reprint, New York: Sourcebook Press, 1970), p. 54.

subject rather than force a discussion which would lead to charges of obstructiveness without leading to practical gains. "What we are doing now will lay the foundation of a further movement when advisable, and will prepare for that moment much greater support in the country than we should have if we attempted it at present."[17]

The country was certainly not prepared to give serious consideration to the question of increased political participation by women. In measured tones the *Spectator* dismissed the first suffrage petition. Admitting that perhaps twenty women in the country might be politically capable, it argued that these were remarkable exceptions and that the general effect of women on political discussions was "thoroughly bad—unreal, tawdry, dressy."[18]

Bodichon began to revise her Kensington Society paper on the women's franchise during the summer of 1866 in hopes of publishing it in the *Cornhill* or the *Fortnightly*. Keeping the issue in the public mind and accustoming influential men and women to the idea of even a limited extension of the franchise to women was her goal. By nature impulsive and far more advanced in politics than Davies, she was extremely practical about feminist possibilities. She relied on Davies's cautious advice to temper her prose. As a collaboration, the work of Bodichon and Davies on the suffrage and female higher education benefited from the fortuitous balance of two contrasting natures. If Bodichon soared too high, Davies quickly brought her down to earth. At the same time, Davies's timid but curiously stubborn nature was prevented from declining into single-mindedness by Bodichon's ability to soften and inspire.

Ultimately the suffrage and higher education campaigns split, but during 1866 and 1867 the feminists continued to work simultaneously on both fronts. Bodichon planned to present a suffrage paper at the Social Science Association meeting in Manchester in October 1866. Her first pamphlet on the subject, *Objections to the Enfranchisement of Women Considered*, was published in a small edi-

---

17. John Stuart Mill to Darby Griffith, 9 June 1866, *The Later Letters of John Stuart Mill, 1849–1873*, ed. Francis E. Mineka and Dwight N. Lindley, 3 vols. (Toronto: University of Toronto Press, 1972), 3:1175.

18. *Spectator*, 9 June 1866, p. 630.

tion during that summer. Davies suggested modifying this paper to stimulate discussion at the social science meeting. Bodichon rewrote the essay and presented it as Davies wished, concentrating on the arguments "for" with a new title, "Reasons for the Enfranchisement of Women."

Bodichon sent early drafts of her essay to Helen Taylor for comment. She suggested that the time had come for an essay on the suffrage in book form and asked Taylor to make the attempt. She reasoned that a discussion in book form would be widely reviewed and extracted, which would provide much needed publicity at this early stage of the suffrage campaign.[19] Taylor did publish a brief article on the female franchise in 1867,[20] but the important initial publications were left for Bodichon to write.

By mid-August 1866 Bodichon and Davies realized that no major forum was immediately available for a suffrage paper. The *Cornhill*, the *Fortnightly*, and *MacMillan's* would not publish an article by Bodichon, whom they considered too radical. Davies was not sanguine about the possible reception of a paper at Manchester: "Lord Shaftesbury is to be President this year. He is not particularly good for us, as regards politics, but he is favourable to the employment of women, and may perhaps take a good turn as to education."[21] It was decided to avoid connecting the suffrage paper with Mill's name. Bodichon hesitated, but Davies insisted that associating the presentation with Mill would diminish its importance. She reasoned that Mill had not made suffrage for women his first concern and argued that his name would invariably mix their cause in the public mind with other political issues, doing irreparable harm.[22]

In September 1866 a setback for female franchise supporters came in a strongly worded article in *Blackwood's*. Margaret Oliphant dismissed the implications of the suffrage petition, repeatedly misstating the number of women signatories as twenty, not fifteen hundred, and poking fun at Mill, whom she characterized as a phi-

19. Barbara Bodichon to Helen Taylor, n.d., Mill–Taylor Correspondence.
20. Helen Taylor, "The Ladies' Petition," *Westminster Review* 87 (January 1867): 29–36.
21. Emily Davies to Barbara Bodichon, 16 August 1866, Girton College Archives.
22. Emily Davies to Barbara Bodichon, 21 August 1866, Girton College Archives.

losopher inexperienced in the ways of ordinary women.[23] She insisted that only a few women were interested in nondomestic functions. These were unnatural women in whom God's purpose was defeated. She went further, denying not only the possibility of women voting, but also ploughing, carrying guns, and making speeches. She even insisted that women were not sent into the world to produce poetry or excel in the fine arts.[24] She asserted on behalf of her sex complete contentment with the place that God had decreed for women in the world economy, woman's natural sphere.[25]

Oliphant's article was not merely a forceful indication of the depth of resistance to women's political activities. It was a reminder of how restricted a conception of the female role was still held by a large proportion of the British population. The campaigns between 1850 and 1866 had made some progress toward educating and employing limited numbers of women, but no substantial breakthrough would occur until societal ideals for feminine behavior changed perceptibly. The change would be unconscious and subtle. The cumulative effect of feminist efforts and other reform movements resulted by the century's end in a new feminine ideal, not openly articulated, but reflected in the press and other indicators of shifting public opinion. It was clear in September 1866, however, that the arguments for woman's place in the home had not exhausted themselves, nor had the emotional commitment of antifeminists moderated over the years.

The article in *Blackwood's* disturbed Bodichon, who contemplated sending a letter of correction to the magazine.[26] She chose not to rebut Oliphant directly but to present positive arguments for reform instead. On October 6, 1866 her "Reasons for the Enfranchisement of Women," was read before the Social Science Association in Manchester. It was a well-thought-out, succinct statement of the arguments for extending the franchise to women who were

23. Margaret Oliphant, "The Great Unrepresented," *Blackwood's Edinburgh Magazine* 100 (September 1866): 367–79.
24. Ibid., p. 376.
25. Ibid., p. 379.
26. Emily Davies to Barbara Bodichon, 17 September 1866, Girton College Archives.

freeholders and householders. The strongest argument for giving a limited population of women the vote was the increased influence they would exert on public opinion.[27] Giving some women votes would tend to make all women take national affairs seriously, increasing their sense of responsibility and enlarging the pool of talent available for solving the pressing social problems facing Parliament. Bodichon insisted that the issue was not a party matter and that it was impossible to predict the effect such a franchise reform would have on party politics. She characterized the change as the correction of a "special legal disability," noting that no class of persons might bring forward a more just claim to exercise the privilege of electors.

Bodichon's limited claim for female suffrage was all but ignored. Hers was the only paper presented on the topic at Manchester. There was little interest expressed during the conference and only a brief extract of her paper was published in the year's *Transactions*. Public lack of interest was disheartening, but not astonishing. The paper had at least one effect of lasting importance. Lydia Becker (1827–1890), a Manchester woman of scientific tendencies, who had had no prior connection with feminist circles, heard Bodichon's paper and later described it as "an era in her intellectual life."[28] By January 1867 Becker had formed the Manchester Women's Suffrage Committee.

Bodichon was pleased by women's response to her paper. In October 1866 she wrote to thank Helen Taylor for a letter praising the essay and to let her know that she had received numerous cards and letters offering support for the movement. She admitted to a lack of confidence in her essay, which she felt was poorly written, "not strong as it ought to be—nor strong as my feeling about this matter."[29] She planned to have the essay reprinted as a pamphlet for widescale distribution. She was pleased that Elizabeth Wolstenholme had requested three thousand copies of the pamphlet be

27. Barbara Bodichon, *Reasons for the Enfranchisement of Women* (London: J. Bale, 1866), p. 6.

28. Strachey, *The Cause*, p. 106.

29. Barbara Bodichon to Helen Taylor, 21 October 1866, Mill–Taylor Correspondence.

mailed to female householders in Manchester along with copies of a new suffrage petition.

On October 20, 1866, Bodichon met with a group of women at Elizabeth Garrett's London home to form a new provisional suffrage committee. There was some difficulty over the secretary's responsibilities. Emily Davies was persuaded to accept the position with the proviso that Mrs. J. W. Smith (the eldest Garrett sister) would hold the public title, thereby protecting Davies's name so that her higher education projects would not be tainted. Bodichon withdrew her own name from the committee's official roster, insisting, "work as an outside well-wisher is my forte."[30] She was drawn back into the official circle shortly thereafter to serve as nominal secretary on the death of Mrs. J. W. Smith.

The divisions that would eventually destroy this committee surfaced almost immediately. Helen Taylor objected to having men on the committee and Mill agreed with her. Bodichon felt that Mill and Taylor were mistaken and that an exclusively female organization would be unsuccessful. She dismissed Taylor's apprehension that men would get the credit for the movement and deplored the loss of "educational utility" if women were prevented from working with men. Bodichon believed that Taylor was losing sight of the true aim of their work in her insistence on exclusive management of activities by women: "After all what we aim at is getting the suffrage and I think we shall get it 10 years quicker by working the association with a small committee composed of men and women."[31] Her experience of the American woman's movement had convinced her of the foolishness of excluding men. She admired American feminists, but felt that their tactics had gained nothing, while British methods had achieved a great deal. American feminists had wasted their forces. They had been impractical, "1st by trying to get too many things at once 2nd by not working with men 3rd by being too sentimental."[32] Since Clementia Taylor and several other female committee members agreed that men should participate,

---

30. Ibid.
31. Barbara Bodichon to Helen Taylor, November 1866, Mill–Taylor Correspondence.
32. Ibid.

Bodichon suggested that a woman treasurer and secretary would give sufficient female character to the organization.

Men were included in the 1866–67 committee, and, having temporarily resolved their differences, the suffragists proceeded toward presentation of new franchise petitions. On November 2, 1866, Bodichon wrote Taylor that a modified version of "Reasons for the Enfranchisement of Women" would be published in Jessie Boucherett's new journal, *The Englishwoman's Review of Social and Industrial Questions*. Bodichon was concerned about the new magazine, which had only sold 250 subscriptions and needed 600 to avoid financial loss. She confided to Taylor that the last time she had seen Boucherett the latter had been preparing to sell some diamonds, "which she said were no use to her, to get money for that (the *Englishwoman's Review*) and the franchise."[33]

Bodichon left England in December 1867 for six weeks in Spain and expected to winter in Algiers as was her custom. Severe Algerian fever forced her to spend a recuperative period in France during March, returning to England in early spring, 1867. During her absence the suffrage committee worked actively. In January 1867, Bodichon's "Authorities and Precedents for Giving the Suffrage to Qualified Women," appeared in the *Englishwoman's Review*.[34] Signatures were collected for two types of petitions, one bearing only the names of female householders who sought the franchise, the other including names of all interested men and women.

Bodichon had been named committee secretary in February 1867 without her knowledge. The committee had only learned of her illness after designating her secretary and could neither withdraw her name from official notices nor write to explain the difficulty. When her fever abated she had written to assure Davies she did not mind the committee's action, but Davies felt compelled to apologize and explain that only formalities had been undertaken in her name. Davies had arranged for the committee to circulate about ten thousand of each of Bodichon's pamphlets to support the petition

33. Barbara Bodichon to Helen Taylor, 2 November 1866, Mill–Taylor Correspondence.
34. Barbara Bodichon, "Authorities and Precedents for Giving the Suffrage to Qualified Women," *Englishwoman's Review of Social and Industrial Questions* 1 (January 1867): 63–75.

campaign: "They seemed to be just what was wanted. Sir Thomas Erskine May thinks *Reasons* 'unanswerable.' There is a strong let-ter from Kingsley too, which I must show you when you come to England."[35]

Illness kept Bodichon in Hastings throughout the spring and summer of 1867. Her participation in committee affairs during this period was limited to correspondence. She influenced events indi-rectly, but most effectively through the thousands of copies of her essays distributed throughout the country. On March 28, 1867, H. A. Bruce presented a petition with 3,559 signatures. Mill presented a similar petition with over 3,000 signatures on April 5, and on April 8 Russell Gurney presented the women householders' peti-tion, with the signatures of 1,605 women qualified as forty-shilling freeholders, or ten-pound leaseholders, copyholders, or occupiers in boroughs.[36] This group of petitions was greeted with some respect, however grudging. Even the *Saturday Review* was forced to admit that "when Mr. Mill makes a legislative proposal, something may probably be said in its defense," although it quickly reasserted its contemptuous dismissal of the issue: "But Mr. Mill himself can hardly be surprised at finding his proposal for giving votes to women so generally treated as a joke."[37]

Mill went further than petitioning in his second suffrage effort. On May 20, 1867, he moved an amendment to the Representation of the People Bill "to leave out the word 'men' in order to insert the word 'person' instead." Thus the question of granting the suffrage to women was debated in Parliament for the first time.[38] The amend-ment was rejected by a vote of 73 to 196, but the results did not dis-appoint Mill or the suffrage committee. Mill expressed surprise and pleasure at the large showing for women, which seemed to promise consistent future progress.[39] His speech impressed the House and raised the issue of women's rights, if only momentarily, above the

35. Emily Davies to Barbara Bodichon, 21 March 1867, Girton College Archives.
36. Blackburn, *Women's Suffrage*, p. 60.
37. *Saturday Review*, 30 March 1867, pp. 385–86.
38. *Hansard's Parliamentary Debates*, 187 (1867): 817.
39. John Russell, Viscount Amberley, *The Amberley Papers*, 2 vols. (New York: W. W. Norton, 1937), 2:36.

level of laughter and ridicule. Answering critics who said that the
exercise of the vote would interfere with woman's domestic function, he pointed out that physicians, lawyers, and merchants were
no worse at their tasks because they voted. "I know there is an obscure feeling—a feeling which is ashamed to express itself openly
—as if women had no right to care about anything except how they
may be the most useful and devoted servants of some man. . . . We
talk of political revolutions, but we do not sufficiently attend to the
fact that there has taken place around us a silent domestic
revolution."[40]

The arguments against extending the franchise to women demonstrated the same attitude underlying opposition to every previous
appeal for wider opportunities and fuller rights for women. There
was in 1867 no demand for the extension of the suffrage to married
women, nor was there any suggestion that the further right not
merely to elect but to be elected should be granted. Bodichon,
whatever her personal conviction, had recognized the wisdom of a
restricted demand and insisted since 1865 that the campaign be
carefully structured toward gaining "the possible." Yet the expressed
opposition centered largely around the undesirability of giving to a
married woman a power which would allow her to act as an independent human being. The preservation of family unity was the
prime concern of the debate. It was asserted that limited franchise
extension could not be permanently contained and that inevitably
married women would be sullied by the vote. One member expressed the majority opinion: "A man qualified to possess the franchise would be ennobled by its possession; woman, in his humble
opinion, would be almost debased or degraded by it. She would be
in danger of losing those admirable attributes of her sex—namely
her gentleness, her affection, her domesticity."[41] The emotional
antagonism which had greeted Bodichon's married women's property campaign was muted in the reaction to Mill's amendment in
1867, but the basic fear remained. Reform was rejected largely be-

40. *Hansard's Parliamentary Debates*, 187 (1867): 817.
41. Ibid., p. 833.

cause members read domestic revolution between the lines of Mill's arguments, ignoring the carefully structured attempt by suffragists to reassure them with temperate language and limited franchise claims.

Bodichon and Davies agreed that the division had been good despite the amendment's rejection. They had expected rather less and found the vote encouraging.[42] Suffragist efforts did not diminish after this first parliamentary campaign, but organizational strains took their toll among the leadership. The provisional committee that had operated since 1866 dissolved in early June 1867. The question of male participation on suffrage committees surfaced again, the radicalism of some committee members exacerbated the situation, and by June 3, Davies suggested that it might be best to have a parting of the ways. She wrote advising Bodichon to send her a letter resigning the secretaryship and calling for the dissolution of the committee. Davies would then arrange a meeting to discuss Bodichon's resignation and the status of the committee. Davies informed Bodichon that Lady Goldsmid, Miss Manning, and Elizabeth Garrett, "the quiet section," agreed on the necessity of dissolution. She did not favor splitting into two committees, theirs moderate, the other under the leadership of Clementia Taylor and Helen Taylor. That kind of division would make their disagreements public and give credence to the argument that women could not work together.[43] Bodichon agreed, and a meeting was held on June 13, at which Helen Taylor remained adamant on the principle of male exclusion. The committee dissolved and a new suffrage organization formed on July 5 at Aubrey House with Clementia Taylor in the chair. Bodichon and Davies did not join the new London National Society for Women's Suffrage. They were convinced that excluding men from the managing committee was a mistake, but even more they were concerned that the suffrage issue would become wholly identified with the extreme section of the Liberal Party and that the new committee would operate completely among people

---

42. Emily Davies to Barbara Bodichon, May 1867, Girton College Archives.
43. Emily Davies to Barbara Bodichon, 3 June 1867, Girton College Archives.

already sympathetic to reform. Davies, more pessimistic than Bodichon, predicted gloomily: "Conservatives and moderate Liberals will be treated, I am afraid, as hopelessly blind and stupid, and our chance of success will be very much injured, to say the least."[44]

Davies withdrew from suffrage activities completely. Bodichon, who had exerted only intermittent leadership during late 1866 and 1867 because of illness and commitments in Algiers, did not make her break so final. She continued to correspond with Lydia Becker, Clementia Taylor, and Helen Taylor on suffrage matters throughout the years. A revised and enlarged edition of one of her suffrage essays appeared in 1872, entitled *Reasons For and Against the Enfranchisement of Women*. Published by the renamed National Society for Women's Suffrage, it was widely distributed to stimulate continuing parliamentary efforts to gain the franchise for women.

Bodichon was, by 1867, ready to relinquish the suffrage effort to new leaders. She was by no means a conservative of Davies's type. Davies considered the radical elements of feminism "uncongenial" and once clear of the suffrage committee she vowed never to work with them again: "The more I see of them, the worse they appear, qua Radicals. No doubt some of them have domestic virtues."[45] Bodichon did not share Davies's sentiments. In July 1869 she attended the first large public gathering on women's suffrage and then wrote enthusiastically to Helen Taylor about the diverse nature of suffrage support. She was particularly pleased that women of all classes had attended the demonstration and that many moderate middle-class women continued to press for the franchise.[46] She believed personally in the most sweeping social reform. Indeed, by nature and background she had a great deal more in common with radical Clementia Taylor than with conservative Emily Davies. Yet she chose to withdraw from the formal suffrage committee structure with Davies and turned her efforts to the field of women's higher education, although not for want of interest in the franchise nor for lack of sympathy with Mill's and Taylor's ideology.

44. Emily Davies to Miss Manning, 14 June 1867, Girton College Archives.
45. Emily Davies to Anna Richardson, June 1867, Girton College Archives.
46. Barbara Bodichon to Helen Taylor, 1 August 1869, Mill–Taylor Correspondence.

In 1869 Bodichon published a third edition of her *Laws Concerning Women*, revised to reflect her conviction that franchise reform was of prime importance to women.[47] The issue of the vote, ignored in the two earlier versions of her work, was now treated as the most crucial legislative question affecting women's status. Married women's property reform was mentioned, but the central focus of the work was on the franchise disability. Full citizenship and public participation were rights and privileges women could no longer be denied.[48] Bodichon's revised edition was well received by the *Westminster Review*. Describing her as "unresting" and "single-minded" in her dedication to social reform, particularly feminist projects, the reviewer congratulated her for her courage and the moderation of her pamphlet. Her contribution to codification of the English law concerning women was applauded, while the work was characterized as well-planned and demonstrating "a naturally keen juridical instinct."[49]

When Mill's *Subjection of Women* was published in 1869, Bodichon was profoundly moved, believing that it summarized and argued more eloquently and effectively than ever before the basic injustice of the inequality between the sexes. Mill's object, clearly stated in the work, was to convince society that the principle of the legal subordination of one sex to the other was wrong and constituted one of the chief obstacles to the improvement of the human condition. He declared that social relations should be based on an acknowledgment of the perfect equality of the sexes, "admitting no power or privilege on the one side, nor disability on the other."[50] *Subjection* had been written in 1861, although not published until 1869, but Mill's sentiments had been familiar to Bodichon since her reading of *Political Economy* in 1849. They mirrored her own intense belief in complete sexual equality and demonstrated the radical nature of her personal viewpoint. She wrote to Helen Taylor in

47. Barbara Bodichon, *A Brief Summary in Plain Language of the Most Important Laws of England Concerning Women*. 3d ed. (London: Trubner, 1869), p. 18.
48. Ibid., pp. 19–20.
49. "Politics, Society, Voyages and Travels," *Westminster Review* (July 1869): 118.
50. John Stuart Mill, *The Subjection of Women* (London: Oxford University Press, 1963), p. 427.

August 1869, primarily to thank her for supporting the idea of a women's college in a letter to the *Spectator*. She was particularly pleased that the rift in feminist ranks appeared to be diminishing: "There is nothing which has given me so much pleasure for a long time, it is such a delight to have the approbation of people one religiously respects."[51] She tried to thank Mill through Taylor for writing the *Subjection*, but found herself unable to express her feelings. Overcome by emotion at the thought of the effect that Mill's book would have on future generations, she could only assert her conviction that the *Subjection* constituted a perfect expression of feminist ideals.[52]

Bodichon shared Mill's commitment to the removal of all legal and social disabilities from women. Absolute equality of opportunity and freedom of action were her ultimate goal. Why then did she turn from franchise reform? Why not devote all subsequent efforts to this most advanced outpost of women's struggle? Her experience with parliamentary activity during the 1866–67 effort had taught her a great deal. Pragmatic from the moment of establishing the first suffrage committee, she had never underestimated the years that would have to pass before the law was modified by even a syllable. In 1869 the municipal franchise was extended to women ratepayers, but those women who imagined that they would get the parliamentary vote with similar ease were gravely mistaken. Lady Amberley echoed Bodichon's assessment when the storm of criticism broke over Mill's *Subjection*: "No reform was ever made without talk and without boring people out at last, and so I suppose we must be discussed and turned inside out for the next twenty years and then lawmakers will begin to see they had better give in and let us manage our own affairs and keep our own property and be guardian to our own children."[53]

In the suffrage effort, as in previous feminist campaigns, Bodichon's role had been unique. She was an innovator, anticipating change and serving as a catalyst, but she could not devote patient

---

51. Barbara Bodichon to Helen Taylor, 1 August 1869, Mill–Taylor Correspondence.
52. Ibid.
53. Amberley, *Amberley Papers*, 2:282.

attention to the day-to-day detail necessary to complete franchise reform. Her enthusiasm was dampened by the petty differences that were so much a part of organization life. Bessie Parkes had recognized when the *English Woman's Journal* was dissolving that societies and committees were not always successful agents of change. Parkes suggested that some of the momentum for reform was actually lost in the friction within organizations.[54] Bodichon was constitutionally unable to devote her energy to working around those strains. In 1867 she experienced satisfaction that female suffrage had become a viable, if distant goal and turned from it to join the new experiment in higher education for women.

54. Parkes, "Review of the Last Six Years," p. 368.

VII

HIGHER EDUCATION
FOR WOMEN:
GIRTON COLLEGE

The establishment of Girton College, Cambridge was Bodichon's last major feminist project. Her role in this campaign was a new one. Girton was a true collaborative effort. Bodichon and Davies partnered the project, though each contributed in very different ways. Bodichon came to the enterprise with her usual restless energy. It became the most fulfilling endeavor of her life and sustained her through years of poor health from 1877 until her death in 1891.

It has been said that the fundamental issue of feminism, which became clearer throughout the nineteenth century, was the drawing out of women into "the sexless sphere of disinterested intelligence," resulting in the conception of "autonomous personality."[1] Sometimes obscured by campaigns for subordinate ends (the right to vote, to control their own property after marriage, and to graduate), the struggle of women to exert themselves as individuals, to break away from their separate sphere, was clearly the basis for all feminist activity. While every effort by the organized women's movement contributed materially and cumulatively to the creation of a new feminine ideal by the century's end, the improvement and expansion of female education must be acknowledged the most important agent of change, because it altered woman's own nature, enlarging her concept of self.

Bodichon and Davies had been early advocates of improved edu-

---

1. George Malcolm Young, *Victorian England: Portrait of an Age*, 2d ed. (London: Oxford University Press, 1953), p. 91.

Girton College, Cambridge (Mistress and Fellows of Girton College)

cation for women and girls. The absolute neglect of girls' schooling
had been described by Bodichon in her "Middle Class Schools for
Girls," in 1860. Her first reform endeavor had been the coeducational experiment at Portman Hall. As early as 1851, when she visited her brother at Cambridge, the dream of a college for women
had inspired her.[2]

Bodichon's experience at Bedford College in 1849 sharpened her
vision of what might be possible, but demonstrated all too effectively how ill-prepared girls were. They could barely absorb a secondary education and were singularly unfit to teach others, even af-

2. Barbara Bodichon to Emily Davies, 1868, Girton College Archives.

ter the best efforts of instructors at Queen's and Bedford. The opening of the North London Collegiate School for Women by Frances Mary Buss in 1850 and the Ladies' College at Cheltenham by Dorothea Beale in 1858 did little to improve the situation. These institutions were, like Queen's and Bedford, secondary schools. They managed with difficulty to train girls as governesses or teachers for girls' academies. But training was not education, the curriculums were disorganized, and the faculties of uneven quality. In the ten years that had passed since the opening of Queen's, female education had advanced only superficially. Schooling was still haphazard and it was by no means generally accepted that girls needed more than a smattering of accomplishments to prepare them for life.

Arguments until 1858 had centered around the use that women might make of schooling. Proponents of improvement concentrated on the plight of financially distressed gentlewomen or the emotional frustration of other idle though wealthy females. Those who opposed more education dismissed it as a waste, an unnecessary expenditure on girls whose only purpose was to marry. By 1858 a subtle change entered the discussion. The idea that educated wives and mothers might benefit a household was given increasingly serious consideration. In that year Emily Shirreff, a future mistress of Girton College, but by her own admission a firm believer in the superiority of men over women, published *Intellectual Education and Its Influence on the Character and Happiness of Women*. Outlining a course of intellectual and moral development for women, the book expressed Shirreff's conviction that society's basic error rested in the valuation of the usefulness of knowledge. For Shirreff the prime purpose of education was the systematic and harmonious development of every individual. The elementary principles of education should be the same for all and the use to which knowledge might be put, once acquired, was totally irrelevent.[3] Shirreff dismissed "worldly utility": "The human being remains a mutilated creature if the capacities of his mind are left dormant. . . . The education of

3. Shirreff, *Intellectual Education*, pp. 6–7.

women has no firm standing on any other grounds. Fashion and custom may make certain acquirements desirable, but the *necessity and consequent duty* of education lies in that broad principle alone."[4] A new justification had been made for female education. Bodichon and Davies shared Shirreff's moral commitment. Over the next ten years they mingled arguments of utility with discussions regarding society's moral responsibility to develop all human potential. By 1869 they had succeeded in persuading a variety of social and political interests of the need for a college for women. So, in an atmosphere of controversy and with no clear agreement on the nature of women's higher education, Girton College was founded.

In 1862 Elizabeth Garrett applied to take the matriculation examination at London University. She could not attend medical school without a university degree. When Garrett's application was denied, Emily Davies launched a campaign to force the University to change its policy. The effort was unsuccessful, but before it was over Davies and Bodichon had mobilized friends from a variety of social and religious circles on its behalf. They agreed that this was a point worth fighting for. Davies was buoyed by her brother Llewellyn's support, since he generally discouraged her feminist aspirations. He brought Frederick Denison Maurice's circle into the campaign. His sister contacted Quaker friends, while Bodichon wrote to a number of influential Unitarians.[5]

The optimism of 1862 was premature, but the abortive effort proved how effectively Bodichon and Davies could pool their talents. They had access to legislators and writers of every political and religious conviction. They managed to reconcile these disparate interests so that they joined in support of the continuing struggle for women's higher education. By 1863 Davies had published an article in the *Victoria Magazine*, "Women and University Degrees," and had enlisted Bodichon's participation in a committee to open university local examinations to women. The local examinations

4. Ibid., pp. 8–9.
5. Barbara Bodichon to Emily Davies, Early 1862(?), Girton College Archives.

had been established in 1857 and 1858 by Oxford and Cambridge to provide secondary schools with standards for their graduates. Davies was only peripherally interested in the examinations, viewing their opening as an opportunity to establish the precedent of girls taking the same tests as boys.[6] It was difficult for the committee to find a sufficient number of female candidates to make the unofficial experiment when Cambridge finally agreed in 1863. Davies was forced to concede in "Women and University Degrees" that the greatest value of degrees for women might be indirect. They would raise the standards of excellence of primary and secondary schools for girls and force improvement in the preparation of teachers for those institutions.[7]

In 1864 Davies presented a paper at the Social Science Association conference, "On Secondary Instruction as Relating to Girls," reiterating Bodichon's 1860 arguments about the deficiencies of middle-class girls' schools. In 1865 Cambridge officially opened local examinations to women and Oxford followed in 1870. The deplorable state of girls' schooling was underlined by the results of the Schools' Inquiry Commission which operated from 1864 to 1867. The Taunton Commission (established to inquire into the "whole subject of middle class education") did not include girls' education within its scope. Since the subject was not expressly excluded from its charge, Davies and Bodichon organized a petition asking that women be heard. The Commissioners agreed and a number of women, including Davies and Buss, testified. Davies mailed Bodichon a copy of their evidence, as well as a group of Assistant Commissioner D. R. Fearon's questions to comment on. Davies was optimistic. She was particularly pleased by the readiness of schoolmistresses to organize for future educational reform efforts.[8]

The report of the Commission, published in 1868, recognized the need for reform of girls' education. The commissioners cautiously but officially affirmed that there was "weighty evidence" supporting contentions that essential learning capabilities were the

6. Emily Davies to Anna Richardson, 12 July 1862, Girton College Archives.
7. Davies, *Questions Relating to Women*, p. 56.
8. Emily Davies to Barbara Bodichon, 1866, Girton College Archives.

same in both sexes.[9] The cause of many deficiencies in girls' schools was found to rest in the poor quality of the teachers, who had not been taught and therefore could not teach. Somewhat timidly the commissioners gave their blessing to the opening of local examinations to girls and suggested vaguely that institutions were needed for the higher education of women.

Davies was involved in the improvement of teaching standards even before the commission's report was published. In March 1866 she organized the London Schoolmistresses' Association, which she led for more than twenty years. By January 1867 it was clear to her and to Bodichon that the only remedy for the poor quality of female teachers was the establishment of a women's college. Davies had tried to convince Bedford and Queen's to fill the gap by raising the admission age and setting up entrance examinations, but they refused, afraid that registration would drop sharply.[10] Cambridge seemed the most encouraging atmosphere in which to begin, and Davies suggested to Bodichon that they form a college committee to raise the £30,000 necessary to establish the institution. She sent Bodichon a proof of a proposed program for the college. She speculated about fund-raising and asked Bodichon to consider a personal contribution. Once Bodichon endorsed the plan, Davies planned to approach Lady Goldsmid, Russell Gurney, and others who might be influenced by her opinion.[11] Since Bodichon was ill with fever no reply came from Algiers for some time. In March she sent an encouraging answer, but expressed more concern over suffrage matters than the college.[12] She returned to England in May but did not become totally involved in the college project until Davies spent a month with her at Scalands in August. By that time the provisional suffrage committee had dissolved and she was partially recovered from the effects of fever.

Davies was concerned about Bodichon's health. The Algerian fe-

9. Schools Inquiry Commission, "Report of the Commissioners," *Parliamentary Papers* (1867–68), vol. 1, p. 553.

10. Davies, "Family Chronicle," p. 521.

11. Emily Davies to Barbara Bodichon, 29 January 1867, Girton College Archives.

12. Barbara Bodichon to Emily Davies, March 1867, Girton College Archives.

ver had been severe and social obligations made convalescence difficult. Barbara could not seem to regain her old vitality.[13] Her generosity with time was no longer a matter for amused indulgence. She could no longer give unstintingly of self. George Eliot bluntly advised her best friend: "The physician's opinion would, I should think, be conclusive for all rational people. I presume you give up the idea of pleasing *all* the world rational and irrational!"[14] Bodichon was only forty and it was not until ten years later that she suffered a disabling stroke. However, she never recovered fully from the fever of 1867 and this altered her pattern of feminist activities. But she gave generous financial support to the college project, and from 1867 she was the principal sounding board for Davies's ideas. She contributed her own unique approach to the curriculum in terms of physical education and was responsible in great part for the physical environment of the institution. She became intimately involved in student problems, served for a time as headmistress, and was called upon throughout the early years to mediate when difficulties arose between faculty and students. However, her role was primarily supportive. Her diminished physical resources meant that Davies assumed responsibility for directing the project, writing articles, heading meetings, and prodding reluctant allies. For the first time in her life Bodichon, recognizing her limitations, assumed a secondary leadership position. In 1869 she insisted to Helen Taylor that credit for establishment of the college should not be hers. She did not feel she should be called the "originator" of the institution, although she admitted that her commitment to university education for women went back to her 1851 visit to Cambridge. She insisted that she could not have carried out the plan without Emily Davies: "I am not strong enough or orthodox enough."[15]

During the August 1867 visit to Scalands, Davies and Bodichon planned a fund-raising and publicity campaign and discussed the membership of the first working college committee. Because of her reputation for unorthodoxy Bodichon was not officially a member

13. Emily Davies to Anna Richardson, 24 August 1867, Girton College Archives.
14. George Eliot to Barbara Bodichon, 27 July 1867, *George Eliot Letters*, 4:378.
15. Barbara Bodichon to Helen Taylor, 1 August 1869, Mill–Taylor Correspondence.

of the committee until February 1869. It was decided at Scalands that the membership should include no one "specially known as advocating the rights of women." The members were chosen carefully in order to win the confidence of "ordinary people."[16] Just as in 1856 Bodichon's name had been kept out of public statements by the Married Women's Property Committee, so in 1867 her advanced opinions on equality of the sexes were considered a liability to the campaign for a women's college.

However, Bodichon worked privately to attract funds and amass support within her social circle. By the end of October 1867 she had decided to contribute £1,000 to the venture and wrote Davis about her concern for the "sanitarian" aspects of the curriculum. She had strong views on the importance of exercise, diet, and physical environment in the education of young women. She gave Davies permission to publicize her intention to make a generous contribution, contingent upon the development of a program to insure the physical and emotional well-being of the students: "I desire to see some one in power who has made the physical constitution of women a study and if I give my £1,000, as I am not rich, I must be sure it is used in accordance with my best judgment of what will really promote the great object we have in view, the ennobling, morally, intellectually and physically one half of humanity."[17] Although Bodichon was quite wealthy, £1,000 was a considerable contribution and the conditions attached to her gift demonstrated her lifelong insistence on value for her money. She knew that her ideas about health and environment were important and determined to insure their being carried out.

Bodichon offered to intercede on the college's behalf with George Eliot and to arrange for Davies to visit Eliot. Poor health still restricted her activities a great deal and she was forced to ask Davies to send back her letter, so that she could forward it to Eliot to prepare her for the visit. "I am not well yet and have promised my doctor to write no letters."[18] Eliot agreed to see Davies, assur-

16. Davies, "Family Chronicle," pp. 538–39.
17. Barbara Bodichon to Emily Davies, 31 October 1867, ibid., p. 540.
18. Ibid., p. 541.

ing Bodichon that the better education of women was an object she could support.[19]

Eliot talked with Davies several times about the proposed college. Eliot subscribed fifty pounds to the project and made suggestions regarding the curriculum. In March 1868 she described her reasons for approving of a women's college, emphasizing the idea that thorough higher education ought to instill "the gospel that the deepest disgrace is to insist on doing work for which we are unfit —to do work of any sort badly."[20] In August 1868 she advised Davies on the preparation of a paper for presentation to the next Social Science Association conference. She insisted that objections to higher education for women must be dispelled with assurances that true union and understanding between men and women would come only if both sexes had access to the same fund of knowledge and truth.[21] Eliot's support for the college was her strongest feminist commitment, though it was, like all her others, a private one. When Mrs. Nassau Senior questioned her about her ties to the college after its opening in October 1869, she wrote a compelling letter in favor of the experiment. She admitted having no personal knowledge of Charlotte Manning, its first headmistress, and explained that she had no "practical connexion" with the institution other than her advice to Davies about the curriculum. She asserted yet again that there was no subject about which she was more reluctant to make public statements than the woman question. However, she expressed her strong conviction that women should have the same access to knowledge as men. She felt responsible to take action to promote that end: "It is not likely that any perfect plan for educating women can soon be found, for we are very far from having found a perfect plan for educating men. But it will not do to wait for perfection."[22]

Eliot's support surprised Davies. She wrote Bodichon that she would not have been shocked if Eliot had been against the idea: "In

---

19. George Eliot to Barbara Bodichon, 16 November 1867, *George Eliot Letters,* 4:399.
20. George Eliot to Barbara Bodichon, 28 March 1868, ibid., 4:425.
21. George Eliot to Emily Davies, 8 August 1868, ibid., 4:468.
22. George Eliot to Mrs. Nassau Senior, 4 October 1869, ibid., 5:58.

fact the only thing that ever surprises me is to find anybody for it."[23] Bodichon and Davies were somewhat discouraged by the apathy which greeted the college proposal. Fund-raising was painfully slow, and after one particularly tiresome dinner party Bodichon reassured Davies that her faith in the project was unshaken and her optimism unimpaired.[24] Davies replied that she did not doubt Bodichon's conviction, but feared for her overenthusiastic nature: "I thought you were more discouraged than need be by other peoples' coldness, because you expected more from them than I did. You go about bravely talking to people and expecting sympathy from them, when I should not open my mouth, and so you get the cold water showered upon you."[25]

Bodichon was well enough to join Davies in a round of fundraising public relations efforts by early 1868. Rebuffs were common. Charlotte M. Yonge, respected author and pillar of the Anglican church, sent a chilly reply to a solicitation for her support. She objected to bringing women together for formal education outside the home. She refused to aid the project and suggested that female minds should be molded by "sensible fathers," not women's colleges.[26]

Anthony Trollope's Lecture on Higher Education of Women, published in 1868, echoed the sentiments of Yonge's letter. Trollope denied that the improvement of education for women could result from campaigns to achieve the political privileges, social standing, or educational systems that men enjoyed.[27] He outlined a scheme for self-improvement that must have horrified the college committee. Davies had instilled in the group her unswerving conviction that only examinations and degrees on precisely the same terms as men could produce educated women.

Not all receptions were hostile. Davies was pleased by the reac-

23. Emily Davies to Barbara Bodichon, March 1868, Girton College Archives.
24. Barbara Bodichon to Emily Davies, 1868, Girton College Archives.
25. Emily Davies to Barbara Bodichon, March 1868, Girton College Archives.
26. Muriel Clara Bradbrook, "That Infidel Place": A Short History of Girton College, 1869–1969, (London: Chatto & Windus, 1969), pp. 24–25.
27. Anthony Trollope, "Higher Education of Women," Four Lectures (London: Constable, 1938), pp. 76–77.

tion at the Social Science Association conference to her paper on the college proposal. The press was polite and the respectable membership of the college committee forced the *Times* to admit that the project must at least be given serious consideration.[28] However, fund-raising was inordinately slow. Only £2,000 had been pledged after more than a year's work, and this included Bodichon's £1,000.

During this period other educational experiments began which caused Davies anguish and led Davies quickly to open a modified version of the college at Benslow House, Hitchin in October 1869. In 1868 Lectures for Ladies were organized by Anne Jemima Clough throughout the north of England. From these lectures was developed the North of England Council for Promoting the Higher Education of Women, with Josephine Butler as president and Clough as honorary secretary. The Council began to press for special examinations for women, a concept which was anathema to Davies but which appealed to a number of educational reformers. Davies was infuriated by the enthusiasm generated by the idea of special tests and declared: "We do not want to have certificates of proficiency given to half educated women."[29] Bodichon and other committee members favored the immediate opening of classes in Cambridge, but once again Davies was adamant. She agreed with Bodichon on the necessity to make a prompt temporary beginning in rented quarters, but felt that a Cambridge location would be unsuitable. She was certain that the proximity of the men's colleges would prove a distraction and give rise to gossip damaging to the cause of higher education for women.[30] A respectable compromise was found in a house in Hitchin, midway between London and Cambridge. Eighteen young women took the entrance examination at London University in July 1869, and three more were examined in early October at Bodichon's Blandford Square home. On October 16, 1869, Davies welcomed the first five students to the college at Hitchin.

The curriculum at Hitchin reflected Davies's stubborn resolve to

28. Bradbrook, *"That Infidel Place,"* p. 27.
29. Davies, *Questions Relating to Women*, p. 125.
30. Emily Davies to Barbara Bodichon, 23 November 1868, Girton College Archives.

give the women exactly the same course required for Cambridge undergraduates. The women were expected to prepare first for the
Little-Go or Previous Examination, at the same time working for
the Tripos or Final Examination. The Little-Go had just been re-
formed and included additional mathematics, which taxed the un-
derprepared women severely. They were under pressure of time,
since Davies insisted that the course must be completed in exactly
the same time allowed to men. Whatever the difficulties, the
schedule was met. Within two years all five students had passed the
Little-Go and in 1873 two of them passed the Tripos in classics and
one in mathematics. The students were allowed to take the examinations only unofficially and by courtesy of the examiners. They
were not members of the University and they could not be awarded
degrees.

The rigorous discipline of the program was a strain. A diet of
boiled beef and mutton was inexpensive and nourishing, but Bodichon feared it added to the monotony of college routine.[31] She
sent framed sketches to brighten the college, invited students to
Scalands for holidays, and visited often in an effort to lighten the
atmosphere. In March 1871 a potential student mutiny caused an
uproar. Absolute respectability and ladylike conduct by the students was necessary in an institution closely watched by critics
hoping for unfeminine lapses. In search of diversion the students
planned an amateur theatrical, which necessitated their appearing
in male attire. A flurry of letters between Davies and Bodichon at-
tested to the seriousness of the situation. The entire college project
could be jeopardized by this kind of activity. Bodichon consulted
George Eliot and Elizabeth Blackwell. Both counseled that the
project be stopped. The students were stubborn and vowed to go
on. To avoid the scandal of bringing the matter before the entire
college committee, Bodichon sought to mediate the dispute. Davies
was certain that her opinion would carry more weight with the students than anyone else's.[32] The visit was successful. The students

31. Barbara Bodichon to Emily Davies, March 1870, Girton College Archives.
32. Emily Davies to Miss Manning, 17 March 1871, Girton College Archives.

agreed to cancel the theatrical, and Bodichon made an especially strong impression on one of the rebels, a Miss Gibson, with whom she met privately to discuss not only the theatrical but the young woman's unusual style of dressing, consisting of simple loose gowns. Davies wished Gibson to adopt a more conventional manner of dressing, but Bodichon, rather than censuring her choice, complimented the fashion and asked for the pattern.[33]

Bodichon's unselfconscious friendliness won the students' confidence. They accepted her blunt advice because she seemed more than any committee member to understand their independence and applaud their tentative gestures toward modernity. Relieved that scandal had been avoided, Davies felt nonetheless that Bodichon's unorthodox views were not always in the college's best interests. The contrast in their natures was sharp and Davies complained more than once about Bodichon's tendency to sympathize with the students: "I think Madame Bodichon goes too much by the temporary opinions and tastes and requirements of the existing generation of students."[34] Their differences of opinion and personality benefited the college, however, because each appreciated the other's talents and because they managed on most occasions to incorporate something of both their natures into the final product.

Once the student rebellion of 1871 was over, Bodichon and Davies began to plan for a permanent site for the college. Bodichon invited Davies to Scalands in September 1871 and they spent the visit talking about the college building and garden. A site was purchased about two miles from Cambridge at the junction of the Girton and Huntingdon roads, and the architect Alfred Waterhouse was employed to draw up plans.[35] A subcommittee on building was appointed in October 1871 with Bodichon as the chair. The lease on the Hitchin building was to expire in 1873 and the growing student body was rapidly overflowing the building. Throughout 1872 Bodichon and Davies discussed details of the physical plant, includ-

33. Stephen, *Emily Davies and Girton College*, p. 244.
34. Emily Davies to Miss Manning, 3 January 1875, Girton College Archives.
35. Emily Davies to Anna Richardson, 27 September 1871, Girton College Archives.

ing coal cellars, materials for curtains, the planting of trees, and gifts of books for the college collections.

The fund-raising campaign had realized only £7,000 and despite careful modification of Waterhouse's plans it was necessary to borrow money to proceed with construction. The popularity of Henry Sidgwick's Cambridge lectures for ladies was in part responsible for the fund-raising problems. Davies refused Sidgwick's offers to join the two experiments in 1869, rejecting any proposal that entailed special treatment of women students. By 1871 Anne Jemima Clough, Sidgwick, and Millicent Fawcett had established a competing college for women. This experiment in Cambridge proper eventually became Newnham College.

Financial restrictions did not deter Bodichon and Davies. Convinced that a permanent building would help establish the college's reputation, they gathered gifts of furnishings and equipment from friends and family and were rewarded by the opening of Girton for the October term of 1873.

In the *Fortnightly* of July 1873 Emily Shirreff had clearly outlined Girton's objects in a strong appeal for funds. She noted that the college was founded for three purposes. First, it was to prove that women were capable of completing a difficult program of mental work judged by the same standard as men's work. Its second object was to train women teachers at the same level as men. Its third aim was to provide a structure for female education so that girls' schools would work toward a standard of excellence to be measured in a college entrance examination. Her article provided a succinct summary of the college's history and pointed toward its future goals.[36] Girton was no longer an experiment. Four years had turned it into a small but permanent institution.

By January 1874, despite the lack of basics such as a bell or a lock for the main door, Davies could write Bodichon in Algiers that they would certainly show a profit by June which could be used to pay off

36. Emily Anne Eliza Shirreff, "Girton College," *Fortnightly Review*, n.s. 14 (July 1873): 87–93.

the debt. Bodichon's absence was a continuing source of anxiety for Davies. During her yearly visits in Algiers Bodichon's time was taken up with her painting and her duties as the center of an active colonial social circle. She participated in her husband's projects for improvement of Algerian environmental conditions and joined in his studies of the peoples of the area. Davies needed Bodichon's advice on the financial and curricular problems that arose on a daily basis at Girton. She complained about the difficulties of handling college affairs through their irregular correspondence.[37] The college grew substantially during 1874 and Bodichon drew up a variety of new plans for consideration by the general committee when she returned to England in early March 1875.

Girton's small success was mirrored elsewhere. Llewellyn Davies had become principal at Queen's College and planned to reform the institution. He aimed at modeling it on King's College, combining in one institution a school for girls under eighteen and a college which they could attend after passing a rigorous entrance examination.[38] By the end of 1874 Bodichon and Davies felt secure enough about Girton's future to plan for enlarging the college and to ponder the more distant goal of university degrees for women. Bodichon had abandoned earlier feminist campaigns when they reached this more mundane stage of development. She did not shift her focus this time, however.

In 1873 Girton became the center of Bodichon's personal attention as well as her primary public project. In July of that year she met Phoebe Sarah Marks, a nineteen-year-old student recommended for a Girton scholarship. Marks, the daughter of poor Jewish immigrants from Poland, spent her girlhood in the London home of her aunt and uncle, Marion and Alphonse Harton. Marks was a brilliant student of mathematics, and when Davies received an inquiry from her about the college, Bodichon invited her to Blandford Square to discuss her wish to attend Girton. The interview on the evening of July 29, 1873 marked the beginning of a

37. Emily Davies to Barbara Bodichon, 6 January 1874, Girton College Archives.
38. Ibid.

warm relationship. Bodichon treated Marks as a daughter and became wrapped up in her career and family.

Marks filled a gap in Bodichon's life. Barbara's poor health was making Algerian trips increasingly arduous. Eugène Bodichon's own health was failing and he came to England infrequently; indeed, his wife's anxiety about him was strong enough to send her to Algiers in 1873 and 1874 despite doctor's warnings. In August 1873 George Eliot expressed her concern to Bodichon over her proposed travel plans.[39] The journeys were hardships now, not the adventurous wanderings that had brightened the early years. Eliot was relieved when Bodichon returned safely from an Algerian visit in 1874: "I am delighted to hear so good an account of the Doctor, and I trust that your soul is at rest now from any gnawing anxieties."[40]

The childless Bodichons derived great satisfaction from Marks's presence in their family circle. For ten years beginning in 1873 until she married, Marks spent all her holidays and most weekends at Scalands. Eugène Bodichon's few visits in the seventies were spent teaching her Breton folk songs and listening to her sing the Hebrew hymns her mother taught her in childhood.

Marks did not enter Girton until 1876 because of financial difficulties and the responsibility of caring for her widowed mother and mentally ill sister. However, from the summer of 1873, Bodichon lent money, sent gifts, made arrangements for easing her family situation, and enlisted friends in support of her new protegée. George Eliot responded warmly to Bodichon's descriptions of Marks: "To hear of good young things growing up is the best of news . . . you will let me know what is to be done for this nice girl."[41] Eliot invited Marks to visit her often and when *Daniel Deronda* was published in 1876, many speculated that Marks was the original for the character of Mirah. Bodichon wrote Marks in April 1876 that Mirah had been developing in Eliot's mind for many years before Marks made the writer's acquaintance, but there is strong internal

39. George Eliot to Barbara Bodichon, 23 August 1873, *George Eliot Letters*, 5:428.
40. George Eliot to Barbara Bodichon, 16 November 1874, ibid., 6:90.
41. George Eliot to Barbara Bodichon, 23 September 1874, ibid., 6:83.

Hertha Ayrton (Sarah Marks) (Mistress and Fellows of Girton College)

evidence in the novel that Eliot used many of Marks's physical traits and mannerisms in drawing Mirah's character.[42]

Bodichon gave Marks advice on diet and dress and taught her a great deal about college administration. She and Marks held lengthy discussions about spiritual uncertainty and the reality of prejudice in an unjust world. When Marks complained that some-one else had been offered a school appointment she had applied for, Bodichon suggested that her full black hair might cause objection and reminded her that she might earn fifty pounds more per year if she put it in a net when she went out to give lessons.[43] During the summer of 1876 they discussed "birth and pedigree." Marks was horrified by the bigotry of a family who had employed her as a sum-mer tutor, and during afternoon tea with them one day she blurted out the fact that she was of Jewish origins and that her father had been a watchmaker and peddlar. They promptly let her go. Bodi-chon gave the agitated girl a mixture of practical advice and warm support:

> I think you told your friends about yourself too soon. You should have been sure they liked you and thought you a lady first! It is quite right to tell if it seems important; but I think it is better to say to some of your true friends (like Mrs. Lewes and me) that you do not wish to make a secret of your parent-age. Dr. Bodichon insists that your Jewish birth is noble par-entage. Yours is an unmixed race; you are not mongrel as we are. Be content to say you are pure breed and become in your-self a true gentlewoman.[44]

An agnostic, Marks had given up the Jewish religion at sixteen and wrote Bodichon in October 1875 of her need for moral direc-tion. Orthodox religious connections did not enter into their dis-cussions. Both Bodichon and Marks demonstrated a decided lack of interest in denominations, but Marks's search for moral guidance

---

42. Evelyn Sharp, *Hertha Ayrton, 1854–1923* (London: Edward Arnold, 1926), pp. 38–39.

43. Ibid., p. 46.

44. Ibid., p. 52.

was basic to their talks about the goals of education. During 1875 Bodichon deplored the lack of moral direction in the teaching at Girton, but admitted: "The College cannot do much more than give *quiet liberty* and *opportunity.*"[45]

In October 1876 Marks was finally able to enter Girton, but her first term was ended abruptly by illness. She was forced to spend several months resting in the country, at Scalands and in rooms at Eastbourne, supported by Bodichon's financial help. In May 1877, while Marks was at Scalands with Bessie Parkes Belloc, Bodichon went to Zennor, near St. Ives in Cornwall, to nurse an old friend, Jessie Merton Mario. On May 4, 1877 Bodichon sent Marks an interesting description of a new machine, a typewriter she had just purchased, complaining that the inked ribbon "is the devil to manage because it gets ruffled and cross."[46] This was the last letter she wrote before a sudden stroke paralyzed her a few days later.

Bodichon had been moderately active despite bouts of illness that troubled her from 1867. She was dedicated to the success of Girton, although she brought to this project only a fraction of the energy that had galvanized the feminists of the fifties. Her life between 1873 and 1877 was relatively quiet, punctuated by details of college business, but centering on domestic matters. The stroke she suffered at fifty effectively ended her feminist activities.

By July 1877 George Eliot could rejoice at Bodichon's renewed ability to speak.[47] In August of that year Eliot received the first letter Bodichon wrote in a shaky hand.[48] However, a succeeding series of small strokes made her a semi-invalid until her death in 1891. She remained at Scalands, where friends like Bessie Belloc and Girton students provided a constant stream of visitors carrying news of current campaigns. In 1878 George Henry Lewes died and in 1880 Eugène Bodichon made his last journey to England, "a little wandering in his mind."[49] He died in Algiers in 1885. Bodichon

45. Ibid., pp. 288–89.
46. Ibid., p. 60.
47. George Eliot to Bessie Parkes Belloc, 10 July 1877, *George Eliot Letters*, 6:392.
48. George Eliot to Barbara Bodichon, 2 August 1877, ibid., 6:398.
49. Barbara Bodichon to George Eliot, 1880, George Eliot Letters, Beinecke Library, Yale.

retained her spiritual optimism and unorthodoxy throughout these years. When in 1880 George Eliot astonished and horrified old acquaintances by marrying John Cross, more than twenty years her junior, Bodichon wrote a characteristically intense and unqualified letter of support: "Tell Johnny Cross I should have done exactly what he has done if you would let me and I had been a man. You see I know all love is so different that I do not see it unnatural to love in new ways—not to be unfaithful to any memory. If I knew Mr. Lewes he would be as glad as I am that you have a new friend."[50]

Six months later George Eliot was dead.

The end of Bodichon's life was not merely a succession of deaths and illnesses. In 1878 she learned with satisfaction that London University had admitted women to degrees. In 1882 she began a night school at Scalands for the boys and young men of Hastings. In 1885 Marks married Professor W. B. Ayrton, FRS, and in 1889 their daughter, Barbara Ayrton Bodichon was born. The baby gave special pleasure to Bodichon, who dubbed her "the little professoress."[51] In May 1891 Bodichon suffered another stroke. She died on June 11, 1891, leaving a legacy of £10,000 to the product of her last campaign, Girton College.

50. Barbara Bodichon to George Eliot, 8 May 1880, *George Eliot Letters,* 7:273.
51. Sharp, *Hertha Ayrton,* p. 123.

CONCLUSION

Barbara Bodichon was born shortly before the passage of the Reform Act of 1832 and came of age in 1848, the year revolution swept Europe and Chartism was at its height in England. She was publicly active for a quarter of a century between 1850 and 1875, a period George Kitson Clark has dubbed the "High Noon of Victorianism."[1] During these twenty-five years of social and political peace and economic prosperity, strong spiritual and social forces operated below the surface, establishing foundations for the sharp changes that characterized the last three decades of the nineteenth century.[2]

It is against this background that Bodichon worked, her character embodying the curious mixture of "progress and survival" identified with the mid-Victorian period. Acutely aware of the value of money, she could with perfect consistency declare, while preparing her will in 1878, that she was morally bound to leave the money inherited from her father to her family, while at the same time asserting that she had absolute liberty to give the money she had earned by selling her paintings (the work of her own hands) to Girton College.[3] Convinced of the evils of overlegislation, her reform efforts aimed at removal of legal and social disabilities, rather than at the creation of administrative superstructures or increased government intervention. Highly principled, emotional, and indi-

1. George Kitson Clark, *The Making of Victorian England* (Cambridge: Harvard University Press, 1962), p. 31.
2. Ibid., p. 58.
3. Stephen, *Emily Davies and Girton College*, pp. 310–11.

vidualistic to the point of eccentricity, her life tempts the writer to appraisals in flamboyant prose.

It would be easy to focus on Bodichon's singularity or to drama-tize the romantic and melancholy aspects of her life. One might portray a young Barbara Bodichon as Romola, the heroine George Eliot admitted she had invested with her best friend's physical and emotional attributes:

> The hair was of a reddish gold color, enriched by an unbro-ken small ripple, such as may be seen in the sunset clouds on grandest autumnal evenings. It was confined by a black fillet above her small ears. . . . It was a type of face of which one could not venture to say whether it would inspire love or only that unwilling admiration which is mixed with dread; the question must be decided by the eyes, which often seem charged with a more direct message from the soul.[4]

One might emphasize the effect of emotional difficulties, drawing attention to Bodichon's domestic disappointments. A young cousin expressed something of the emptiness of her personal life in verses composed shortly after her death:

> Those curtains where they fall
> Might almost drop apart and she walk through
> And very sight recall
> The robes line and the slow walk once I knew,
> The face, both sad and bright, the gold hair
>   bound with blue.
>
> The ghosts of sad thoughts press
> On one another in this empty spot
> Of grief for childlessness
> Of sorrow heavy on an innocent lot,
> And of a genius little known and soon forgot.[5]

4. George Eliot, *Romola* (New York: Merrill & Baker, n.d.), bk. 1, chap. 5.

5. Undated poem attributed by the archivist to an unnamed Bonham-Carter cousin who was a student at Girton College at the time of Bodichon's death. Bonham-Carter Family Papers.

The quaint or picturesque aspects of Bodichon and feminism are enticing. The modern reader is drawn to those qualities and anecdotes contributing to the creation of yet another Victorian oddity. This kind of analysis would be unfair to Bodichon and would yield an inaccurate trivialization of the role of feminism within the context of mid-Victorian reform.

Bodichon's significance in British feminism is clear. When she reached her majority in 1848 there was no organized women's movement. She activated feminism through the publication of *Laws Concerning Women* and the organization of the first committee dedicated to removing female disabilities from the law. She was an organizer first and foremost, although a writer of merely mediocre talent. Bodichon was a catalyst for the movement. She inspired her friends and utilized her family heritage of wealth and political acumen on behalf of her sex. For several generations the Smiths had devoted their energies to political campaigns to remove social and religious inequities from English law. Bodichon continued that tradition. She was one of the first women to enter the public arena. She worked to abolish prejudicial disabilities just as William and Benjamin Smith had participated in efforts to abolish slavery and religious discrimination and to extend education and the suffrage. She chose to champion women, whose legal and social status reflected the most basic societal sanction of injustice.

That Bodichon was an eccentric cannot be denied. Her dress, lifestyle, and impatience with social niceties encouraged public criticism. Her participation was often hidden by her coworkers to protect the reputation of various feminist undertakings. But despite personal foibles and a public career checkered by physical and mental illness, she must be acknowledged as the originator of organized feminism in England.

Raised in the Smith family tradition of rationalism, religious toleration, and social responsibility, Bodichon became the center of an upper-middle-class circle of women whose families were intimately associated with every major social and political reform effort of the sixties and seventies. Feminism was closely linked to social reform through the National Association for the Promotion of Social Science. The Association was involved in housing and educational reform. It helped shape public policy in prison reform and industrial employment as well. Its efforts in law reform were particularly important to the continuing campaign to change women's legal status. The Association was not directly involved in efforts to expand the suffrage. Feminist ties to the general suffrage reform effort of the mid-sixties were based, rather, on a close association with John Stuart Mill. The effort to improve higher education for women was part of the general trend toward professionalization that characterized the third quarter of the nineteenth century. Both the attempt to improve the quality of women teachers and to open the universities and the professions to women reflected a general concern with improved educational standards, a concern clearly demonstrated in the reports resulting from a series of government investigations of the issue.

Bodichon's career epitomized a radicalism which might best be described as progressive conservatism, a social philosophy which resulted in societal changes built on middle-class reform movements. Thus Bodichon and feminism may be seen in the context of other reform movements, electoral, educational, and professional—a unique, but not an isolated phenomenon. This radicalism was not based on any advanced code of personal behavior, the characteristics of individual reformers notwithstanding. Rather, it reflected the combined strands of humanitarianism and an increasing scientific professionalism. The Victorian amateur inspired by Evangelical or Unitarian tradition to social welfare efforts joined with the new professional by the 1860s to create a broad-based middle-class effort to shape public policy.

For G. M. Young, the prime function of the nineteenth century was to disengage the disinterested intelligence, to release it from the entanglements of party and sect and sex.[6] Mid-Victorian feminism created the impetus and structural apparatus to free women from social and legal restriction. The movement initiated by Bodichon's married women's property campaign was painfully slow.

6. Young, *Victorian England*, p. 186.

There was little change in the feminine ideal until the end of the century. Indeed, women were not given the vote until after the First World War. However, the feminist circle that coalesced around Bodichon during the 1850s represented the first concrete action by women on their own behalf. The Married Women's Property Committee was the first organized feminist endeavor and in creating it Bodichon launched the movement that eventually released women from their separate sphere.

Feminist progress continued during the last quarter of the nineteenth century. Although events were not exciting or sensational, education and employment opportunities gradually expanded during the period. The Married Women's Property Act was finally passed in 1883. Feminist committee structures expanded and the political activities of suffragists such as Millicent Garrett Fawcett reflected a growing sophistication in the movement. The changing British economy altered the situation of working women at the turn of the century. The woman worker was not a new phenomenon; women had provided over a third of the total workforce since the mid-century. What was new was the variety of jobs offered women and the fact that trade unions were beginning to organize them.[7] By the time the Pankhursts began the suffragette movement in 1906, feminism had broadened its ranks. The middle classes had been joined by increasingly assertive working-class women. The Pankhursts' militant suffrage campaign shocked traditional suffragists but brought the issue enormous public attention. The Pankhursts dismissed gradualists for their timidity and inability to cause rapid political change. Whether militancy or World War I or fifty years of organized committee work was primarily responsible for the granting of female suffrage in 1918 has been argued at length. Limited franchise did come immediately after the war, however, and by 1922 Nancy Astor was serving as the first woman M.P., chosen as a Conservative for the Sutton division of Plymouth at a by-election made necessary by her husband's accession to the peerage.

7. David Morgan, *Suffragists and Liberals* (Totowa, N.J.: Rowman & Littlefield, 1975), p. 21.

By the time that Barbara Ayrton Gould, daughter of Bodichon's protégée Hertha Ayrton, became a member of Parliament in 1945, almost one hundred years had elapsed since Bodichon's coming of age. During that time feminism had emerged as a major factor in societal reform. Looking back we can identify the Married Women's Property Committee as its first formal structure and recognize Barbara Bodichon as its earliest organizing agent.

Bodichon's feminism was radical in that she believed in complete sexual equality in the home and in the state, but her tactics were pragmatic. She would not have been comfortable in the ranks of the militant suffragettes. The Pankhursts' methods would have struck her as self-defeating. She could appreciate the value of public attention, but despite a personal tendency to flamboyance, she was careful to avoid notoriety which she was certain would undermine any reform effort. Where would Bodichon stand among the feminists of our own day? Certainly she was completely convinced of the need for equal education and employment opportunities for women. Equal pay for equal work would have been her slogan. She was the first writer to recognize the value of woman's work within the home and to attribute an economic value to the tasks of wife and mother. It is not possible to gauge Bodichon's reaction to each of the questions facing women in the late twentieth century. What we can be sure of are the criteria by which she would evaluate current issues. She believed in the removal of all disabilities affecting women. Absolute equality of opportunity for men and women in all areas of public and domestic life was her eventual goal. To achieve that equality she believed in the art of the possible, the necessity for organization and education to gain public consensus. Her goals and methods remain alive in the modern feminist movement.

BIBLIOGRAPHY

MANUSCRIPT SOURCES

Columbia University: Bodichon–Blackwell letters.

Fawcett Society Collection, City of London Polytechnic: Bodichon letters. Davies letters.

Girton College Archives: Bodichon letters and notebooks. Davies letters. Davies "Family Chronicle."

Greater London Record Office: Bodichon estate documents and letters.

Hampshire Record Office, Winchester, Eng.: Bonham-Carter Family Papers.

London School of Economics: Mill–Taylor letters.

MacCrimmon Collection, Tallahassee, Florida: Sixty-five Bodichon letters from the private collection of Barbara S. MacCrimmon.

Beinecke Library, Yale University: Bodichon letters and diaries. Eliot letters. Chapman letters and diary.

WRITINGS OF BARBARA BODICHON

A Brief Summary in Plain Language of the Most Important Laws of England Concerning Women. London: Holyoake, 1854.

A Brief Summary . . . 2d ed. London: Holyoake, 1856.

Women and Work. London: Bosworth & Harrison, 1857.

An American Diary, 1857–1858. Edited by Joseph W. Reed, Jr. London: Routledge & Kegan Paul, 1972.

With Eugene Bodichon. *Algeria Considered as a Winter Residence for the English.* London: Published at the offices of the *English Woman's Journal,* 1858.

With Eugene Bodichon. "Slavery in America." *English Woman's Journal* 2 (October 1858): 94–100.

Women and Work. New York: C. S. Francis, 1859.

"An American School." *English Woman's Journal* 2 (November 1858): 198–200.

"Slave Preaching." *English Woman's Journal* 5 (March 1860): 87–94.

"Algiers: First Impressions." *English Woman's Journal* 6 (September 1860): 21–32.

"Middle Class Schools for Girls." *English Woman's Journal* 6 (November 1860): 168–77.

"Cleopatra's Daughter, St. Marciana, Mama Marabout and Other Algerian Women." *English Woman's Journal* 10 (February 1863): 404–16.

"Of Those Who Are the Property of Others and of the Great Power that Holds Others as Property." *English Woman's Journal* 10 (February 1863): 370–81.

"Six Weeks in la Chere Petite Bretagne." *English Woman's Journal* 11 (May 1863): 188–97.

"Accomplices." *English Woman's Journal* 12 (February 1864): 394–400.

Objections to the Enfranchisement of Women Considered. London: J. Bale, 1866.

Reasons for the Enfranchisement of Women. London: J. Bale, 1966.

"Authorities and Precedents for Giving the Suffrage to Qualified Women." *Englishwoman's Review of Social and Industrial Questions* 1 (January 1867): 63–75.

"A Dull Life." *MacMillan's Magazine* 16 (May 1867): 47–53.

Reasons for and against the Enfranchisement of Women. London: n.p., 1869.

A Brief Summary . . . 3d ed. London: Trubner, 1869.

Reasons for and against the Enfranchisement of Women. 2d ed. London: n.p., 1872.

"A Conversation on the Enfranchisement of Female Freeholders and Householders." *Englishwoman's Review of Social and Industrial Questions.* n.s. 4 (April 1873): 105–11.

PRIMARY SOURCES

Sources chosen for this section include letters, memoirs, and works by figures central in mid-Victorian reform and Bodichon's personal life. Items have also been chosen to illustrate the range of feminist and anti-feminist sentiment throughout the period.

Allingham, William. *Letters.* Edited by H. Allingham and E. Baumer Williams. London: Longmans, Green, 1911. Reprint, New York: AMS, 1971.

Betham-Edwards, Matilda. "Girton College." *Fraser's Magazine* 91 (May 1875): 561–67.

———. *Mid-Victorian Memoirs.* London: John Murray, 1919.

———. *Reminiscences.* Rev. ed. London: Unit Library, 1903.

Blackwell, Elizabeth. *Pioneer Work in Opening the Medical Profession to Women.* London: Longmans, Green, 1895; Reprint, New York: Sourcebook Press, 1970.

Bodichon, Eugène. *De l'Humanité.* Brussels: Lacroix, 1866.

———. *Etudes sur l'Algerie et l'Afrique.* Algiers: Privately printed for the author, 1847.

———. *Of Humanity.* Abridged translation. London: Holyoake, 1859.

Bray, Charles. *The Industrial Employment of Women.* London: Longman, 1857.

Buchanan, Barbara Isabella. *Buchanan Family Records.* Cape Town: Townsend, 1923.

Butler, Josephine, ed. *Woman's Work and Woman's Culture.* London: Macmillan, 1869.

"Capabilities and Discapabilities of Women." *Westminster Review* 67 (January 1857): 23–40.

Cobbe, Frances Power. "Social Science Congresses and Woman's Part Therein," *MacMillan's Magazine* 5 (December 1861): 81–94.

Davies, Emily. *The Higher Education of Women.* London: Alexander Strahan, 1866. Reprint, New York: AMS, 1973.

————. *Thoughts on Some Questions Relating to Women, 1860–1908.* Cambridge: Bowes & Bowes, 1910. Reprint, New York: AMS, 1973.

Eliot, George. *George Eliot Letters.* Edited by Gordon Sherman Haight. 7 vols. New Haven: Yale University Press, 1954–55.

Ellis, Sarah Stickney. *The Daughters of England.* London: Fisher, Son, 1842.

————. *The Women of England.* London: Fisher, Son, 1839.

Gaskell, Elizabeth Cleghorn. *The Letters of Mrs. Gaskell.* Edited by J. A. V. Chapple and Arthur Pollard. Cambridge: Harvard University Press, 1966.

Greg, W. R. "Why Are Women Redundant?" *National Review* 14 (April 1862): 434–60.

Howitt, Mary. *Autobiography.* Edited by her daughter Margaret Howitt. 2 vols. Boston: Houghton Mifflin, 1889.

Jameson, Anna B. *Sisters of Charity and The Communion of Labour.* Boston: Ticknor & Fields, 1857.

————. "Woman's Mission and Woman's Position." In *Memoirs and Essays.* London: R. Bentley, 1846.

Law Amendment Journal, 1855–1857.

Malleson, Elizabeth Whitehead. *Elizabeth Malleson, 1828–1916: Autobiographical Notes and Letters.* Edited with a memoir by Hope Malleson. London: Printed for private circulation, 1926.

————. "The Portrait of a School." *Journal of Education* 18 (September 1886): 357–59.

Martineau, Harriet. "Female Industry." *Edinburgh Review* (American ed.) 109 (April 1859): 151–73.

Mill, John Stuart. *Autobiography.* Indianapolis: Bobbs-Merrill, 1957.

————. *The Subjection of Women.* London: Oxford University Press, 1963.

National Association for the Promotion of Social Science. *Transactions.* 1857–1885.

"The 'Non-Existence' of Women." *North British Review* 22 (August 1855): 288–302.

Norton, Caroline. *English Laws for Women in the Nineteenth Century.* London: n.p., 1854.

————. *A Letter to the Queen on Lord Chancellor Cranworth's Marriage and Divorce Bill.* London: Longmans, Brown, Green & Longman, 1855.

Oliphant, Margaret. "The Condition of Women." *Blackwood's Edinburgh Magazine* 83 (February 1858): 139–54.

————. "The Great Unrepresented." *Blackwood's Edinburgh Magazine* 100 (September 1866): 367–79.

————. "Laws Concerning Women." *Blackwood's Edinburgh Magazine* 79 (April 1856): 379–87.

————. "Mill's 'The Subjection of Women.'" *Edinburgh Review* (American ed.)
    130 (October 1869): 291–306.
Owen, Robert. *The Life of Robert Owen*. 2 vols. London: Effingham Wilson, 1857.
    Reprint, New York: Augustus M. Kelley, 1967.
Parkes, Bessie Rayner. *Essays on Woman's Work*. 2d ed. London: Alexander Stra-
    han, 1866.
————. "A Review of the Last Six Years." *English Woman's Journal* 12 (October
    1864).
Perry, Sir Thomas Erskine. "Rights and Liabilities of Husband and Wife." *Edin-
    burgh Review* (American ed.) 105 (January 1857): 94–106.
"The Property of Married Women." *Westminster Review* 66 (October 1856): 181–
    97.
Rossetti, Dante Gabriel, *Letters of Dante Gabriel Rossetti*. Edited by Oswald
    Doughty and Robert Wahl. 4 vols. Oxford: Clarendon Press, 1965–67.
Shirreff, Emily Anne Eliza. "Girton College." *Fortnightly Review* 14 (July 1873):
    87–93.
————. *Intellectual Education and Its Influence on the Character and Happiness of
    Women*. London: John W. Parker & Son, 1858.
Shirreff, Emily Anne Eliza and Maria G. Grey. *Thoughts on Self-Culture Addressed
    to Women*. Boston: William Crosby & H. P. Nichols, 1851.
Smith, Sidney. "Essay on Female Education." *Edinburgh Review* 15 (January 1810):
    299–315.
Taylor, Helen. "The Ladies' Petition." *Westminster Review* 87 (January 1867): 29–
    36.
Wharton, John J. S. *An Exposition of the Laws Relating to the Women of England*.
    London: Longmans, Brown, Green & Longman, 1853.
Wollstonecraft, Mary. *Vindication of the Rights of Women*. New York: W. W. Nor-
    ton, 1967.

SECONDARY SOURCES

Annan, Noel Gilroy. "The Intellectual Aristocracy." In *Studies in Social History: A
    Tribute to G. M. Trevelyan*. Edited by J. H. Plumb. London: Longmans, Green,
    1955, pp. 241–287.
Banks, J. A. and Olive Banks. *Feminism and Family Planning in Victorian England*.
    New York: Schocken Books, 1964.
Best, Geoffrey. *Mid-Victorian Britain, 1851–1875*. London: Weidenfield & Ni-
    cholson, 1971.
Blackburn, Helen. *Women's Suffrage*. London: Williams & Norgate, 1902. Re-
    print, New York: Sourcebook Press, 1970.
Bonham-Carter, Victor. *In a Liberal Tradition*. London: Constable, 1960.
Bradbrook, Muriel Clara. *"That Infidel Place": A Short History of Girton College,
    1869–1969*. London: Chatto & Windus, 1969.
————. *Barbara Bodichon, George Eliot and the Limits of Feminism*. James Bryce
    Memorial Lecture. Oxford: Oxford University Press, 1975.
Branca, Patricia. *Silent Sisterhood: Middle Class Women in the Victorian Home*. Pitts-
    burgh: Carnegie-Mellon University Press, 1975.

Burton, Hester. *Barbara Bodichon*. London: Constable, 1949.

Davis, Richard W. *Dissent in Politics, 1780–1830: The Political Life of William Smith, M.P.* London: Epworth Press, 1971.

Dicey, Albert Venn. *Lectures on the Relation between Law and Public Opinion in England during the Nineteenth Century*. London: Macmillan, 1917.

Fawcett, Millicent Garrett. *Women's Suffrage*. London: T. C. & E. C. Jack, 1912. Reprint. New York: Sourcebook Press, 1973.

Fulford, Roger. *Votes for Women*. London: Faber & Faber, 1957.

Garnett, Richard. *The Life of William Fox, 1786–1864*. London: John Lane, 1910.

Haight, Gordon Sherman. *George Eliot, A Biography*. Oxford: Oxford University Press, 1968.

———. *George Eliot and John Chapman*. New Haven: Yale University Press, 1940.

Hayek, Friedrich August von, ed. *J. S. Mill and Harriet Taylor*. Chicago: University of Chicago Press, 1951.

Hewitt, Margaret. *Wives and Mothers in Victorian Industry*. London: Rockliff, 1958.

Holt, Raymond V. *The Unitarian Contribution to Social Progress in England*. Rev. ed. London: Lindsey Press, 1952.

Kamm, Josephine. *Rapiers and Battleaxes: The Women's Movement and Its Aftermath*. London: George Allen & Unwin, 1966.

Lowndes, Marie A. *I Too Have Lived in Arcadia*. New York: Dodd, Mead, 1942.

MacGregor, O. R. *Divorce in England*. London: Heinemann, 1957.

Neff, Wanda Fraiken. *Victorian Working Women*. New York: Columbia University Press, 1929.

Pinchbeck, Ivy. *Women Workers and the Industrial Revolution, 1750–1850*. New York: F. S. Crofts, 1930.

Reiss, Erna. *Rights and Duties of Englishwomen: A Study in Law and Public Opinion*. Manchester: Sherratt & Hughes, 1934.

Rodgers, Brian. "The Social Science Association, 1857–1885." *Manchester School of Economic and Social Studies* 20 (1952): 283–310.

Rover, Constance. *Women's Suffrage and Party Politics in Britain, 1866–1914*. London: Routledge & Kegan Paul, 1967.

Sharp, Evelyn. *Hertha Ayrton, 1854–1923*. London: Edward Arnold, 1926.

Stenton, Doris Mary. *The English Woman in History*. London: George Allen & Unwin, 1957.

Stephen, Barbara. *Emily Davies and Girton College*. London: Constable, 1927.

Stewart, W. A. C. and W. P. McCann. *The Educational Innovators, 1750–1880*. 2 vols. London: Macmillan, 1967.

Strachey, Ray. *The Cause*. London: G. Bell & Sons, 1928.

Vicinus, Martha, ed. *A Widening Sphere: Changing Roles of Victorian Women*. Bloomington: Indiana University Press, 1977.

Webb, Robert Kiefer. *Harriet Martineau: A Radical Victorian*. New York: Columbia University Press, 1960.

Woodham-Smith, Cecil. *Florence Nightingale, 1820–1910*. London: Constable, 1950.

Woodring, Carl R. *Victorian Samplers: William and Mary Howitt*. Lawrence: University of Kansas Press, 1952.

INDEX